THE SOCIOLOGICAL TOOL BOX
and
THE DICTIONARY
of SOCIOLOGICAL TERMS

Daryl P. Evans

Gar Sum Koo
Christian McCallister
Ericka Treslo
with
Clay Bartel

Purdue University

The McGraw-Hill Companies, Inc.
Primis Custom Publishing

New York   St. Louis   San Francisco   Auckland   Bogotá
Caracas   Lisbon   London   Madrid   Mexico   Milan   Montreal
New Delhi   Paris   San Juan   Singapore   Sydney   Tokyo   Toronto

McGraw·Hill

A Division of The McGraw·Hill Companies

The Sociological Tool Box and The Dictionary of Sociological Terms

McGraw-Hill's Primis Custom Publishing consists of products that are produced from camera-ready copy. Peer review, class testing, and accuracy are primarily the responsibility of the author(s).

1 2 3 4 5 6 7 8 9 0 BBC BBC 9 0 9 8

ISBN 0-07-230244-5

Editor: Dee Renfrow
Printer/Binder: Braceland Brothers, Inc.

TABLE OF CONTENTS FOR THE SOCIOLOGICAL TOOLBOX

....

Sample Exams

<u>SYLLABUS</u>

<u>Course</u>: Introductory Sociology -- Soc. 100
<u>Place</u>: The Class of 1950 Lecture Hall
<u>Professor</u>: Dr. Daryl Evans
<u>Professor's Office</u>: Stone Hall, Room 351
<u>Office Phone</u>: 496-2834
<u>Office Hours</u>: Tuesday and Thursday 10:30-11:30; And By Appointment.
<u>Consultation Hours</u>: There is a room adjacent to our classroom in the Class of '50 Lecture Hall in which I will be available to talk with students right after both the 12:00 class and the 3:00 class. I will show you where this room is.
<u>Teaching Assistants</u>: You will meet the persons assisting in this course and be provided with a listing of the times and locations of their office hours as soon as these are set. We will set these to maximize the coverage that meets your needs.

<u>Required Reading Material</u>:

   <u>Elements of Sociology Through Theory</u> by Daryl Evans, with Christian McCallister. New York: McGraw-Hill, Fifth Edition, 1998. The book was designed specifically for this course. The overheads follow the lectures very closely. Many people take their class notes on the overhead pages.

   <u>The Sociological Toolbox/The Dictionary of Sociological Terms.</u>, by Daryl Evans, Gar Sum Koo, Christian McCallister, Ericka Treslo, with Clay Bartel, New York: McGraw-Hill, First Edition, 1998. This contains chapters on how to get along in college, particular reference tools you will need in college, historical perspectives on the people we will study in the textbook, a special chapter on the contributions of women to sociology, important studies that have been done in sociology, sample examinations, chapter summaries concerning the textbook and <u>The Dictionary Of Sociological Terms</u>, among other things. The book was designed specifically for this course. <u>The dictionary contains a list of terms, all of which, you will be responsible for knowing</u>.

<u>Assignments in Books</u>:

   I will try to let you know every day where you should be reading for the next few classes. If I forget, please remind me.

<u>Objectives of the Course</u>:

   <u>1</u>. To provide an overview of sociology.   We will investigate the primary approaches to the theory and practice of sociology.
   <u>2</u>. To explore the relevance of sociological thought and practice in our world. This course is meant to be practical as well as mentally stimulating.

3. To examine the basic principles of human group interaction and to teach the fundamental vocabulary of sociology.

Instructional Philosophy:

There is broad range of interests in the class. Some students are curious about sociology, while others may be here only to satisfy a requirement. Some students are career-oriented in their learning; others are not. Some students learn for the pure enjoyment of it; others seem to study primarily to take tests and obtain grades. Many students blend these orientations with a complicated set of other motivations. I am aware of your differing degrees of interest in sociology and the various paths that have brought you here and which you will pursue in the future. I respect that diversity of motivation.

Everyone associated with the class would be pleased if those of you who are interested in sociology end up feeling that you have learned as much as you can assimilate during the semester. It also would be very satisfying to us if those of you who are not so keen on the prospect of taking a sociology course find that the subject is more interesting and worthwhile to your own lives than you imagined it could be.

The best outcome in this course comes to those students who actively participate in thinking about the ideas and issues we discuss, and keep an open mind. I hope you will find the range of ideas broad, and the presentation of these ideas fair and engaging.

No other discipline asks, and attempts to answer in a scientific way, more difficult questions than sociology. Sociological issues are at the heart of our civilization's survival, and probably the survival of our species. All human activity occurs within a social context. We are all part of an enormous social web of interaction and mutual dependence. If you can imagine the society as a huge web, everything that happens on one part of the web has rippling waves of consequence or undulations that all of the people on the web feel. Everything social is connected to everything else. A recognition of this should provide common ground and mutual purpose for all of us.

Grades:

1. Grades will be based on a point system.
2. There will be three examinations; each question on each of the exams will be worth 5 points.
3. The first examination will be worth the least number of points. The second examination will be worth more points than the second. The final examination will be worth the greatest number of points. For example, there might be 40 questions on the first exam, 50 on the second exam, and 65 on the final. I don't know exactly how many yet because I have not made out the questions yet. This situation favors the student because, as you get better at taking the exams, you have a greater possibility to enhance your grade.

4. The grade for the course will be based on the total sum of points a student earns during the semester.

5. I cannot say now how many possible points there will be just yet because I have not made up the exams yet. In the past, however, students usually have been able to accumulate a maximum of somewhere in the neighborhood of 650-800 total points, depending upon how much material we cover. The amount of material we cover depends to a significant extent on how fast you want me to cover the material. We will establish an optimum speed for all students so we don't go too slowly for the people who move through the material easily and quickly and don't go too fast for the students who find the material more challenging or would prefer to savor it more through discussion.

6. The exams are not cumulative However, you would be expected to know the dictionary terms you studied in earlier exams or quizzes for later exams or quizzes. In other words, students will be expected to learn the "language" of sociology and retain it.

7. The exams will include true-false and multiple choice questions.

8. Grades will be based on a curve. If we all do our jobs well, the curve should be skewed towards "As," "Bs," and "Cs."

9. There is no extra credit option for students. Students are much better off studying the considerable material for which you are responsible rather than going off on "side trips."

10. Remember, I do not **give** you a grade; you **earn** it. I cannot turn in an "A" for you just because you "studied a lot," "thought you knew the material," "liked the course and really got a lot out of it," "came to class every day," etc. I have to assess your performance. This keeps our standards at Purdue high and gives credibility to letters of recommendation I write and the reputation of the school when you encounter prospective employers and other situations based upon the quality of your education.

11. Once a grade has been earned by a student, I do not negotiate it. I can't. If I did it for one person, I'd have to do it for a thousand. We are, however, willing to go over exams, check for errors, and the like and give you all the help we can to give you a chance to improve your understanding and your grade.

Examination Dates:

The dates for the first and second exams will be decided as the semester progresses. This will give us time to make sure we have a chance to go over the material carefully and for us to look at everyone's exam schedules in other classes. I will try to schedule the exams on dates that are convenient to the greatest number of students. **The decision will be made by majority rule of the students in attendance on a pre-arranged decision date.**

The **Final Examination** will be announced approximately mid-semester. The final exam schedule is made up by a computer that tries to minimize the number of students who have three exams in one day or time conflicts because of other classes' exam schedules. **I have no control over the final time and cannot schedule it the week before final exams. So, please make your travel plans to correspond with the time of the final, or, if you need to make them before that, to correspond to the last day of finals.** Someday, university officials will come to understand that grading a thousand people is different than grading forty and they will cut the big classes some slack. Until then, what we have tried to change and cannot change, we endure.

Policy on Missing Exams:

It is inadvisable to miss an exam in this course. **But, if you have to, please do not call the Department of Sociology and Anthropology on the day of an exam if there is a reason you cannot make it. Obviously, this can keep the office staff from their duties. If you are ill, or some other misfortune befalls you, and you will not be able to make it to the scheduled exam, just talk to me at the next class period you do attend and I will put you in touch with a teaching assistant who will help you.**

Attendance:

Because much of the material on exams comes from lectures and other class activities, it makes good sense to attend class. Information is covered in lectures that is not referred to in the reading material. **It will make a big difference in how well you do in the course if you come to class.** I do take attendance several times during the semester to get a general idea of who is attending class on a regular basis and who is not.

.*****EXTREMELY IMPORTANT******

If you do not want to be in class, do not come to it. I always treat students with courtesy and respect. It makes life easier for all of us when you reciprocate. Next to students who cheat or plagiarize, the thing that most angers me are people who walk out of class during class. If you have to leave for a good reason, let me or a TA know; otherwise I'll be just as rude to you as you are being to me.

*****EXTREMELY IMPORTANT PART TWO*****

I have a covenant with all students that they will have an orderly classroom. It is really not my nature to have to police the room for talkers. The teaching assistants don't like to do that either. We want you to learn and have fun doing the learning. However, if you are disruptive, you will receive a form to fill out that has an accompanying brochure that spells out your rights and responsibilities under University rules. It is humiliating to get one of these forms and just about as humiliating to have to give one. So, if you are given to yapping in class, give everybody a break -- yourself, the people around you, the teaching assistants, me, the Department Head, The Dean of Students, and all the other people you will inconvenience if you forget your dignity and maturity when you walk in the classroom.

Students With Special Needs:

Students with special needs related to disabilities, test-taking circumstances, travel plans, etc. should report them to me either now, or as the need arises. You also can take up special needs and circumstances with the Office of the Dean of Students, Helen B. Schleman Hall of Student Services. The people in that office are friendly and very good facilitators of student needs.

Tape Recording Lectures:

Students may tape record any lectures they wish. The lectures also will be recorded by The Center for Instructional Studies and be in a special place in the Undergraduate Library. One of the teaching assistants archives these tapes so you will have a general idea of what is on them.

Class Participation:

1. If you have something to say, wait for an appropriate pause and ask the question or make the comment. I encourage participation and try to elicit comments and clarification in the course of most class sessions. I always repeat student questions and comments so people who are not within the immediate hearing range know what we are talking about.

2. Please do not be worried about asking "dumb questions." If you are confused, chances are there are many other people who also are confused and will welcome your efforts at clarification. I assure you that you will never be made to feel silly for asking a question. Questioning ideas is an essential part of the learning process and we respect your inquiries.

Caveats:

Caveat Number One:

I will be showing many video clips to introduce and/or clarify sociological principles. Insofar as many of these clips are from contemporary movies, some of the language might be crude and offend your norms of conversation and not be in keeping with the professional standards of language I attempt to adhere to in the classroom. My philosophy on this is that I always am going to choose the best video clip to illustrate the material, even if it has some very unsavory language or unsettling substantive content.

I have a standing policy that, if you can find a better video clip to illustrate the same point I am trying to make, I will adopt it. Period. We must be sensitive to people with strong beliefs and values, be they religious, political, racial, ethnic, or deal with any other aspect of the fundamental tolerance of other people's morality. But I am trying to adapt to the way people learn at the turn of the millennium and this is college -- a place for adult education and freedom of speech and thought. Now that you have been forewarned, if you think you are going to have a problem with this aspect of the course, come and let me know; I'll try to help you get into another class.

Caveat Number Two:

Occasionally, because life does not work out just as we have planned it, we have to make changes in the what has been specified in this syllabus. If this is the case in our class, you will be apprised off those changes during class lecture periods; they will be written down on an overhead projection; and you will be given a "hard copy" notice of the change on paper in the form of an "Addendum or Amendment to the Syllabus." If you do not happen to be at class when such changes are announced, I always will attempt to repeat an announcement about the changes several times on several successive days. If you miss this because you are absent from class for long periods of time, or because you are not paying attention to what is going on in class, surely you understand that the responsibility lies with you. There are no "boys" and "girls" in this class -- just men and women.

Sequence of Topics to be Covered:

Caveat Number Three:

The course will unfold very much as it does in the outline to follow below. However, I continually research new lectures and restructure the course. Thus, I will not feel locked into this outline just for the sake of being locked into something.

It is possible that we will not get through all the material listed below. I would rather cover what we do, well, rather than rushing through it for the sake of saying it was covered. The time frame of our progress will depend, to a significant extent, on how fast you want to go. The more we discuss ideas, the slower we will go.

1. Theories of **Social Change**.

2. Positivism: **Auguste Comte** and One-Sided Sheep.

3. Radical Sociology: **Karl Marx** and the Economic and Political Basis of the Social Bond. "Can this Guy Possibly Be Right; and What if He Is?"

4. Do the Weak Pollute Our Species? Social Darwinism in the Thought of **Herbert Spencer**. "Can This Guy Possibly Be Right; and What if He Is?"

5. Is Deviance Normal? Are even our most intimate activities socially-determined? The Development of Sociological Method and Theory in the Works of **Emile Durkheim**.

6. The Roots of Modern Society. Power, Bureaucracy, and the Socio-Religious Basis of Economic Organization in the Works of **Max Weber**.

7. The Triumph of "Objective Culture." The Sociology of **Georg Simmel**.

8. The Importance of Symbols in Social Life. Do we see ourselves as we see others to be seeing us? The Ideas of **George Herbert Mead, W.I. Thomas, and C.H. Cooley**.

9. Concluding Remarks: Where Do You Go From Here?

Finally, I believe it is important that you understand that this kind of survey course is designed to provide you access to a very broad range of ideas. I try to present them in as even-handed a manner as possible. Try to understand, however, what the word "professor" means: one who professes. I certainly will not do that nearly as much in this 100 level course as I would in a higher division course, in which a greater number of students are more prepared to exchange ideas critically with one who professes. Conversely, I hope you understand that the class would be pointless if I dished out pabulum that pleased everyone all the time.

I hope everyone in the course will work to make this semester memorable, joyful, stimulating, and practical. I look forward to all of us learning and having a good time doing it. Welcome.

Dr. Evans

6

WELCOME TO THE SOCIOLOGY TOOLBOX

SOME THOUGHTS ABOUT HOW TO GET ALONG IN COLLEGE

In the next pages, I will be sharing what I believe to be practical ideas for your stay in college. The one thing I do not want to do in sharing this advice is to be patronizing to you or be preachy. I have great respect for students and know that the last thing many of you want or need is unsolicited advice. So for those of you who do not feel you need to read the following, I understand. However, I believe that there will be so many subjects touched upon that a person new to college would not know about that, even those of you who have your act totally together will find things in the forthcoming pages that will be of help in getting along in college. The one thing I can say with certainty is that the main reason I have written this section is because I care about you and want you to make the best of the Purdue experience.

DREAMS

Many of you are new to the college experience. And probably more than a few are excited to be here, but overwhelmed with all the things a student has to think about given all the excitement going on around you. Many of you are more advanced in your college career, but have only figured out part of the things a student has to figure out in learning how to get along in college. To those of you who know you have things figured out, I both envy and congratulate you.

This workbook is a first effort to give you more than a mere textbook. Because the classes I teach are large, I have for years wanted to write a monograph about how to get along in college for students. I have been a professor for nearly twenty years and teaching in higher education for twenty-six and surely, the most conspicuous thing I have noticed about the down side of being a student is that many people never learn how to get along in college. And by the time many people start to figure it out, they are getting ready to leave and it is too late to put their skills to the task of making the college experience the best it can be.

As fate would have it, I found time to make a segment of the Sociological Toolbox include some of what I think are important tips to help you make sense out of what will be one of the most remarkable experiences of your life. I still remember one of my professors telling me that my undergraduate years would probably be "the best years of my life." And even though I've had a wonderful life, I think he was right . . . so far, anyway.

First, lets think about what college can be at its best. At its best, it can be an opportunity to help a dream come true for you. Some of you have dreams of how you want to live your life that you have thought about for years. You are the lucky ones, even though you may find that circumstances might not let those dreams come true, either because you change your aspirations, or because you have to change them because of circumstances beyond your control.

One of the beauties of college is that it is a wonderful place to give birth to dreams -- a chance to get on a pathway that becomes a highway to a life as exciting, and yet full of peace of mind and satisfaction as a human can have. So, if you don't have a dream yet, you can help to maximize the college experience and perhaps have an educational triumph just by looking for that dream. Yeah; you have to study a lot and you should lead a balanced life in the social sphere, and about a million other important things. . . . But you have to make a lot of time to search for the dream because the dream you should be looking for is <u>you</u> at <u>your</u> <u>best</u>.

What is one way to start the search? Answer two important questions. First, what do you want out of life? That's the more selfish of the two questions, but even those people who are the most generous of spirit in the world are to a significant degree driven by self interest. Second, what do you want to give back to life? If and when you can answer that one, you are really onto something because that is going to provide you with as much satisfaction as if the more self-interested part of your dream for yourself comes true.

CYNICISM AND THE DREAM

Let's face it. There gets to be a lot of cynicism on the part of many people who are connected with higher education. It's easy to see that things don't always work the ways the brochures tell you they will. Sure, you will see things and meet people -- some of whom will be your teachers -- who will make you feel as though the search you are on for an education is just a process of cramming for tests so you can earn certain grades that will become part of a transcript that might result in a degree. If cramming, regurgitating facts and ideas on tests, promptly forgetting what you learned for the test, and getting ready to cram for the next one gets to be habitual for you, then college becomes more like a silly ritual. If you are in college, you have the means to achieve an education, but if you find yourself just going through the motions of educating yourself rather than really becoming an educated person, how pointless.

What is the point of questions such as what you want out of life or what you're prepared to give back to it then? **You** are. No one but you has your unique set of qualities. No one can maximize the potentials that lie within you as well as you can. That diploma is not without meaning; it can open doors for you. But the diploma pales by comparison when it is held up to what a person can become when a person becomes educated. Being a "graduate" is just a word. Being an "educated graduate" is being a strong force in the world.

For every question that has to do with what courses you took and what grades you earned, there are a whole set of questions that are much more important. For example, what did you learn? What did you retain? What did you figure out today that will make you a better person -- giving you the capacity to pass what you've learned on as competence, love, wisdom, or something else that draws people to you? Of course, a degree is part of your dream, but your dream will always be more important than your degree.

FINDING THE DREAM

Do you sometimes feel so overstimulated that all you want to do is deaden your senses? Unless you are a phenomenally calm person, how could you help but be overstimulated in our world? Just the technological revolution we are going through right now seems impossible to keep up with. You've heard the term "Renaissance Man." It just means that there were times in history when a person could be a generalist and maybe have the talent to know a great deal about the art, science, humanities, and other knowledge of the times.

Look at us now. How can an individual be a "Renaissance Person?" To know the bare essentials of a small part of life requires incredible specialization. The truth be known, what did most of us come to college for? To specialize. But when we aim the camera of specialization in one direction, we, of necessity, aim it away from many other areas about which we may be curious -- away from other real and potential passions. And as we attempt to decide where to point the camera, some of us become so overstimulated that we go numb. And that numbness is the dream killer. The way to avoid numbing out is to look for something -- to aim that camera in the direction of something about which we have a passion.

Let me tell you a story about myself, which I will tell very few of so as not to bore you to tears. I was lucky because I knew I wanted to be a teacher when I was an undergraduate. And I was lucky because I knew I either wanted to teach economics or sociology by midway through my undergraduate degree. And by the time I finished my undergraduate years, I knew I wanted to teach in higher education -- the university level. All in all, I was a lucky guy. Right?

Well, sort of. When I graduated, I took some jobs in the private sector of business just to make sure that I wouldn't be missing out because people in business made a lot more money than professors. And to become a professor, I had to go to about seven more years of school, during which I ended up getting a lot of loans and so on. Moreover, I knew that it would be very difficult to find a job as a professor. There were way more people obtaining the necessary degree to do what I wanted than there were jobs "doing" professional sociology.

But finding a job was only the beginning of a stressful process. If a person found an academic job, the person had six years to make a lot of "publish or perish" contributions to the sociological discipline, be a good teacher, provide service to the university community and the community at large. If a person does these and about a thousand other things, that professor can come up for what is called "promotion and tenure." If one doesn't get promoted and tenured, the person gets fired, and, if you're lucky, you may be given a year to find another job in a market still glutted by people -- many of whom are young (less expensive to hire) and do not have the stigma of not having earned tenure. I got lucky and found a nice job and earned my tenure, etc.

The reason I told you this story is because the one thing that pulled me through every one of the hoops I had to jump through -- some of which were OK, and some of which I hated -- was the dream I had. As long as I was working toward something for which I had a passion, there was much less anxiety in my life than there would have been if I had compromised my idea of what I wanted to do both for a living and for a life.

In 26 years of university teaching, I've never let the dream go and I've never felt like I didn't want to go to work. The moral of the story, of course, is that life is very nice when you get to do something for a living for which you have a passion. And the bottom line on this is that it will be difficult for you to enjoy your professional life unless it is something for which you already (today) have a passion or feel one developing. That's why you have to ask what you want out of life and what you intend to put back into it, and ask those questions now. In other words, if you don't feel the passion to fuel the dream, it is wise to start your search today.

INVENTING YOUR FUTURE

Having a dream and achieving it was a good deal less difficult when I was a student than it may be for you. The world was much less complex then. Professions and occupations didn't change so fast as they do now. For example, what if you gamble on doing something that doesn't even exist by the time your educational period to do it is over? Technology changes the environment so quickly every day and the explosion of knowledge is so huge, a person has to be realistic in the choices he or she makes and practically has to be a fortuneteller.

So, if you are going to be the kind of student who just hopes there will be a rewarding job waiting out there for you when you graduate, you have to look at educational choices that teach you to maximize your adaptability. Just as one example, languages make us more adaptable in a world that has developed a global culture.

If you want to pursue the dream "your way," you need to equip yourself with the skills and the courage to invent your own future. In basic terms, this means that you need to be both adaptive and creative. And the way one does that is to look at the whole university as a huge institution in which you can shop for your future. Just imagine if you spent as much time deciding what you want occupationally or professionally as you do shopping for commodities such as shoes, CDs, and whatever other commodities for which you have a passion. Take it as a rule of thumb: if you take more time shopping for commodities than you do shopping for your future, your priorities are wrong if you want to make the best out of the university. And remember: a university education is one of the most expensive purchases you will make. It would be a shame to throw your money away in trivial pursuits.

As you search for your dream at Purdue, your academic advisors are going to help you. Your teachers are going to help you. Your family and friends are going to help you. In other words, you will have formal and informal support groups to help you to fashion your dream. The formal support apparatus is large. But you have to initiate the process of using those support groups, especially if you are going to see what the university has to offer. Indeed, one of the very nice aspects of the university is that there are many "futurists" working here. The "cutting edge" nature of these people's work probably can help you to prognosticate with them what's likely to be "out there" occupationally in the long haul and what you can enjoy doing for a lifetime.

It is the proximity to such "futurists" that is a good portion of what you are paying for as you move through the university. Not to avail yourself of a search for your dream with such people is a terrible waste of your money and time. Use Purdue to the utmost. There are many people waiting here just to help you. And in your periods of lethargy, you may be missing that one perfect point -- that moment -- when you choose the path best taken.

PROFESSORS

Scarcely anyone ever tells students about professors. As a consequence, much of what students come to know about even the most friendly and accessible professors is based on stereotypes -- usually inaccurate generalizations about a diverse group of people. What are you really going to find out about the people who teach you?   Well, the first thing you are going to find out that they are a diverse group of humanity with all the strengths and foibles of any group of people. The thing you may not always see is how much most of your professors want to and can help you. We don't always remember to tell you that, but you'll just have to trust me: the vast majority of professors I know respect their students and care about them and very much want to help you make your dreams come true. But rather than going on about that, let's get practical.

In addition to helping you learn certain subject matter and trying to advise you when you ask for help, what do you think will be the most important practical thing a professor can do for you? That's easy. They are going to be able to write you letters of recommendation if you go about cultivating such letters. How do you do that?

LETTERS OF RECOMMENDATION

Think about it; let's say you graduate and are seeking a job. What do we know about our society? It's highly bureaucratized. What does that mean to you in your job search? It means that, for most jobs, people are going to get a sense of who you are on paper before they ever meet you. So what kind of paper is that going to be? You'll have a resume. You'll have a transcript of grades. You'll usually have an application in which you describe why you want a certain job and/or what you want to do with your life. You may have some standardized tests like MCATs if you want to go to medical school, or LSATs if you want to go to law school, or GREs if you want to go to graduate school. And all of you will be expected to have letters of recommendation. So let's think about such letters for a while.

What is a good source of a letter of recommendation? A good friend of the family who is a person of power and integrity? That's not bad, but people expect a friend of the family to say something good about you so such letters don't always have much persuasive power. Your minister, priest, or rabbi if you have one?   That's not bad, but unless you are going into ecclesiastical life, it has been my experience that, whether they ought to or not, people don't always put too much stock in such letters. Employers? Employers are a good source of letters of recommendation because they can comment on work habits, reliability, your ability to get along with other people, etc. Make sure to obtain such letters while you can as many people who have been your supervisors in jobs move on to other jobs and may be difficult to find when you need the letter. What about professors as recommenders?

Professors are usually a good source of a letter of recommendation because they often can talk about many aspects of your skills and character, they usually don't disappear to other jobs, and they typically write many letters of recommendation. The issue is, how are you going to cultivate a letter of recommendation from a professor? Let me suggest one way this can be done that can result in a useful letter.

Let us say you are a first year student. Is it too early to start thinking about letters of recommendation? Quite the contrary. You are going to run into some people in your first or second year of college who you are going to like as professors and in whose classes you are going to do well. Let's say you are in a class of 500 people, though. If you wait until your senior year, about the only thing the professor is going to be able to say about you is where you placed in the class out of 500 people. Even if you did very well, that can result in a weak letter. So let us try something.

If you have decided that you eventually are going to want a professor to write a letter of recommendation, you have to let him or her know. And here is one way to do that. First, make an appointment with the professor. Most professors are very good about keeping their office hours, but people give special attention to appointments. Second, before the appointment give the professor the following information: 1) a short agenda for the appointment; 2) a single page (typewritten) letter telling the professor a bit about yourself -- your family, where you are from, your interests, etc.; 3) a single page (typewritten) describing what you are considering doing with your professional life and why, or, which subject or subjects interest you the most in school and why; and 4) a transcript (even if it only has one semester on it). If you do these things, you can have a much more focused meeting. If you hit it off with the professor, he or she probably will start a file on you to refer to and to add to as you go through college. Along with the initial contact, there is another important thing you can do.

Agree that you will periodically keep in touch so that you can keep the professor apprised of what is happening with your professional aspirations, grades, activities, etc. Now think about how much easier you have made the ultimate job of writing a letter of recommendation for the professor. With each successive visit, you give the professor more information. By the time the letter needs to be written, the professor actually knows you. They will be able to tell stories about you, which most people who read letters of recommendation usually like. The professor will be able to demonstrate that you were thinking about your dreams early in your college life rather than doing it at the last minute. Last minute dreams give the impression that you are willing to take anything that is out there for a career. And many professors who get to know you as a student and a person can tell you about scholarships, research opportunities, and the like.

So, just as soon as you identify a professor who can be of help to you with your aspirations, make sure to try to make contact. Because professors are people, some may not respond to your efforts. But unless they specifically tell you to leave them alone, keep trying. On the day of your first contact, they may just be having a bad day.

Now remember what I've told you; your letters of recommendation are going to be about as important to you as your transcript and your degree, assuming your transcript is not terrible, and your degree is from an excellent university such as Purdue. The way I have described cultivating letters of recommendation is surely not the only way, but it is a way and I know it helps me a great deal when a student asks me for a letter of recommendation if we -- the student and I -- have cultivated that letter over a period of years.

Oh, and by the way, if you are going to ask a professor for a letter of recommendation, I consider it to be rude if a person does not give me at least two weeks of lead time to write the letter. If you come cruising into a professor's office two days before the letter is due, they may look at you as though you are wacky, or, they may just write it and give you a lousy letter. Remember, professors are busy people and they write lots of letters of recommendation, so give them a break so they have time to write a letter they have time to think about. And if you can give a professor more than two weeks during the spring semester, that is even better, because we write many letters just before seniors graduate.

Not incidentally, there is another factor that can really help a letter of recommendation; that is if you have worked on research with a professor. Doing so can be one of the most practical things you can do. Let's look at how you might cultivate research opportunities with professors.

CULTIVATING RESEARCH OPPORTUNITIES

At a research university like Purdue, every professor is going to be doing research, and probably have a lifelong intellectual and research project. Such is an expectation of one's employment at the university. Now I know there are students who think some professors see undergraduate education as a necessary evil to allow the professors to conduct their research. There may be a few professors like that around the university, but, so far, I haven't met one at Purdue. Most professors see their research as a means to do a better job of teaching at the graduate and undergraduate levels. But most professors do care about their research for other reasons -- mainly because they are trying to answer very difficult questions about very important things.

Now just imagine if you could have the opportunity to work with a professor or a research team that cares a great deal about an important research investigation. You are probably saying to yourself, "Oh, I'd never have such an opportunity; I'm just an undergraduate." You'd be surprised. If you are an excellent student who has a bent for research, there is a pretty good chance you could become involved in an advanced research project where you don't learn by taking tests, but you learn by doing. So, for those of you who have the abilities and who care about such things, how do you facilitate getting involved in research?

Like most things associated with students and professors, you are probably going to be drawn to the professor in a class. Most professors talk a little or a lot about their research in classes so you will have a basic idea of what their intellectual project is. Let's say you find a professor's research fascinating. What should you do? The obvious thing is to let them know. How do you do that? A good thing is to write them a note and explain what there is about their work that you find interesting. If you are not exactly sure what the researcher is doing, most departments on the campus keep a file of professional resumes in the main office. By the way, we don't call resumes "resumes" in Academia. We call resumes *curriculum vitae* or "CVs" for short. So what you could do if you think you are interested in a professor's research is to look at his or her CV and find the most recent publications. Read a couple of these and you will find out if you are interested in the same thing the professor is researching, although, unless you are an advanced student, you may not understand all of the details of the article.

Once you have gotten a general idea about the professor's research, if you still find it interesting, you will want to make contact. Make an appointment and let the professor know that you would like to talk with them about their research and if there is anything you might do to help. If there is no chance of you getting involved in the research, the professor will probably let you know right away. Chances are, if you have a chance of getting involved it will probably be at a very fundamental level. To put that another way, you might end up cleaning up a lab, or running errands, or doing some fairly inglorious tasks. That might seem as though it is beneath you, but you have to consider what is as stake. Think about it.

First, most researchers are going to want to check you out to see if you are really serious about research and whether you have basic strengths of character and skills to be involved in research. Second, you have to remember that, in helping with research, you are going to be taking up some of the researchers' time. You may be helping them, but they are going to have to teach you things and a lot of those things may be at a much higher level of inquiry than a person is going to get in a regular classroom/lab situation. In effect, if someone takes you on as a research helper, you may be getting the most sophisticated level of your education for free. Third, remember that most research is funded by the government, or foundations, or other sources. If you "pan out" as a good research helper, you may find that, at some point in time, the researcher may be able to offer you some funding to act in some research assistant capacity. Fourth, if you do further your education in a research capacity and do a good job as a research assistant, imagine how much more substantive a letter of recommendation a professor is able to write. The researcher will get to know you under all kinds of conditions and can address the "real you" in letters on your behalf. In a world where many letters of recommendation scarcely say anything about a person, a really substantive letter can be every bit as important as your transcript.

As I say, getting involved in research as an undergraduate is not for everybody. But for those people who have the abilities and commitment, it may be the one most important things you can do during your undergraduate years. And when you are at an excellent research university such as Purdue, you are going to want to use the people and facilities of the university to maximize what you get out of your education.

DUMB THINGS TO DO WITH REGARD TO PROFESSORS

Just as professors can do an enormous number of things to help you, they can fail to help you or hurt you if you do certain really dumb things that some students do. Some of the things are obvious; some more subtle.

CHEATING

The two most egregious things a student can do with regard to a professor is to cheat or plagiarize. We shouldn't even have to talk about cheating -- and for most of you it is not an issue. But in the last two decades I have seen a growing sense among students that nearly everybody cheats at one time or another. Well, of course, everybody doesn't. You have got to understand that and the fact that there are professors who would stop at nothing to get you thrown out of the university and make sure you don't get into another one for what to you and some other students may seem to be the slightest transgression. Because there are no slight transgressions when it comes to cheating. We shouldn't even have to mention cheating, but we know it happens. Trust me, though; there are hundreds of reasons not to cheat and I cannot think of a single good reason to recommend cheating. Not one. Enough said.

PLAGIARISM

There is a certain kind of cheating that particularly makes professors mad. It is called plagiarism. It simply means stealing a quote without giving the proper attribution to the source from which it was taken. Believe it or not, some college students don't know how serious plagiarism is. For example, you might think that if you copy a paragraph out of a book and put it in a term paper that is no big deal. Not so. Professors are so steeped in the idea that it is wrong to steal an idea or quote that most will think it a horrible academic transgression. Over the years, I have met many students who honestly did not understand that plagiarism was wrong. Imagine their surprise when they are caught for taking a quote or idea without attribution and discover that the professor wants to drum them out of the university. What makes plagiarism particularly dumb is that if a student uses a quote with the appropriate citation, a professor who is reading the work will like that. So it is just the matter of the proper citation.

Most professors do not care if a student uses a lot of quotes in their written work. If someone does care, he or she will probably tell you. So don't ever be so stupid as to put a quote in a paper without citing the quote. Such a thing can result in an academic misconduct charge. And that can, in provable instances, result in a student being dismissed from the university. I know that there are many sources from which a person can take quotes. And I know the temptation is sometimes great to copy a whole paper from a single or a few sources. And I know that it is possible that the professor may not have read the sources and thus not know that plagiarism has taken place. But please don't ever make yourself vulnerable to a plagiarism charge. Over the years, those of us who read lots of papers have a pretty good idea when we are reading something a student has not written. And since a proper citation is so easy to provide, there is no point in doing anything that can result in academic troubles or potential blemishes on your reputation. Such things can plague you for a lifetime.

ADDRESSING PROFESSORS IN A TOO FAMILIAR WAY

One of the things that professors sometimes fail to do is to tell students what to call us. Some professors prefer to be called "Professor." Since most of us have a doctoral education, some professors prefer to be called "Dr." Some people are satisfied to be called "Mr." or "Mrs." or "Ms." or "Miss." Many of your instructors will be graduate students who do not have their doctorates yet so the Mr., Ms., etc. route is the best. Some of your professors will tell you it is okay to call them by their first name, although that is rare. All in all, it can be pretty awkward trying to figure out what to call your instructors. Thus, many students may communicate in a very cryptic way in which they don't call the instructor anything, which makes for mighty impersonal interactions.

There are three pretty good ways of figuring out what to call your professors. First, ask them what they want to be called? Second, check out your syllabus and see if the professor has called him- or herself "Professor" or "Dr." or has a "Ph.D.," "Ed.D." or the like after their name. If they have a degree designation after their name, they probably expect you to use that designation. So, for example, if the professor has a Ph.D. after his or her name, they probably want to be called "Dr. So and So." Third, when in doubt, call the person "Professor."

Most professors are not stuffy about what you call them. I would not have even brought this subject up except that some students, not having been told what to call a particular professor, may make the mistake of using the person's first name or calling them "Doc" or the like. In most cases, professors won't take much offense. However, you may be talking to the one person in the university who doesn't like that degree of familiarity in their interaction with students. Better safe than sorry.

And by the way, you want to be careful in addressing administrators as well. For example, if you happen to be at the Dean of Students Office and be talking with the Dean or one of his Assistant or Associate Deans, out of respect, call the person "Dean" and, if they want you to call them something else, they will let you know.

REALLY DUMB QUESTIONS TO ASK PROFESSORS

This may just be a personal prejudice of mine because I expect college students to be bright folks who have enough sense to consider what they are communicating to others. And when students ask me these dumb questions, I don't get mad. But I sure know some professors who do get angry. What are the offending questions? Let's take the first one. Pretend you are going to have to miss class for some reason. You want to let the professor know that you will be gone and are curious about what material you will miss in class. And so you ask, "I'm going to be unable to attend class on Friday; is anything going to be happening?" The other side of this dumb question occurs when you have missed class and want to know what has happened in class, and you say, "I was gone on Friday, did anything happen in class?"

Your intentions might have been good in asking such questions, but I have heard professors explode at students when they ask them. When you ask the "did anything happen?" question, what do you expect the professor to say, "oh no, we just slept like we always do." Or, "oh no, I gave my usual dull, lackluster, substantiveless, boring lecture." Obviously such questions imply that nothing ever happens in class. Well, maybe that is the case. But even if that is the case, don't ask the question.

Now, if you really want to ask the questions right, there is a way to do it. One way is: "I've looked at the syllabus and see what we will be covering on Friday. I can't make it to class;

is there anything else I should be covering in my studying?" Another way: "I missed class last Friday and saw by the syllabus what we had covered in class; was there anything else that came up in class that I should be thinking about in my studying?" When you do this, rather than insulting the professor by implying that nothing ever happens, you have acknowledged that, often times, more happens than is even in the syllabus and you'd like to be sure that you don't miss any of the material. This can make for a much better relationship with the professor than if one takes the dumb and dumber route.

GRADE-CRAZED STUDENTS

There is no question that earning grades in a university setting has its importance, albeit grades are not necessarily the most important thing there is to obtaining an education. Think about it: would you rather learn a huge amount in a class in which your earn an "B" or waste your time, learning nothing in a class in which you learn an "A." That is a tough one, huh? For my part, because undergraduate transcripts usually have a "shelf-life" of about three or four years, I'd take the "B" and the richer learning environment. No matter, though; that is not going to be my point. The real point is that grades are often arbitrary means to much more important ends. What ends, you say? Education. Knowledge. Career. Wisdom. And many other important values. So when grades come to be ends in themselves, they become rather dysfunctional. Let us start with a couple of questions.

The first question: How many of you would rather know the questions that are on a test so you can look up the answers, rather than know how to answer the questions because you have studied for the test and understand its underlying principles? If you answer that you want to know the underlying principles through your study, then you have maintained your perspective. The point of education is learning basic principles, facts, and how to think critically. Grades, on the other hand are simply means to induce you to study and to asses how well you have studied. Now, if in the example above, you chose having the answers to the questions so you can obtain a good grade quite apart from understanding the underlying principles, you have made the grade an end in itself. The problem, of course, is that when you get out in the "real world" you may have a history of good grades but lack good sense and a good education. Let me tell you a story that might illustrate what I am talking about.

I taught at the University of Kansas for fifteen years, during which time I was on the medical school admissions committee. Needless to say people who want to become physicians have to have good grades. But shortly after assuming my role on the committee, I began to notice a very strange phenomenon. Some students who had come to the university with a wonderful passion for medicine and a profound commitment for healing began to forget those feelings and became "grade-crazed." For some, the grade lost its role as a facilitant to learning what doctors need to know and the grade became an end in itself. It was sad to watch the people all but jettison their passion for medicine and replace it with a passion for grades. Perhaps a more specific story will illustrate.

One day I was walking across the campus with another professor who was also on the medical school admissions committee when we were approached by one of his students who

17

seemed to be in an agitated state. The student approached the professor holding a test paper upon which the student had earned a "B" -- missing an "A" by a couple of points. It was clear from the outset that the student wanted those points and wanted that "A." The professor, a man known for his fairness, examined the student's paper to make sure a mistake had not been made in grading. Indeed, it had not; thus, there was nothing the professor could do to raise the grade. Despite this, the student kept, first pleading, then arguing with the professor for the points. Although the professor was not one to show his anger, I could tell he was becoming quite miffed at the student. And the student's performance went on way beyond the level of appropriateness. Quite simply, the student had become grade-crazed. The grade, rather than what it facilitated, had become an end in itself. I'll always remember how pathetic the situation was. For one thing, the student intended to use this professor as a referee to gain admission into medical school. Moreover, the professor was on the admissions committee. You can imagine what the professor thought about the student's maturity and impulse control by the time this little scene played itself out.

So what had the grade-crazed student done? He had lost what, until then, had been a good letter of recommendation. He had prejudiced his admissions opportunity both with the other professor and me. And he had done it for two points on a test.

Please don't get the point of this story wrong. If, in the university, you are not treated fairly in matters of grading and assessment of your performance, it is your right -- actually your responsibility -- to argue your position. Universities are forums of institutionalized doubt and, moreover, professors certainly do make mistakes. Most professors will respect a cogent argument. But don't prejudice your dreams by taking leave of your senses. In the long run, that two points would have meant nothing in that student's life. And yet, he made it make so much more than it needed to be.

GRADES, PROFESSORS, PHONES, AND STANDARDS

One of the things that often happens to students is their wish to check a grade with a professor or the professor's teaching assistant because the student finds that he or she didn't receive the grade he or she had expected. Most professors are quite willing to go over a test, term paper, or the like to verify that a mistake has not been made. Frequently, when a student asks about a grade, the student does not necessarily want to check the grade over so much as to talk the professor into a higher grade, although there are many legitimate inquiries made. Let's look at some of the factors that should and should not go into a grade check.

If you want to check a test, term paper, etc., do not expect that the professor can talk with you over the phone about the matter. Set up an appointment. We are duty-bound to maintain absolute confidentiality in matters relating to your grades. Hence, even if we know you, we are not supposed to talk with you about your grades over the phone. Most of the time, we really have no way of knowing if it is you or not. Thus, if we are talking with someone who is posing as you, we would be in breech of our guarantee of your confidentiality. So if you want to check a grade, make sure to make an appointment to come and visit and we can look things over carefully and see what happened that did not meet your expectations.

Now there are some special circumstances where grade checks are difficult. For example, let's say it is the end of the spring semester and you have left campus, gone home, and received your report card and see that something just doesn't seem right. Well, if we cannot talk about the specifics of grades over the phone, what are we going to do. Simple. Send a letter to the professor explaining your concern. Give as many specifics as you possibly can -- for example, what your other test grades were, where you were on the grading scale, and so forth. If you have these documents, Xerox them and send them along in the letter. Most professors stay in town during the summer months to research and write and will respond to your letter with the information you need. Just remember to include your name, address, phone number, and the dates you will be at those locations so the professor can contact you.

What happens if the professor leaves town right after finals? Suggest that the letter be forwarded and be patient. In some cases, you may not be able to do a grade check until the first week of the fall semester if the professor is out of the country over the summer. If that is the case try not to worry as professors are required to keep documentation of grades for a lengthy period of time so they can have access to your records and accord you the respect you deserve.

One very important thing concerning checking a grade with a professor is to remember how most of us regard grades. Any university that wants to award you a degree worth the paper upon which it is written has got to maintain high standards. Think about it: to compromise our standards for anybody is to compromise them for everybody. Purdue is an excellent university with very high standards and a lot of difficult classes. For the students who want to work hard and make the best of the university, this is very good because a Purdue degree means something. Imagine if we were to slack on our standards in even one of our colleges. If that happened and you go out with a Purdue degree to compete for career opportunities with persons from other excellent universities, people will know. And you will be at a competitive disadvantage. So when you think about those really hard professors, don't disparage them because they are challenging. Be grateful that they are not letting you waste your money on a second-rate education.

I always remember the issue of standards when I write a letter of recommendation. If people think that I am an easy mark to write glowing things about any student who comes along, then a good letter from me doesn't mean anything. And grades are the same way. If every student in every class I teach could earn a high "A," I'd be the happiest guy in the world. But it doesn't happen that way. However, some students give one the impression that they paid their money, so they want their "A." Sorry; we have to maintain standards. I can't tell you how many times students have said to me things such as, "I came to class every day," "I really knew all the material," "I studied all the time," "I really liked the class," "I really liked you," "I learned more out of this class than any of my others," and so forth. Those are really nice things to hear. But the only way any Purdue professor is going to assess you for a grade is on the basis of your performance.

Well, you've probably heard about all you want to (or more than you wanted to) about professors. But let me leave you with one more bit of information about professors that students hardly ever understand and that -- once your understand it -- can have practical ramifications for you. To wit, this whole business of Assistant Professors, Associate Professors, and Full Professors can really be confusing for students. It basically has to do with "pecking order," or as we call it in sociology, "status hierarchy." Let's look at it for a minute and see what it can mean for you.

THE STATUS HIERARCHY OF PROFESSORS

You are going to have a bunch of different levels of instructors while you are at the university. Probably you will have some graduate students teaching you. Almost always, these people will have a masters degree or the equivalent. They are due the same respect as any instructor. In other words, Purdue does not let people teach classes unless those people are seen to have the full weight of the university behind them and are deemed worthy of your respect. Because someone is a graduate student, you should not assume that they will be "less" of a teacher than someone with higher credentials. Some graduate student instructors are extraordinary teachers and could well be some of the best instructors you will have in the university. Some have wide experience and most work very hard to give you a good educational experience. Of course, some graduate student teachers may be getting some of their first teaching experiences and learning the kinds of things that will help them to improve. If that is the case, you can make their jobs a lot easier by letting them know when they are doing a good job and giving them constructive criticism if they ask for it.

The next level up from graduate student instructors are some Visiting Professors. These people are usually at the university for a year or two. Typically, they do not have tenure at Purdue and are not on a so-called tenure track, which we will talk about in a subsequent paragraph. You can't always assume this about Visiting Professors though. Some Visiting Professors are very distinguished and usually famous people who are taking leave from another university to take advantage of some of the special qualities of Purdue.

Next in the academic pecking order are Assistant Professors. Typically, Assistant Professors are people who have their Ph.D. or the equivalent and are on what is called a tenure track appointment at the university. What this means is that they are working on their teaching, research, and service expectations at the university so they can earn tenure at the university. When a person earns tenure, that usually means that they have proven themselves to be a very good teacher, scholar, and provider of service to the university and community, and that they have a fairly high degree of job security. When a person earns tenure, they are usually promoted from the position of Assistant Professor to the position of Associate Professor. Typically, to be promoted a person has to have made substantial contributions to their particular discipline (sociology, for example) and have established a national and oftentimes international reputation as a scholar.

The next step up the status hierarchy in the academic world from Associate Professor is promotion to Full Professor. Full Professors usually have extensive experience in their discipline and are widely known in their discipline for their contributions both nationally and internationally. Many Full Professors have edited some of the most prestigious journals in their discipline. Most Full Professors have administrative experience, such as having been the Chairperson or Graduate Studies Director in their department and have probably, at one time or another served on most of their department's and the university's most important and powerful committees. If you are trying to study aspects of the history of the university or trying to understand the dynamics that make a university run, most Full Professors are pretty good sources of the history and the culture of the university.

About the highest a person can move through the professorial hierarchy of the university as a professor is to be named a Distinguished Professor. Put bluntly, Distinguished Professors are famous. Their position typically is called an endowed Chair in a particular discipline. So, for example, you might hear that one of your professors has an endowed chair in electrical engineering. This usually means that they are paid from a special fund that has been set up for people who make extraordinary contributions in their area. Such an endowment may come from a foundation, a business in the private sector, or special funds that have been set aside by university benefactors.

When we talk about the pecking order of instructors in the university, it is pretty difficult to make generalizations that are going to be relevant to you. There are many great teachers at all levels. Everybody will be doing some kind of research, and, at a place such as Purdue, the research will not be trivial. So what is relevant to you?

First, it is probably safe to say that, if you are seeking a letter of recommendation, a greater number of people in your discipline are likely to know professors from the Associate and Full Professor ranks than from the ranks of Assistant Professors, although many Assistant Professors have a lot of contacts. Second, a letter of recommendation from a graduate student instructor probably won't carry the weight of a letter from the ranks of professors. Third, letters of recommendation from Full and especially Distinguished Professors will probably have quite a bit of clout, not only because these scholars are more established in the discipline, but because they always have a very wide range of contacts. Of course, it may be difficult to obtain a letter of recommendation from the more established persons in a discipline because they will be very reluctant to put their reputations on the line unless you are an extraordinary student.

I've just touched the tip of the iceberg as far as what students ought to know about professors in the university. So why don't you help me make this section of the toolbox better. It is easy to do this by writing down questions you are wondering about and I'll contact you if I know the answer and include the topic you brought up in the next revision of the toolbox. For now, though, let's get on with some other practical factors that can help you make the best of the university.

JOB EXPERIENCE AND VOLUNTEERISM

When it comes to obtaining a job in the "real world," I'm sure most of you have heard the cliché about how you can't have the job unless you have the experience and you can't have the experience unless you've had the job. It is a dilemma. But college provides all kinds of opportunities to get experience that is regarded highly when you do step out into the occupational world. Probably the best experience you can have is to work while you are going to college. Given the expense of college and the return of many so-called nontraditional students to the university, we know that many students do work while they are going to college. One of the things that students often don't consider is whether they might be able to find a job while going to college that will provide skills for their chosen profession when they get out of college. Clearly the easiest jobs to come by while in college are in service industries such as the fast-food industry. Those are good honest jobs that give a person experience in many of the skills and expectations that will be part of any job a person will later seek. However, one of the things I have noticed about students is that they don't know what to do to find a job in an area that will be related to the subject they are studying. Let's think about it.

Say you want to be a pharmacist. Obviously it makes a lot more sense for you to work in a pharmacy than at a McDonald's. Of course, it may be a good deal more difficult to find a job in a pharmacy than in a McDonald's, but if you take the path that is more difficult to travel and persevere, eventually you are going to find something suited to your long-term goals. When this happens, you are going to be getting a free education, good experience, and cultivating a good source of letters of recommendation. Obtaining a job relevant to your long-term goals may just be a lot more hassle than getting a run-of-the-mill job. But let's think about how you can go after a job that is special to your aspirations..

Say you've decided you want to be a veterinarian. The first thing I'd do is see if there are any jobs in the School of Veterinary Medicine. And, if that meant cleaning out cages, that is as good as any place to start. If the School does not have anything for you, make sure to put in an application and check back periodically to see if anything has opened up. Persistence usually pays off.

Of course, there are probably a lot of opportunities in the community working with animals. How do you go about scouting those out? First, I'd write a one or two page letter about why you want to be a veterinarian. Second, I'd have somebody you trust -- maybe a professor -- read it to see if it makes sense. Third, I'd look in the phone book for every veterinarian, pet store, grooming emporium for animals, animal shelter, or anything else that has to do with animals. Fourth, I'd Xerox enough copies of your letter to send or deliver to every place on your list. At the places that look the most appealing, I'd make an appointment to deliver the letter in person and see if there might be somebody there who you could talk with about your job possibilities. Fifth, I'd mail the rest of the letters off with a return phone number and address. Sixth, I'd put an add in the local and university newspapers explaining that you would like to find a job working with animals. Seventh, I would follow up the letters you sent out with a call. All this may take a lot more work than answering a want-add to flip-burgers (and I definitely don't say that with any scorn or sarcasm), but I'll lay you odds you'll find a job working with animals. And because pathways do tend to become highways, you may find yourself in the ideal work position for what it is you will be studying in the university.

Your work life can be a wellspring of experience, contacts, letters of recommendation, etc., but there is another thing that can be a great source of experience -- volunteering your help to your community. Let's get specific again. You have decided you want to be a clinical psychologist. You're only a first year student and you are saying to yourself, "Where am I going to get any experience?" I know what I'd do. There is an excellent crisis center in this town that deals with all manner of crises. The center does very good training sessions to prepare student/volunteers to deal with all manner of crises. Once you've been trained, you will get a wealth of experience. Again, you will have made contacts. You may get a line on a job. And you will come to know people who can write letters of recommendation for you. You've established another resume line. And, most important, you have helped some people who are going through rough times.

We're going to talk about resumes later. But, for now, think about this. Almost everything I have discussed so far has been something that can prove useful as an entry on your resume. And virtually everything I have discussed is something you can do your first year in college. I can't believe it when I run into seniors who still haven't gotten around to making their resumes and are ready to go out on the job market. As I said, we'll discuss resumes later. But keep in mind; that is going to be one of the first pieces of paper people in the job world see before they ever see you. And that resume is going to be important. So even if you are a first day freshman and all you can put on the resume is your name address and phone number, start that resume now, revise it every month, and if you find that you don't have anything to put on it, think about what that is going to mean in terms of the practical concerns you are going to face after graduation.

PROFESSIONAL ASSOCIATIONS AND CLUBS

In the university and in the broader world there are clubs and professional associations for just about any interest a person can have. I won't go on about the clubs and honoraries around the university. For example, though, in my department, there is a sociology club and an honorary. People get together to have fun, talk sociology, eat, discuss job prospects, and a plethora of other things. If you go to the club, you'll find out about the honorary and what the qualifications are for it. Obviously, if you are thinking about doing something such as going to graduate school in sociology, having been in the honorary can help you get into the university of your choice.

Clubs and honoraries are good, but the thing that impresses me the most as having very deep practical value is belonging to national associations associated with what you are pursuing as a course of study. And these associations are usually really a good deal for students professionally and financially. Let me give you an example. The major association for sociologists in the United States is The American Sociological Association. If one is a professor, it costs quite a bit to belong to the association, but one does get newsletters, journals, and access to all kinds of good and important information and literature. For a fraction of what it costs a professor to join, a student essentially gets all the same material, information about meetings, job prospects, and the like. Just think about this for a minute.

Whether you want to be a sociologist or an engineer or a mathematician or a physicist or go into food science, etc., there is going to be at least one and probably more national and

23

regional professional associations that are going to give students a big break on membership fees. So why would you want to join?

First, you are going to be reading the same material your professors are reading so you can carry on intelligent conversations with them about the profession. Second, you are going to have a lot better idea about what is going to be happening in the profession in the forthcoming years. Remember when I told you earlier that a person almost needs to be a fortuneteller in today's rapidly changing technological environment and job market to tread a sensible path. Well, most professional associations can help you be that fortuneteller with their forecasts about the future prospects in the profession. Third, most of the professional associations have competitions such as paper-writing or problem-solving competitions for their student members. Frequently, these are accompanied by cash prizes or scholarships. Fourth, you might find that you want to attend a regional or national meeting of one of these associations where you can really find out what the profession is about and meet some other students with whom you can communicate. Fifth, membership in these professional associations looks very nice on a resume. And, in most cases, you can enjoy the benefits of membership for just a few bucks.

LANGUAGES

Over the years of my teaching, I've heard more than a few students complain about the language requirements of a good liberal arts education. Some people can't seem to figure out why language studies are included in collegiate education since so many people in the world speak English and we can get translations for just about anything we want to read and translators when we travel. I've heard smart students say the language requirement is just a carryover from the Renaissance when people were supposed to be multi-lingual to be educated. And I can't tell you how many students have confided in me that they took four semesters of a language and can't remember much more than a phrase or two.

My view is that, if we didn't need language studies, we wouldn't have them except for language majors. But your language requirement may be one of the most important things you will get to do at Purdue. First of all, we do need language studies. Just because many of our international neighbors learn English, it doesn't mean that everybody on the planet wants to or will learn English, or, will speak it even if they know it. Second, we essentially live in a bilingual country if you consider just all the people who speak Spanish as a first language, not to mention all the other beautiful languages people speak in this cultural melting-pot we call The United States. Third, if you are going to be any kind of professional, businessperson, scientist, agronomist, etc. in this world, you are going to be about 100 times more effective if you are bilingual. Fourth, you are going to learn your own language a lot better if you learn to speak and write in other languages. Fifth, you definitely are going to enjoy travel a good deal more if you speak the language of the countries you visit. And I could go on for paragraphs with other reasons why languages are important. But let's not take up more space talking about all the practicalities of language study. Let's look at why language study can be fun and make your undergraduate years much more valuable.

Most of you have got to take a language. So why not make the best of it? There is probably nothing dumber you can do than study a language halfheartedly for four semesters and waste all that time and money. So get yourself a plan. Let me suggest one. Is there anywhere in the world you'd like to travel -- or you think you'd like to travel -- where the people don't speak English? Maybe you've made a friend of an international student and would like to go visit them in their homeland. Maybe there has been a place that has sounded really magical to you to which you've always wanted to go. Maybe you have other reasons. Now here's the plan.

Your freshman year, go to the office of the study abroad programs. You'll be surprised at how many amazing places Purdue is networked in with for foreign studies. Talk to a counselor in the study abroad program. Start thinking about where you might like to study if you don't already know. Set up a timetable so that you can coordinate your language studies on campus to act as a preface to your study abroad semester(s). Now look what you've gone and done. You've given yourself an inducement to actually learn a language and a chance to go somewhere long enough to use it so you won't lose it. But you've really done something a lot more important. Look at it this way.

You can probably learn as much in six months of international travel as you can in all the rest of your college experience. It is amazing what going to other cultures can teach us. That's why a well-travelled person is usually about twice as interesting as a person who has never traveled.

Now some of you are probably saying: "Oh, I can't afford to go study in another country because of the cost or because it will slow down my degree progress." My response to you is that you cannot afford not to take advantage of this opportunity. It costs much less than you might think to study abroad. Your degree, at worst, might get slowed down by a semester, but probably won't. And, if you don't take the opportunity to travel and study abroad while you are in college, you may not get the chance to do much traveling after you graduate. Moreover, you become bilingual, which is a very nice resume line indeed.

Just to get the ball rolling, go to the nearest post office and pick up a passport application and get yourself a passport. It's the best means of identification in the world. It hardly costs anything. And you can't go most places in the world without one. Let me give you another tip on travel. This one has to do with international students.

INTERNATIONAL STUDENTS

Let's pretend that you have been studying engineering for several years and, in the course of that study, have been learning Japanese. You get a chance to go study and work in Tokyo for a year. You fly to Japan, get plopped down in the middle of Tokyo, go to where you will be staying, check out the places you will study and work, and generally stay very busy for a period of time. Then life starts to take on its routines. If you are lucky, you will have made some friends by now. And, if you are really lucky, they will be the kind of friends that show you around Tokyo and other parts of Japan. But what if you are not lucky in that way. It could get pretty lonely couldn't it ? Well, you are not in Tokyo right now; you're in the relative comfort of West Lafayette. But you can be sure there are some students here from Japan and all other parts of the world and some of them might just be feeling a bit lonely. So what are you going to do about it? Are you going to try to befriend people from other cultures when there are so many of them around or are you going to miss that opportunity?

This is not an issue that just has to do with human kindness and showing that Americans are good hosts. There are some very practical ramifications to befriending international students. First of all, if you are studying a language and you befriend someone who speaks that language and is trying to learn the finer points of English, both of you get free tutoring. And, believe me, it can make a huge difference in how much you can learn. That is all well and good, but the part I like most about meeting international students/scholars is showing them around our country and helping them understand our culture. This is where things become particularly nice and promising for the future.

To put it simply, if you have exposed your country and culture to an international friend and decide you would like to travel to their country, you can practically be certain the person will muster every resource at their disposal to make your stay in their country a wonderful experience. To be at a place such as Purdue, that has people from literally every place on the globe, and not to make those international friendships is a shame. Chances are you probably will not have so many opportunities again. So, if you've a mind to, show our friends from around the world what good hosts we can be. In the long run, I'll bet you get more out of the effort than you put into it.

SERVICE TO THE UNIVERSITY

Earlier I talked about volunteerism and how that can help you and others. Let's talk now in practical terms about how you can do service on behalf of the university that benefits both the university and you. You will have hundreds of opportunities along these lines so I won't get into trying to cover the options. Let's just say you ought to render service as a good citizen of the university. What I want to talk about here is a special kind of service -- one that students don't often think about, and the kind of service that will probably pay big dividends for you. I am talking about service on college and university committees.

As you doubtless know the university has many faculty and administrative committees. Many of these committees are very productive and powerful. What students oftentimes do not know is that quite a number of the university's committees have positions for student representatives. For example, I am on The Advisory Committee For Disability Issues and we have student representatives who attend our meetings and vote.

Being on a university committee not only gives you a chance to serve the university, but it typically affords you a great deal of insight into how the university works, puts you together with important contacts on the faculty and administration, and may lead to opportunities that students usually don't have. Moreover, such service is a very nice addition to your resume.

The problem with getting on university committees is finding those that have student members. One way to start hearing about such committees is to serve on student committees. Another thing you might want to do is go to your respective college and/or to the office of the Dean of Students to inquire as to what committees have student representatives. Further, you might leave a note with the appropriate person in these offices explaining your wish to serve the university and explain the kinds of things that are most interest you. You can also find out what committees may be known to the people in the student government offices and in the offices of The Exponent.

HONORS CLASSES

One of the things many students don't know about when they first arrive at Purdue is the wonderful honors program. There are special honors classes in virtually all departments. In some cases, a student can take a regular class for honors credit. And there are an extraordinary number of very interesting activities that go along with being part of the honors program. The Honors Office in the College of Liberal Arts is in LAEB right across from the Dean's Office on the first floor. The people there are friendly and knowledgeable. If I were a student pursuing a dream of excellence, I'd look into honors as soon as I arrived at Purdue and got settled. Obviously, from a practical standpoint, graduating with honors is very special and gives you many advantages as you pursue your career choices.

THE LEARNING CENTER

There are hundreds of things I could tell you about that are dedicated to helping students reach their study and other goals around the university. There are very nice computer labs, writing labs, and all manner of practical opportunities for you. To talk about one place is not fair to all the others. But since learning is what Purdue is about, I feel that I would be remiss if I did not talk about The Learning Center. It is located in LAEB on the third floor, south wing.

For years, I have had various students come to me and tell me they don't know how to study. Frankly, when I was earlier in my career, I thought that was a bunch of bunk. I don't think that any more. I think there are students who make it all the way to college and are virtually devoid of the study skills necessary to graduate. And I do not say that with any malice to those people; indeed, I feel a lot of compassion for them. That's why I am mentioning The Learning Center. It is just what its name indicates -- a place where students can learn how to learn. It is has excellent facilities, a great staff, and operates all kinds of important workshops. Examples would be speed reading, notetaking, test taking, time management, etc.

One thing to make sure you understand about The Learning Center is that it is not just for students who may be struggling with their studies. You could be the best student on campus and still go over to The Learning Center and pick up skills that would make you a better student. Another nice thing about The Learning Center is that if you are looking for some help in an area in which they don't provide services, the staff can probably tell you where on campus you can go to get the help you need.

MAKING YOUR RESUME

I hope some of the topics I have touched upon in this segment of the <u>Toolbox</u> will be of help to you in getting along in college. I'll try to share other tips as the semester rolls along. And, as I said earlier, please don't hesitate to let me know about topics that I have not covered or topics about you would like more coverage. For now, though, let us finish this portion of the <u>Toolbox</u> by considering what you might do if you decided to make yourself a resume.

First, I want to repeat an earlier comment. You ought to make your resume as soon as you possibly can, even if you have hardly anything on it when you start. And take ten seconds just to check it out everyday to see how it might have changed and to enter the changes. Believe me, it really can be a hassle if you need a resume and have to generate it from scratch in a day or two. You always end up missing important things and it usually doesn't have that professional quality that a resume that has been nurtured has.

So, how do we get started? Obviously, you need to think about the look of the document. Usually, people use a ten or twelve point font. The ten point font will help you to get a bit more information on a page. This is important because many people at the university who are going to offer you advice on making a resume are going to try to get you to make it no longer than one page. That is all well and good if you only have one page of accomplishments by the time you graduate. The whole one page concept of resumes can really result in silly things, though. I've seen students who easily had three pages worth of notable entries try to put them on a single page. Either it was very difficult to know what they were referring to with certain entries, or you needed a microscope to read it because they had taken the font level so low.

Clearly, you are going to want a certain economy of style in creating your resume so people who are reading many of them from different people in a short time period will get the high points of your life and college career. And one of the most counterproductive things you can do is to try to "pad" a resume to make your accomplishments look greater than they have been. What I would do to avoid a too short or a too long resume would be to take the resume into your counselors every so often and let them have a look. Professors are good at giving you feedback on a resumes. The one bit of advice I'd have for you about the one page issue is: if your accomplishments don't fit on one page, tastefully put them on as many pages as it takes. I've known those rare undergraduates who needed three or four pages to list all their accomplishments. And I hope you are going to be one of them.

As for the resume's contents itself, you'll want your full name; home address; home phone number; school address; school phone number; e-mail address; and fax address, if applicable. Some people put their Social Security Number on the resume as it has become one of those more universal numbers in the last few years. Of course, you always have to consider personal security issues when you give out your social security number.

Once you have your name, address, etc., one of the things many people do is to put a brief set of phrases or a sentence about their professional or life objectives. I have mixed emotions about such statements. Sometimes they sound too grandiose. Sometimes they sound too bland. Sometimes they sound like a cliché. In other words, there are several ways to make such a statement of life or career objectives become counterproductive. If you are going to have such an objective statement, keep it simple, have a bunch of people give you a critical reading of it, and revise it until you get it right.

The next thing people frequently do on a resume is to list some of their high school accomplishments. You really have to be careful about this. Remember when I said earlier that an undergraduate resume usually only has a "shelf-life" of a few years? What I was trying to say is that we live in a world in which people are interested in what we have done lately. Putting a bunch of high school activities on your college resume is a bit like wearing your high school letter jacket around campus. So you are going to have to make some mature judgments about what kinds of high school activities you list on your college resume. Something like being a National Merit Scholar has a pretty good shelf life. Being Editor of your school's newspaper has a reasonable shelf life. Employment activity you had in high school may be as important on your college resume as if you were student body president. In any case, if you are going to put high school material on your college resume, be careful and check it out with your counselors.

A special class of resume line is military service. If you have military service, you'll have to be the best judge of where that goes. Obviously, if you are in R.O.T.C. or the like, that would go under university activities, which would come later in the resume.

The next logical thing you would want on your resume would be what your major or majors are. It is not uncommon for students to obtain a double major in college and often a very sensible thing to do. If you have not chosen a major yet, on the early drafts of your resume, you might just put majors and minors under consideration. If you have already chosen a major and have a G.P.A. in that major, put the G.P.A. by the major and any minor in which you have accrued credit hours. If you have established your overall G.P.A., you usually put that above your major and list the number of hours you have earned in college to that point.

Next on your resume, you are going to want to start listing your academic awards and activities. In the award area, scholarships are very nice resume lines and have a long shelf-life. If you have won any academic awards or been elected to an honorary society, those would also go under awards.

In terms of academic activities, that would include material such as if you are in the Honors Program, whether you have taken any special classes that average students don't typically take, whether you have been involved in a study abroad program, and, most important, if you are involved in research activities. Eventually the study abroad program will probably come under the heading of your language skills. And, if you continue to be a research assistant, that probably will become a category of its own. With the research, you might want to put a sentence about what it is you are researching and the professor(s) with whom you are working.

Although the importance and extent of your language skills is up to you, I'd surely include the number of semesters or years you have in a language or languages. Remember, too, that you may know some other languages. If you can program computers in any languages, those ought to go on the resume. If you can sign in a language such as American Sign Language, that is very important. Indeed, it would be nice if more students would take part of their college time to learn ASL.

Although, technically, they are not languages, you ought to have a section on your resume indicating what kind of software you are proficient with. Some people indicate the degree of their expertise in a particular program. That is oftentimes a pretty subjective judgment, so, unless you are under consideration for a position that requires a specific level of expertise, you can probably just list the programs.

Now that you've listed most of your academic activities, it would be a good time to list your university activities. What you've got to decide is which of these activities fall under the category of service activities and which are mainly social activities. If you are on the student council or serve on one of the university committees I mentioned earlier, or volunteer on one of the university's philanthropic or service committees, those would be more service in nature. If you belong to a fraternity or sorority, or a social club, they are going to be social activities. And if you belong to a religious fellowship or the like, that is going to fall under another category. On early drafts of the resume, I'd put the activities that are close together in purpose close together on the resume under activities. As you approach your senior year, if you have been making the best of Purdue, you'll probably find that you want to break the activities out into subcategories.

If you engage in some volunteer experience in the university or the community that does not fall under any of the aforementioned activities, I'd make a heading for volunteer and/or community service. For example, working for the crisis center is not technically a university activity.

Now we are getting to the point in the resume that is very important -- your work and professional activities and the people who will act as referees in your letters of recommendation. I don't place these toward the end of the resume because they are unimportant. And you may want to put them somewhere earlier in the document. One thing you can be reasonably sure a reader of your recommendation is going to look for is your work history, who your referees are, and, to a lesser extent, if you have any professional affiliations such as the professional associations I discussed earlier in the text. You can give such associations a special section on the resume where it seems to make the most sense to you. As you get more experience and have more professional affiliations, you might want to move the professional associations up earlier in the resume and give the things under it a heading such as "Professional Activities."

As you decide what you want to do about your life in employment, the work history should go first. The first question here is how far back do you want to go? Do you want to list that paper route you had in ninth grade? It does demonstrate that you had initiative even as a kid. When you start listing your work history is really a judgment call that is up to you. And it is another judgment call on how much you say about what you did. Typically, it makes sense to say where and when you worked, your main duties, and, if there is a supervisor with whom you worked still working there, you might want to include that person's name and phone number. If you are going to do that, make sure to let the person know you are going to do it. By the way, for those of you who have worked in circumstances such as the family farm, you might want to list a few more activities than you would in other employment situations.

The second question you might consider regarding work history is do you list the jobs starting in chronological order, or do you list the most recent job first? Again, that is a judgment call. What I would do is try it both ways and see what makes the most sense to you and to other people to whom you show the resume.

The third question you are going to want to ask yourself is if there is any particular skill you learned in any job that you might want to highlight. You could do that by underlining it in the reference or bold-facing it. There are all kinds of things people do with their work experience on resumes, but if you cover what we have above, you'll be in pretty good work history shape.

The next thing you need to do with the resume is decide where you want to put the referees who are going to be willing to write a letter of recommendation, fill out a recommendation form, or give you a verbal reference. Laboring under the assumption that this will definitely be one of the things a reader of your resume will examine, you ought to put the list of your referees where it makes the most sense to you. If most of the referees have to do with your work history, list them close to your work history. If most have to do with your academic life, you may want to list them earlier. If they are a mixture, I'd probably put them towards the end. Make absolutely sure these people know you are going to list them. Call them, visit them, drop them a line. And if it has been a while since you have seen them, give them any written information you can to help them in their recommendation.

Now, is there anything else we should be thinking about to demonstrate what kind of a person you are. One thing that typically makes a person more interesting is if that person has traveled internationally. Every place you have been has been exposure to another culture and to that end, is reflected in you being a more educated person than people who never see the world. And, of course, if your travel has been associated with work, study abroad, military duty, etc., it makes that travel more notable.

Finally, most of you have hobbies, sports, leisure activities, etc. that you like. Although these factors may say a little or a lot about you, they do show you have a life and may shed some kind of light on what kind of life it is. The important thing with your resume is, in relating to the leisure activities, don't ever be frivolous. I have actually seen resumes that are supposed to be serious that had things such as "girl-watching," or "beer-drinking" listed under hobbies. I had little doubt that these were serious activities for the student, but . . . you know; very strange

There are many books dedicated to, or which have sections dedicated to, making resumes. You, doubtless, can pick up some tips in those that I haven't put in these few pages. And you are going to have plenty of time to earn those lines and a lot of fun and work doing it. One thing I want to repeat for the third time though, is start your resume today. Review it. Have others review it. And contemplate it. If your resume doesn't have anything on it but a 4.0 G.P.A., then you are not getting yourself ready for a career.

There is another reason I think people should have their resumes in good shape. It has to do with synergy. And what I mean is that a good resume often leads to a better resume. Let me give you an example. We know that many scholarships only require a small amount of groundwork to be done for a student to apply. And usually, the only groundwork that is any hassle has to do with putting together the activities necessary to have a resume and having one ready. Like so many things in our world, we get so busy that, even if we heard about a scholarship that was perfect for us, we might not have or take the time to create the resume therefore putting us out of the running as a candidate. And like so many things in our world, the speed with which a person responds is almost as important as the substance of the response. In terms of opportunities that happen in a university, a resume (preferably a good one) is almost invariably the key to the opportunity. So it makes good sense to have your act together -- have your resume made and updated.

Insofar as I raised the issue of scholarships, you should know that many of them go unclaimed. So if you want some financial help, I'd pay a lot of attention to the offices on this campus that can tell you about scholarships. Over the years, there have been scores of students who didn't think they could obtain a particular scholarship or just didn't feel like they had time to apply who I have nudged into applying. And, much to their astonishment, many of those students have gotten a scholarship. One more thing about scholarships: if you have one on your resume, you can be sure it is going to be a lot easier to obtain another. Indeed, nothing succeeds like success.

CONCLUDING REMARKS

I sincerely hope that the tips I have passed along to you in the last 25 pages will help you to make the best of your educational experiences at Purdue. If you read the material and act on it and just one nice thing happens to each of you, I'd be a happy guy. Let me know of your experiences of learning to get along in college. I am sure I can use your stories to help other students that follow you, that I can avoid giving others any bad advice I might have given you, and that we can find all kinds of subjects that I did not address that should be addressed to those who follow you.

Finally, remember never to lose sight of the fact that there are hundreds of people who work here at Purdue who would love nothing more than to help you help yourself make your dreams come true. I hope you have more tools now to help you in that endeavor.

THE NEXT SECTION

The following section of the Toolbox really does have to do with tools. In this case, I'm talking about the kinds of things you need such as dictionaries, manuals of style, biographical dictionaries, dictionaries of foreign phrases, etc. Clay Bartel put this together for you, and it is about as good a list of its kind as you will see anywhere.

Essential Tools to Navigate College

By Clay Bartel

The following list is made up of materials and suggestions known to be of help to anyone, especially college students. In college each student chooses a course of study that will probably start him or her on the path to their future. Deciding what path to take is your job, but here are some tools that will make academic life easier and more fulfilling. To do the best you can is all this University asks of you. These tools will make your "best" full of much more information. Please take advantage of these hints and I'm sure you will be happy that you did.

1. **A daily planner**. One of the most essential tools a student can have is good time management! A daily planner is a good way to organize your days and create a schedule to effectively accomplish all the tasks you need to do in one day. Even social schedules can be organized. A devoted student will stick to the schedule they have laid out for themselves and accomplish the things that need to be done and still have time to spare in one day. This can definitely relieve a lot of the stresses of being a student, and make it more **fun.** The "MortarBoard" is a daily planner that Purdue provides at all bookstores for a couple of bucks. This planner has a schedule of University events listed each day. For freshman this is a good purchase, it will help you get aquatinted with the schedule of the year, and you won't miss out on any *planned* fun.

2. **A good College Dictionary**. No one knows everything, and only the ignorant and stubborn are unwilling to admit it. Get a dictionary if you don't already have one! Webster sells hardbacks for $22.00 and paperbacks for $6.00 in any bookstore.

3. **A Thesaurus.** These books can help and accompany a dictionary to further explain meaning, and <u>expand your vocabulary</u>. Usually these can come in a set with a dictionary; it will be cheaper to buy them together if you don't already have one. A good thesaurus will have antonyms as well as synonyms, Webster's New World, 1998 is a good edition. Hardback $18.95 or paperback for $8.95

4. **A writing style manual.** These next two entries are two of the most important books to own to help write essays, term papers and research reports. There are many styles used in documenting your work, and it is different in every field of study. These books give the rules and a guideline of documenting work, even if it is just a bibliography, there is a right way to do it. There are three major book you can choose from, the best is this: <u>The Easy Writer: a pocket guide</u> by Andrea Lunsford and Robert Connors. St. Martins Press. NY. 1997 ($9.00). The <u>MLA Handbook</u> 4th edition by Joe Gibaldi. NY. 1998, ($14.95) is the most standard manual on this campus (The <u>Easy Writer</u> has the MLA format quick reference guide in the back). The next most popular style is the <u>Chicago Manual of style</u> 14th edition U. Chicago Press ($16.95)

5. **<u>Elements of Style</u> by Strunk & White.** ($5.95) This book is essential for every student! It is short and easy to read, but very important. Just like the previous style manuals, this book will help you express ideas in the correct form and manner to be understood. To be understood in this world we have to communicate clearly. This book is a great handbook and guide to clarifying your thoughts to express them as efficiently as possible. This book is **not about** writing your papers for a grade in **school**, but about being able to communicate. Read it, hang on to it!

6. **Familiar Quotations by John Bartlett**. ($47.50) This book is a universal book of interesting and useful quotes by famous people. To quote famous philosophers or writers, orators or politicians, this book has them all easily accessible. For a more affordable book, the Oxford press puts out a book called The Dictionary of Famous Quotes 4th edition ($995). This book will also save you time at the library and make it easy to drop quotes right into your papers.

7. **Dictionary of foreign phrases**. . In many classes there are phrases and ideas borrowed from other cultures, sometimes they are understood in English, and sometimes not. This book explains the nature of ideas and phrases that have been adopted into the English language. (i.e.) *Weltanschauung: world view, of an individual or group*. A good one is the Oxford Foreign Words Dictionary Ed. Jennifer Speake. NY. 1997 ($30.00) paper back:($14.95)

8. **Dictionary of word origins: Etymology**. A dictionary of word origins can be helpful in writing papers also. To state the origin of the word if it is the main topic of the paper is a good starting point and professors love it! There are two really good editions out there; the first is The Dictionary of Word Origins by Jordan Almond. 1996. ($12.95) and the other is True Etymologies by Adrian Room. 1987. ($14.95)

9. **Biographical Dictionary**. This book lists authors of any published work in history. These help when a professor or classmate may mention a book or author that you are unfamiliar with, and if you need to know what that person "did" or who they were, this is the book to look in. A good copy is the Cambridge Biographical Dictionary. Ed. David Crystal. 1996 ($14.95)

10. Sociological Dictionary. For whatever your field of study is or will be there is a "lingo" that the people, especially professors will use. It is in your best interest to get a dictionary for that field. For Sociology there are two copies that Dr. Evans gives his seal of approval; The Blackwell Dictionary of Sociology by Allan G. Johnson. Oxford Press. 1995 ($18.95) this edition contains biographies of famous Sociologists, Penguin Dictionary of Sociology by Stephen Hill, Nicholas Abercrombie and Bryan S. Turner. London 1994 ($13.95) this edition contains bibliographies of famous Soc. Books.

11. A Historical Dictionary. These are a little more rare than the other previous dictionaries. Any good "general" World History book is a good substitute. To be able to look up historical events if you don't already know them is important to understanding the full scope of some classes. Especially in this class historical events have a large impact in the subject of our study, people. People create history and they react to it, it always helps to have a reference book available if the significance of an event is the topic of discussion. The Penguin Series is a good collection of historical events by century, each one costs about $16.50. A concise easy to use version is the Dictionary of American History by Thomas L. Purvis. Blackwell. 1997 ($24.95)

12. Dictionary of Philosophy. As with the dictionary of any field of study, a dictionary of Philosophy can be priceless to a Philosopher. This book is also valuable to every college student who takes a class dealing with theory, like this one. Academics in every area use a sense of Philosophy in their own subject; it permeates all areas of thought and all areas of study. A good version is The Dictionary of Philosophy by Peter A. Angeles. Harper Collins. 2nd edition. NY.1992. ($15.00)

13. A World Atlas. Geography is another subject that not everyone is prolific in, so to compensate for not knowing the exact location of every city, state, and country of the world, an Atlas is good to have on hand. These are also fun to use, and discover places that may have been overlooked before. It is also a good place to start looking for places you may want to travel to in the future. These books can be very intricate and elaborate; a quality book at a good price is Collins Concise Atlas of the World. Collins. 1996. ($16.00).

14. A spelling or "word" book. By about the age of eight, if a person does not have spelling licked, the odds are they never will. In other words if you aren't a great speller, you probably won't become one anytime soon. That's O.K. though, we all have handicaps, and how we overcome those handicaps is a sign of character and ingenuity. Using a "word book", spell check or even getting a friend to "proof read" papers is a way anyone can turn in a correctly spelled paper. Regardless of your major in college, you will have to write at least one paper, paying attention to spelling is necessary for anyone. For in-class writing it is a different story. These books are cheap and easy to find in the dictionary section of any bookstore. The two best and economical I found were, The Word Book II by Kaethe Ellis, Houghton Mifflin Co. Boston. 1983 ($7.99), Webster's Pocket Mispeller 2nd edition. Mcmillian. NY. 1997 ($4.95)

15. A Dictionary of Slang and Euphemisms. As with many of these books on this list this book is a good tool to make your life easier if you are inclined to know everything anybody is talking about and want to know different ways to say things for term papers. This reference is especially helpful if English is not your first language.

A very good copy is the <u>Oxford Dictionary of Slang and Euphemisms</u>. Oxford Press. London. 1996 ($16.95)

16. An Almanac. Almanacs are used in many ways. They are mainly a source of facts about the country for that given year. There are so many facts, too many to list. This book can be useful and fun to read. It is essential for those of you who want to be educated about the world of today. It's a good idea to go to a bookstore and look at one, then decide if you want to own one. There are three comparable editions out there now, <u>The world Almanac</u>. World Almanac Books. 1997, <u>The Wall Street Journal Almanac</u>. Ballantyne Books. 1997, and <u>The New York Times Almanac</u>. Penguin. 1997.

17. <u>The Statistical Abstract of the U.S. 1998</u>. This book is more helpful than you can imagine. I know you all think this list of books is getting quite long, but this is another reference that will save time and money. The Government publishes any statistic you want to know about the U.S. this past year. And if you use the reference section in the Library often to quote statistics in papers or reports, this is a must have book. You can get one at any government print house, or call the local chamber of commerce.

18. A Personal Computer or word processor. With the widespread use of computers these days many students have the opportunity to have a PC. These are truly nice to own, and very helpful in many ways. Computers have word processing capabilities, presentation capabilities, statistical and computational capabilities, but they also allow access to The Internet. The Internet is a huge frontier that many of you have already begun exploring. If you are not familiar with the Internet or the World Wide

Web, you should get aquatinted with a computer as soon as possible. If you are computer illiterate, ask a friend to show you or even sign up for one of the many Computer Science courses here at Purdue University. This resource may become one of the most important to the successful student. With that said about PC's, you may not be fortunate enough to have one of your own, don't worry. Purdue University is lucky enough to offer its students with many Computer labs and lots of software. Every computer here has Internet capabilities and is available to you the student. Look in your "MortarBoard" for location and times for computer labs.

19. **Internet guides**. As with any new technology it is important for people to learn how to use it to fit their own needs. The Internet is compatible for anyone who wants to use it, you just have to learn how to make it work for you. These books are great quick reference guides. These books even detail instruction on designing your own web pages. The "Dummies" collection also has good books to educate the novice Internet user. They can be found at any bookstore or retailer in town. Working the Web: a students guide by Carol Lea Clark. Harcourt Brace College. 1996 ($22.00) is another copy that is very useful. The best book I have run across is The Internet and WWW: the rough guide. Angus J. Kennedy. Penguin. 1997. It is very easy to read and use as a quick reference.

20. **An Encyclopedia CD-ROM**. With the availability of computers on this campus, a CD-ROM is not that hard to come by. Even if you don't have a computer of your own, the labs on campus have the capabilities to run CD-ROM's. An Encyclopedia is especially helpful if it is the only one of these you buy. It is by far the most comprehensive of world events, biography, and Geography. The Encarta edition is

very easy to get at a book retail store, they are a little pricey though, around \$100 for a complete Encyclopedia collection on CD. An investment that is well worth it.

21. **A tape recorder**. Using a tape recorder in lecture is always up to the professor, so be sure to ask before you use one. If it is permitted a tape recorder can do many things for a student. It can be used to take notes in class, record discussions to be played back and transcribed when you have more time, and it can help facilitate memorizing. Tape recorders shouldn't be used in place of going to class, but should help decipher a possibly confusing lecture or discussion. In foreign language study it may help memorizing vocabulary, to hear yourself over and over again, helps to ingrain things into your memory.

22. **Subscription to a weekly newsmagazine**. In college students can get pretty bogged down with their daily activities and accidentally miss the world as it goes by outside of campus. Focusing on studies can sometimes mean that watching the news and reading the papers can get lost in the shuffle. It's a good idea to subscribe to a magazine that you like i.e. *Newsweek* or *Time,* etc. to keep up on the events of the world. These magazines can be a few minutes of quiet time in an otherwise hectic schedule.

Campus Resources:

23. **PU class listings by school**. The little book, which your counselor should have showed you, has a description of all the classes offered in each school. These books are time savers, get one from each school's counseling office and hang on to them. When it comes time to register for the next semester, you will already have them and

decided what classes you want to take. It's a good idea to get other schools books because a lot of the electives that you may be interested in can be offered by a school that is not yours.

24. **Learning Center LAEB 3268**. The Learning Center is a service that Purdue provides to help students achieve more in school. They focus on learning skills and improvement. There are staff members available for appointments or walk-ins. They can help any student who wants to improve his or her learning skills. This is a valuable resource for any student. Go check it out, it can never hurt to try something that can only help you!

25. **Writing Lab HEAV 227**. This is one of the resources at Purdue that does not get used to its potential. The writing lab is a group of English teachers and students who are available to review any writing you would like. They offer suggestions and guidance on form and content. This is a resource that should not be overlooked by any of you!

26. **PU Library system**. If you are not familiar with the Purdue University Libraries, I suggest you go immediately and educate yourself. The Libraries around campus are many, but each one has its own purpose. Your school has its own library, learn it and use it. The Undergraduate library is the general and main library. The Card Catalog is now online; it is high-tech and easy to use. The staff at every library is more than willing to help you get started with any questions you may have. So with all the new resources you have to help you succeed in school the library is the one place that all these things can be found and used.

THE INDUSTRIAL REVOLUTION

PART ONE
1750-1830

WHAT IN THE WORLD?

The Industrial Revolution was a time of dramatic change and transformation, from hand tools and handmade items, to products which were mass produced by machines. Inventions brought on the most drastic changes during both parts of the Industrial Revolution. Machines made life easier. Workers became more productive, and since more items were being manufactured, prices dropped, thus making expensive and hard to make items available to the poor and not just the rich and elite. These changes, generally, improved life. Before the 1750's, life was primitive but simple, which might have been better than sophisticated and complex. Pollution levels in the atmosphere rose, working conditions deteriorated, and capitalists employed greater numbers of women and young children, making them work long and hard hours. Government, technology, the arts, and our way of looking at the world all changed during this period. The Industrial Revolution was a time of change, for the better, or for the worse. The Industrial Revolution took place in two parts over a period of 150 years, both resulting in productive and dire consequences.

The economy in England before the first half of the Industrial Revolution was based upon the textile industry, and most of the innovations during this period were centered around the manufacture and production of cotton cloth. These innovations were introduced between 1750 and 1800, and marked the beginning of the age of the modern factory. Before the mechanization of the textile industry there existed in England a system known as cottage industry.

The cottage industry was a home based system of manufacturing which was widely used during the 1700's and 1800's. Cottage industry basically involved rural families adding to their agricultural income by producing products in the home. A merchant would provide the raw materials, collect and market the finished product, and pay the family a percentage of the price that he received.

This way of industry created many problems for the merchants. Since the workers produced in their own homes, they had many freedoms. They got to set their own pace of work, they often accepted work from more than one merchant, and many hired outside help and apprentices. As a result of these freedoms the merchants had problems regulating standards and keeping schedules of completion. These, and other problems increased costs. So the merchants turned more and more to machinery for greater production and to factories for central control over their workers. Mass production had begun, along with capitalism. Mass production made items that were usually expensive and available only to the wealthy easily affordable to the lower classes, and therefore "the quality of life" improved.

Year after year the demand for cotton cloth became higher, but workers could not keep up with it, and production became lower. Unless a faster method of producing cotton cloth was found, England's economy would be devastated. A solution came during the year 1733 when a British clockmaker named John Kay, invented the flying shuttle The flying shuttle allowed weavers to produce cloth much faster than spinners could supply them with thread Kay was a pioneer, and his invention set the scene for many other inventors to revolutionize the cotton industry.

By the 1750's, the first Industrial Revolution was well under way. At first inventions were strictly limited to the cotton industry. For example, in order to keep up with the speed of John Kay's flying shuttle, two new devices were introduced. One, invented by Sir Richard Arkwright

(1732-1792) in1769, was the water-powered frame, a device that would spin thread by mechanically reproducing the motions ordinarily made by the human hand. The other was the spinning jenny, invented by James Hargreaves (d. 1778) in 1770. The spinning jenny allowed spinning to be conducted on multiple wheels, producing more thread with far less labor. Between 1774 and 1779, Samuel Crompton (1753-1827) developed a machine that combined the spinning jenny and the water-powered frame called the spinning mule. The spinning mule could produce fine yarn for high-quality cloth which before its development had to be imported from India. In the mid-1780's Edmund Cartwright (1743-1823) invented a steam powered loom. This machine wove cloth so quickly that weavers could finally keep up with the large amounts of thread being spun on the spinning machines. At first, many workers did not accept these machines, and between the years of 1811 and 1816, there developed bands of people called "Luddites", who rioted and tried to destroy machinery. Yet, what was inevitable could not be stopped, and the machines made their way throughout the world.

Cleaning cotton was also a tedious and time-consuming job and in 1794 Eli Whitney (1765-1825) invented the cotton gin. This machine made it possible to remove the cotton seeds from the fibers more quickly. Before the invention of this machine it might take one person an entire day to hand pick the seeds from one pound of cotton, after the invention, one person could do the work of fifty in that same one day period. In 1801, Whitney also invented the concept of interchangeable parts which was the first step towards mass production and the assembly line. The further development of these ideas would help usher in the Modern Age of history, over one hundred years later.

Agriculture also became industrialized to meet the increased demand for textiles and other products. Farmers started to raise raw materials rather than food. The farms themselves became larger and organized along the same lines as factories. Standards in farm management improved, as well as the quality of livestock and crop seed.

Many of the new inventions introduced during the Industrial Revolution needed much more power than could be supplied by horses or water wheels. Technology needed a greater and more efficient form of power, and got it in the form of the steam engine.

The first steam engines were made in 1698 but those, and the ones to follow, were inefficient and used a lot of fuel. During the 1760's, James Watt (1736-1819) began work that would vastly improve the steam engine and by 1769, he had a practical steam engine, one that was much more efficient than anything that had preceded it.. Because of Watt's improvements of the steam engine cities were able to grow and move farther away from rivers and other sources of water that had been the main providers of energy.

Robert Fulton (1765-1815), was an American inventor who designed and built the first commercially successful steamboat, which began regular passenger service on the Hudson River in 1807. In 1814, George Stephenson (1781-1848) built the first steam locomotive, a land transport vehicle that could be driven along rails by a steam engine. This invention affected land transportation in the same way that steamships had already begun to affect travel on the water.

Edward Jenner (1749-1823) was one of the most important men in the history of medicine. His idea of vaccinations gave birth to the most effective way to prevent diseases. Jenner noticed that people who contracted cowpox, a milder form of the deadly smallpox, usually did not come down with smallpox. In 1798 he showed that inoculation with cowpox induced a mild disease that produced immunity to smallpox. His discovery paved the way for vaccinations of other deadly diseases.

Elsewhere in science, Rene Antoine Ferchault de Reaumur (1683-1757), showed, in 1752, that digestion was a chemical, and not a mechanical process. Joseph Black (1728-1769) studied carbon dioxide in detail in 1754. Henry Cavendish (1731-1810) isolated and studied hydrogen in 1766. Joseph Priestley (1733-1804) discovered and studied oxygen in 1774 and Daniel Rutherford (1749-1819) identified nitrogen in 1772. Georges Cuvier (1769-1832) was the first to classify fossils. And as a result, he became the founder of the science of paleontology.

In 1765, James Cook (1728-1779) made the first of his three voyages across the Pacific. He circumnavigated New Zealand and landed on Australia. Between 1772 and 1775, in his second voyage, Cook took his ship through southern waters to the Antarctic Circle. During Captain Cook's third voyage, from 1776 to 1779, he sailed the entire north-south length of the Pacific. He discovered the Hawaiian Islands, and was killed there in a fight with the natives. As a result of these voyages, the oceans of the Earth, except the polar regions, had been entirely opened.

Samuel Johnson (1709-1784) prepared the first great English dictionary in 1755. Adam Smith (1733-1790) published *Inquiry into the Nature and Causes of the Wealth of Nations* in 1776, arguing against government regulation of business activity and trade. Thomas Malthus (1766-1814) published *Essay on Population* in 1798, which stated that without famine, disease, and war, the worlds population would outgrow its ability to produce enough food for itself. Jeremy Bentham (1748-1832) wrote *Introduction to the Principles of Morals and Legislation* in 1789, in which he suggested that all legislation should try to do the most good for the most people. Noah Webster (1758-1843) published the first American dictionary in 1806. Jane Austen (1775-1813) published *Pride and Prejudice* in 1813. Mary Shelley (1797-1851) wrote *Frankenstein*, the first modern science fiction story, in 1818. Washington Irving (1783-1859) published *The Sketchbook*, in 1819, which contained the story "The Legend of Sleepy Hollow."

The second part of the Industrial Revolution would prove to be more drastic, not only in inventions, but in social and governmental policies and reforms. Art and culture flourished and were transformed into many different and unique styles. The first half of the Industrial Revolution had forever changed England, and then the World. The World would soon be ready for another change, as life with machinery had now been assimilated into society.

Summary of chapter 1

This is the most metaphysical chapter in the text. It illustrates the most important factor in the development of sociology -- social change. If one can tell the way people explain and relate to social change, one can tell a great deal about these people.

To pass the course, you will have to know the term "social stratification" and all the terms related to it, they are: "hierarchy," "social status," "social role," "role conflict," and "caste system." You can find the definitions of all these terms in the dictionary.

Social stratification has a lot to do with social change. Herbert Spencer believed that evolution, especially natural selection, the "survival of fittest," was the most important factor. While Karl Marx thought social class conflict was the primary reason of the alienation associated with human condition.

So, is change only an illusion? A Greek philosopher named Heraclitus believed there was nothing but change. On the other hand, Parmenides and Zeno argued that our senses tricked us and change is only an illusion. One of Zeno's four paradoxes was like this: since an object cannot move in space and time from point "a" to point "b," therefore, movement is an illusion because change is based on movement. Thus, change must be an illusion. However, Zeno's paradoxes were disproved mathematically only after centuries by James Gregory, that an infinite number of terms added up to a finite sum in a converging series. In addition, according to St. Augustine, most known for his authorship of "The City of God", that the present exists but has no duration.

The three most important models of social change are: 1. linear models; 2. cyclical models; and 3. dialectical models. The linear models are based upon equilibrium theory and thus they tend to see conflicts as undesirable. A linear view of history sees the history of society as going in a straight line, following a fairly "natural" evolution, and may have an end (eschatology). The cyclical view of social change sees historical swings back and forth between periods of different qualities. The cyclical models have cycles that tend to be recurring, in other words, "the more things change, the more they stay the same." The dialectical model was proposed by George Wilhelm Friedrich Hegel. It was based on conflict, and it tends to be revolutionary, and towards social disequilibrium.

These models might be important to you because a person's model of social change is one of the core principles of his or her worldview. This supports what we said at the beginning: if one can tell the way people explain and relate to social change, one can tell a great deal about these people.

Auguste Comte (1798-1857)

FROM THE EYES OF WOMEN:

During the late 1700's and early 1800's, the first matches were lit which ignited numerous women's movements. During the **Age of Reason** (1600's-1700's), educated women were permitted to take part in political and academic debates which helped perpetuate the cause of women's rights especially pertaining to citizenship.

In the **Enlightenment period**, the British activist Mary Wollstonecraft wrote A Vindication of the Rights of Women (1772). This book was in response to Thomas Paine's controversial book, The Rights of Man. Mary Wollstonecraft's book, simply stated that women deserved equality and all the rights which men had, for example the right for women to an education and to take part in politics.

During the French Revolution, one French activist Olympe de Gouge wrote the Declaration of the Rights of Women, in 1791, which was in response to the Assembly's announcement of the Rights of Man. She belonged to the Girondins, a moderate, revolutionary group in France who wanted a constitutional monarchy. The other revolutionary group in France at this time was the radical Jacobins, who wanted to totally demolish the monarchy in France, and desired more rights for women.

Throughout, the Industrial Revolution in the 1800's, women's labor efforts moved from the domesticated homelife atmosphere, into the environment of newly built factories. Working class women had the opportunity to earn wages; however, if a woman was married her husband legally had control over **all** of her earnings. As a result, several women's movements began to flourish including temperance societies and missionary societies. One woman temperance reformer and suffragist was Amelia Bloomer (1818-1894). She held numerous lectures on her causes, and even started a small temperance paper called Lily in January of 1849.

In 1848, Lucretia Mott and Elizabeth Cady Stanton organized the first women's rights convention in the United States. This convention took place in Seneca Falls, New York, over 100 men and women attended. During this convention, a Declaration of Sentiments was adopted which entitled women to receive all the rights and privileges that pertained to them as being citizens of the United States. After the Seneca Falls convention, national women's rights conventions met almost every year from 1850 up until the beginning of the Civil War in 1861. Women delegates at these conventions discussed a variety of rights for women including divorce, property control, and of course suffrage.

Educational Opportunities

In 1819, Emma Willard published a pamphlet titled An Address to the Public, which was specifically created for the members of the New York Legislature to propose a plan for improving female education. In 1821, she founded the Troy Female Seminary (now the Emma Willard School) in Troy, New York. This was one of the first institutions to offer girls a high school education.

In 1833 Oberlin Collegiate Institute (now Oberlin College) opened as the first coeducational college in the United States.

Property Rights

During the 1840's and 1850's, some states permitted married women to make contracts, own property, control their earnings, and even have joint custody of their children.

In 1848, a New York law allowed married women the right to retain control of their own real estate and personal property.

Women Scholars

In 1849, Elizabeth Blackwell was the first woman in the United States to earn a medical degree.

In 1853, Antionette Blackwell was the first woman minister in the United States. She was ordained in the Congregational Church in South Butler, New York. Furthermore, she also was an activist for women's rights, anti-slavery, and temperance. In 1875, she published the book The Sexes Throughout Nature. This book emphasized that the male perspective of Darwin and Spencer limited their analysis of a woman's place in nature. Blackwell felt Darwin offered evidence for female emancipation. Consequently, Blackwell argued, "Evolution has given and is still giving to woman an increasing complexity of development which cannot find a legitimate field for the exercise of all its powers within the household."

Social Facilitation

Bruce Bergum and Donald Lehr reported the presence of others always facilitated performance, this is a phenomenon known as social facilitation. In their experiment, subjects were placed in a booth where they observed a circle of red lamps lighting rapidly in sequence, and they were asked to press a button whenever they saw a light failed to blink on in proper sequence. When subjects were alone in the booth, only half of the subjects would perform the task; while higher scores were consistently obtained when the task was performed in the presence of an observer. Additionally, the accuracy of subjects with a passive audience was consistently better than those who were alone. Thus, behavior is affected by a passive audience as well.

Moreover, Bayer and Chen found that behavior is also affected when one performs a task in the presence of others, who are also engaged in a similar task -- a situation called coaction. In one experiment, Bayer deprived chickens and then allowed them to eat until full. He discovered that chickens would eat half as much when placed in the presence of another chicken that is eating. In another experiment, Chen found that ants digging nests in groups of two or three dig more quickly and more sand per ant than working alone. Consequently, all these illustrate that the presence of others always facilitated performance.

Bandura: Social Leaning Through Observation

The most prominent of all learning theories of personality is the most learning approach developed by Albert Bandura. Bandura believes in the two-way interaction process that the environment is just as influenceable as the behavior it controls. In Bandura's social learning theory, reinforcement is a very important factor. Thus, Bandura himself and Mischel conducted an experiment that demonstrates the acquisition of behavioral characteristics (the willingness to delay gratification in this case) through the observation of models. Typically, the delay of gratification means postponing a small immediate reward in favor of a more valuable delayed reward.

In this experiment, Bandura and Mischel classified a group of fourth and fifth grade students according to whether they preferred a small immediate reward (a small candy bar right away) or a larger delayed reward (a bigger candy bar a week later). Then they exposed the children in the high-delay-of-reward group to an adult model who consistently opted for the immediate-small-reward choice and the children in the low-delay-of-reward group to a model who consistently selected the larger delayed reward.

When the children were given a delay-of-reward test later, those who initially preferred high-delay-reward changed to prefer low-delay-reward and those who initially preferred low-delay-reward changed to prefer high-delay-reward. This results suggest that children may acquire behavioral characteristics through the observation and models.

Summary of Charter 2

The person who named sociology was Auguste Comte He was French and his best known book was the "Positive Philosophy." Comte had made great contributions to the development of sociology, in which it could be seen in his study of social fixity, social statics and social change, social dynamics. He respected science and he believed that scientific revelation would replace religious revelation and revolution. He stated that since the social sciences had greatly improved the human condition, thus social science had the potential to achieve the same goal too. Although Comte was an equilibrium theorist, he thought the French Revolution was crucial. However, he was afraid that the social equilibrium would be destroyed by it. Moreover, Comte was also an organist. Organicism is a biological metaphor applied to the social institutions of a society that, the whole organism will die if one organ of it dies, no matter how healthy its other organs are.

Comte's social dynamics was consisted by his "Law of Three Stages": 1. the theological stage; 2. the metaphysical stage; 3. the positivistic stage. In the theological stage, societies are based on traditional and theocratic principles. There is very little division of labor and diversity in norms. The three basic kinds of norms are: 1. folkways, 2. mores, and 3. laws. In the metaphysical stage, human reason is the basis. There is a much greater division of labor and normative diversity in Gesellschaft than in Gemeinschaft societies. In the Positivistic stage, Comte used the extreme form of empiricism called positivism, in which Comte believed it would be the basis of his utopia. He also discovered that scientific revelation could save us and lead to society improvement. There is widespread division of labor and much diverse norm.

In addition, since Comte was fascinated with science, he had raised some important issues in social scientific inquiry, like observation, experimentation and comparison. Moreover, he also raised some challenges such as correlation vs. causality, reactivity, reliability, validity, isolating variables, controlling variables, and multivariation etc. Please make sure you know all these terms for the exam.

THE INDUSTRIAL REVOLUTION

PART TWO
1830-1900

WHAT IN THE WORLD?

The second part of the Industrial Revolution utilized the power of electricity to aid in the development of technology that would help life in society as well as in the home. Michael Faraday (1791-1867), a self-educated British scientist, showed how to convert mechanical energy into a continuous electric current in 1831. His discovery would, in time, make electricity the product of burning fuel, so that it would be cheap enough for everyday use. Helping to bring the world into the electrical age with Faraday was the American inventor, Joseph Henry (1797-1878). He was the first, in 1831, to construct powerful and practical electromagnets. That year he also invented the electric motor and, in 1835, the electric relay. Electricity improved life by supplying people with light, and a way to power machines.

Communications improved as well, as a result of electricity. Samuel Morse (1791-1872), who began the development of an electric telegraph during the 1830's, patented his invention in 1840. Foe the first time, news was able to travel with the speed of electricity. Alexander Graham Bell (1847-1922) patented the telephone in 1876. This device made it possible to send the human voice over wires. The telephone and telegraph were the first mass communication devices that were available for public use. Now messages could be sent over long distances almost instantly.

Advances in science were also made. Dimitri Mendeleyev (1834-1907) discovered a way to arrange the chemical elements in order of increasing atomic weight in such a way that similar elements fell into distinct rows. He introduced his "periodic table" of the elements in 1869. Antoine Henri Becquerel (1853-1908) found that a uranium compound was the source of unexplained radiation. Some of this radiation was discovered to be speeding electrons. Marie

Curie (1867-1934) called this phenomenon "radioactivity", and in 1898 discovered two new elements that were far more radioactive than uranium, polonium and radium. This discovery earned her two Nobel Prizes, one in physics and the other in chemistry.

Karl Benz (1844-1929) built the first working automobile to be powered by an internal combustion engine in 1885. The internal combustion engine made transportation faster and far less public. A person could own a car instead of using public transportation. During this time a new technology was beginning in the field of transportation, aviation. Two brothers, Wilbur Wright (1867-1912) and Orville Wright (1871-1948), had worked with gliders and were interested in placing internal combustion engines on them. This would turn a propeller and allow the gliders to move in directed flight. On December 17, 1903, at Kitty Hawk, North Carolina, Orville Wright piloted the first heavier-than-air flying machine.

Medicine before the Industrial Revolution was not well developed, and once an infection set in there was nothing a doctor could do, usually, to save a patient. People were living in filth and germ infested environments during the Industrial Revolution, so health was an everlasting issue. Diseases and sickness could not be stopped, controlled, or maintained, and technology and methods of curing diseases were not well developed.

Since technology was beginning to grow, so did the number of weapons doctors had to overcome disease. William Morton (1819-1868) introduced the use of ether as an anesthetic in1846. The X-ray, discovered by Wilhelm Rotentgen (1845-1923) in 1895 was a key factor in diagnosing medical problems faster and with greater accuracy. Louis Pasteur (1822-1895), a French scientist, proved that microbes carried germs, a discovery which led to the use of antiseptics in operations and the treatment of wounds. He also devised a way to heat milk that would kill germs and slow down the fermentation process. This technique of sterilizing milk (and other products) is called pasteurization. These contributions, along with many others, made during the second half of the Industrial Revolution saved countless lives in their time and in ours.

Charles Babbage (1792-1871),as early as 1822, began to toy with the possibility of devising a machine that would solve complex mathematical problems, store partial solutions, and print out final conclusions. With the use of only mechanical devises such as gears and levers, he developed the various techniques of modern computers.

Life was drastically changed during the Industrial Revolution. People were now living and working in cities, which were germ infested, crowded, and very unhealthy. Women and children labored in harsh conditions, working long hours with little pay. In England, Parliament stepped in and put limits on child labor which upset many capitalists who wanted the government to stay out of its matters.

Socialists were reformers who wanted to construct a better life for all people. Among them was Robert Owen (1771-1858), an owner of a textile mill, who urged factory reform and the control of factories by the people who worked in them. He set an example of how mills could be run with decency and consideration for workers. Owen raised pay, improved working conditions, stopped employing children, and even arranged old age pensions and health insurance. Karl Marx (1818-1883), also a socialist, stated that class struggle, or the conflict between the different classes of people, had an impact on the changes that had occurred throughout history. His book, *The Communist Manifesto*, published in 1848, advanced socialist thinking and gave body to much that was to take place later.

During the 1850's, in the midst of the second Industrial Revolution, new ideas and ways to view life changed the way that art was perceived. Various political and social ideas, along with the quality of life, changed the style of art. The styles that came out of this era were Romanticism, Realism, Impressionism, and Post-Impressionism.

Romanticism featured a conception of individual life, society, and the intertwining of nature and humanity. Romanticists tried to picture and capture beautiful things and people, and tried to turn away from the ugly and desolate side of the Industrial Revolution. The Romantic Period painted emotions that society had no control over such as love, religion, and beauty. It showed more of how people look at one moment in time.

Realism, on the other hand, depicted all of the negative aspects of the Industrial Revolution. Suffering and sadness were used to try and capture what was really happening, as it was thought that it would be more effective in convincing people to try and change the conditions around them.

Impressionism and post-impressionism usually tried to capture quick "impressions" of ordinary everyday experiences and events. Impressionist artists were more concerned about recreating how an object or incident looked or sounded than with their personal feelings about the object or incident.

Henry David Thoreau (1817-1862) wrote *Walden* in 1854. Charles Darwin (1809-1882) was a naturalist who put forth his theories of evolution in *The Origin of Species*, in 1859. In this book, Darwin explained how plants and animals changed their characteristics through time due to natural selection. The German philosopher, Friedrich Nietzsche (1844-1900) published the first part of *Thus Spake Zarathustra* in 1883. Mark Twain (1835-1910) published *Huckleberry Finn* in 1884. In 1899, American economist, Thorstein Veblen (1857-1929) wrote *The Theory of the Leisure Class*, a critique of upper-class behavior in which he penned the phrase "conspicuous consumption."

The Industrial Revolution brought on more technology, wealth, and power, but at what cost? People were living in filth, working long hours, and getting very little pay for it. The revolution shaped modern society into what it is today. As Rousseau said, "Civilization spoils people." But did people spoil civilization by creating machines to do our work?

Karl Marx (1818-1883)

FROM THE EYES OF WOMEN:

Suffrage

The women's suffrage movement appeared to dominate the women's rights crusade throughout Karl Marx's life. In 1869, the National Woman Suffrage Association (NWSA) and the American Woman Suffrage Association (AWSA) were formed. The National Woman Suffrage Association was led by Elizabeth Cady Stanton and Susan B. Anthony. The main goal of the National Woman Suffrage Association was to add an amendment to the constitution giving women the right to vote. In addition, this organization was very radical--it demanded equal education, equal employment, and voting rights for women at once. In 1872, Susan B. Anthony and other woman suffragists voted in the presidential election in Rochester, New York; however, Anthony was arrested and fined for voting illegally. It is shocking to comprehend that the right to vote, which many women take for granted today, was actually a highly controversial issue, worldwide, at one time in history.

On the otherhand, the American Woman Suffrage Association was led by Lucy Stone and her husband Henry Blackwell. The main goal of this organization was to persuade the states, individually, to give the right to vote to women. The American Woman Suffrage Association was very moderate, and supported gradual advances such as limited suffrage for women in locally held elections.

Consequently, some small, but significant advances in the women's suffrage movement developed during Karl Marx's lifetime. In 1869, the Territory of Wyoming, gave women the right to vote, and in 1870 the Territory of Utah followed in Wyoming's footsteps by also giving women the right to vote. In 1878, an actual women's suffrage amendment was introduced to Congress; unfortunately, it failed to pass.

One extraordinary woman who actually crossed paths with Karl Marx during his life and made an impression upon him was Flora Tristan (1803-1844). Tristan was an early socialist feminist who believed socialism was the "savior" for women's rights. The optimistic idea of equality meant that women were not to be exploited or oppressed. Hence, women were to be viewed upon an equal playing field with men whether it involved politics or occupations. Tristan believed in a form of Utopian Socialism, and during the 1848 revolution in Paris, several of her ideas were accepted favorably by numerous socialist feminists. Karl Marx actually put some of Flora Tristan's ideas in his book the Communist Manifesto (1848), which he also wrote with Friedrich Engels.

Anti-Slavery Movement

Surprisingly, not only were numerous women committed to the suffrage movement, but there were many women also involved in the anti-slavery movement in America. One of the most famous and courageous women involved in rescuing slaves and a former slave herself, was Harriet Tubman (1823-1913). Tubman was born into slavery in Maryland, and in 1849, her young master died so she seized the opportunity to escape which she did successfully. Tubman went to Philadelphia, Pennsylvania, and soon became employed at a hotel; yet, Harriet never had any formal schooling and she was illiterate.

A year later, Harriet went to Baltimore and helped her sister and two children shed their chains and breathe the air of freedom. Soon Harriet became involved in the underground railroad system with the Quaker Thomas Garrett, and the African-American leader William Still. It is estimated that the underground railroad system helped save between 60-300 slaves. At one point in time there was a $40,000 reward for Harriet Tubman's capture because of all the problems she caused numerous slave owners by helping their slaves to obtain freedom.

Another notable abolitionist and reformer was Sojourner Truth (1797-1883). Similar to Harriet Tubman, Truth was also illiterate all of her life. Truth was once a slave in New York; however, in 1827 she escaped which was the year before the compulsory release of slaves in the state of New York. Truth lectured throughout much of her life and in the 1850's she also started to speak at women's rights meetings. Also, in 1850 she had Olive Gibert write the Narrative of Sojourner Truth. Truth's message was simply stated, "God was loving, kind, good, and all men should love one another."

Another fascinating woman who was dedicated to the women's suffrage movement and the anti-slavery movement was Ida Bell Wells-Barnett (1862-1931). She was once a slave; although, unlike Harriet Tubman and Sojourner Truth she was educated at Rust University which was a freedmens' high school and industrial school that was established in 1866. In 1884 she became an educator, and while using a pen name she also began to write articles for newspapers, which openly condemned the deficient schools accessible for African-American children.

In addition, Ida Bell established numerous valuable organizations for African-American women and men including: the Negro Woman Suffrage Organization, the Alpha Suffrage Club of Chicago, the Negro Fellowship League, the Negro Woman's Club of Chicago, and several anti-lynching societies.

Temperance Movement

During Karl Marx's lifetime, tHe temperance movement first got underway in an organized manner in 1874. This is when the Woman's Christian Temperance Union (WCTU) was founded. In 1883 the temprance movement went interantaitonal when Frances Willard founded the first interantional organization for women called the World's Woman's Christian Temprance Union. This organization was made up of 72 countries and has about one million members.

Women Scholars & Notable Acheivements

In 1865, Mary Walker was the first woman ever to receive the Medal of Honor, which is the highest award given for valor. Mary Walker acceptd this medal for her devoted servieces to the Union army as a medical officer, during the Civil War.

In 1866, Lucy B. Hobbs, was the first woman to become a dentist and receive a D.D.S. degree.

In 1869, Arabella "Belle" Mansfield was the first woman admitted to the (law) bar in the United States.

In 1870, Susan Smith Mckinney Steward was the first African-American woman to earn a medical degeree. She obtained her degree from the New York Medical College for Women.

In 1873, Ellen Swallow Richards was the first female graduate of the Massachuseetes Instiutie for Technology (MIT). She received a bachelor's degree in chemistry and later established home economics as a science and a proffession.

In 1877, Florence Bascom was the first woman addmitted to the University of Wisconsin.

Persuasion: Changing Attitudes by Changing Perceptions

Capitalism puts off crises through many different ways. One way an overproductive economy can deal with its problems is to create a demand for products people did not know they needed through advertising. There is an old economic principle called Say's Law which says "Supply creates its own demand." So, how does that work? Let's have a look at the following study.

Attitudes can be formed in many different ways, such as through social influence, self-perception processes, socialization, and familiarity of the object to the individual. Zajonc has demonstrated that frequency of exposure encourages positive attitudes toward the object. He found that students liked other students depicted in yearbook photographs to which they had been exposed more frequently than those whose photographs they had seen less frequently. This illustrates that frequency of exposure, and thus familiarity, produces positive attitudes. Therefore, advertisers are likely to blitz television and various print media with their name and visual image when introducing a new product, hoping that familiarity will breed increased sales.

Summary of Chapter 3

Karl Marx was a German who received his Ph.D. at the University of Berlin. He was influenced by several people in his life time, such as the German philosopher, Hegel, and the Scotch and British Political Economists like Adam Smith. Marx was a materialist, an activist, an intellectual, a conflict theorist, and a historicist. He believes that the moral order is based upon the material order. Thus, he thought people could not see the world objectively. On the other hand, Marx thought the scholar should talk about and make the world the way it should be.

Marx did not invent communism. His main objective was to provide a critique of capitalism, which was based upon the labor theory of value. Additionally, Marx thought capitalism was unfair to workers, results in the alienation of workers, perverts the idea of the state by making it the servant of the rich, and causes us to come to measure everything in terms of exchange values rather than use values (commodity fetishism). Furthermore, the centerpiece of Marx's whole theory is called the Law of Rate of Falling Profit. And the Polarization of the Social Classes can also be seen as his critique of capitalism. Make sure you understand all these concepts of Marx's critique of capitalism for the exam.

Herbert Spencer (1820-1903)

FROM THE EYES OF WOMEN:

Suffrage

The women's suffrage movement gained a powerful momentum, during Herbert Spencer's lifetime which eventually helped women obtain the right to vote in 1920. In 1890, the National Woman Suffrage Association and the American Woman Suffrage Association united to form the National American Woman Suffrage Association (NAWSA). By the process of combining their efforts, these two associations believed they could become one powerful and persuasive organization. The NAWSA worked diligently by handing out literature which supported their cause, holding individual state campaigns, and of course holding national conventions. Soon other women's social movements, such as temperance organizations and missionary societies, realized that a woman's right to vote was essential if their organizations were going to accomplish their goals. Therefore, social and equal right's feminists both began to support the women's suffrage movement.

The tides began to turn, and the efforts made by the NAWSA and others seemed to be paying off. In 1890, Wyoming entered the Union and became the first state with woman suffrage, Colorado followed in 1893, and Idaho followed in 1896. However, women still needed more--an amendment which allowed women everywhere in the United States the right to vote. In 1893, New Zealand became the first nation to grant women full voting rights, and in 1902, Australia gave women the right to vote in federal elections.

A Radical's View

One radical feminist who made an impact in society, during Spencer's life was Charlotte Gilman (1860-1935). In 1898, Gilman published a feminist manifesto which her reputation was based on. The manifesto was titled <u>Women and Economics</u>, which declared women needed economic independence, and reasoned that financial independence was more radical than woman suffrage. Gilman's next venture was the publication of a monthly magazine titled the <u>Forerunner</u> in 1909. This magazine further discussed the issues of social reorganization and the roles which women play in society.

Not surprisingly, Gilman had a shocking utopian vision: She desired a society that was populated exclusively by women who reproduced solely by the process of parthenogenesis (which is the reproduction by the development of an unfertilized ovum). Gilman's idealistic views were interesting and important for the women's movement to continue their on-going struggle for not only voting rights, but even some basic human rights.

One Notable Achievement

In 1903, Madame Marie Curie was the first woman **ever** to receive the Nobel Prize. She received this award for physics because she discovered radioactivity with the help of her husband Pierre Curie, and colleague Henri Becquerel; however, she was the one who actually coined the term "radioactivity."

Deviance

A classic experiment carried out by Schachter demonstrates the consequences of being considered deviant. In the experiment, three of Schachter's confederates, who pretended to be subjects, were involved in a discussion with other subjects. As the discussion on the prescribed topic began, one of the confederates took a position similar to that of the group. A second confederate took a position deviant from the group and remained steadfast in this dissenting opinion. The third confederate began by taking a deviant position but eventually agreed with the group.

At the end of the discussion, the groups had to assign jobs among themselves, and to rate how much they liked each of the others. They assigned the deviant the jobs that no one wanted, and they all disliked the deviant. Interestingly, the confederate who began as deviant but eventually agreed with the group was not punished. This person was liked just as much as the confederates who had agreed with the group right from the beginning.

Jonathan Freedman and Anthony Doob asked groups of five or six subjects to take a written personality test and then fabricated their results so that one person was shown to have a different score from all the others. This person was the deviant. The experimenters then asked the group to select a member for a learning experiment which would purportedly require the subject to receive occasional electric shocks. Not surprisingly, the groups selected the deviants. Interestingly, when Freedman and Doob arranged the situation so that the selected subject would receive money rather than shocks, the group avoided selecting the deviant for the experiment in this condition. The experiments showed that we always comply with certain group or societal norms because we are afraid that we might be punished or rejected by others if we do not.

Summary of chapter 4

Herbert Spencer's main contribution to the intellectual history of the time was the formalization of a social philosophy called Social Darwinism. It was based upon the principle of "natural selection," or "survival of the fittest." The perversion of Spencer's ideas can be seen in the eugenics movement. Eugenics was developed by Charles Darwin's cousin, Francis Galton.

Politically, Spencer lived at a very exciting time in England. The works of one of Spencer's predecessors, Adam Smith, author of The Wealth of Nations were popular. Smith's views were being challenged by Jeremy Bentham, who founded a school of thought that was called utilitarianism. On one hand, Bentham believed that the best society is one that does the greatest good for the greatest number of people in that society. On the other hand, he claimed that the State should engage in reform with as little interference as possible in citizen's exercise of their individual freedoms. Then, there were the much more liberal, and eventually socialistic views of people like John Stuart Mill.

Philosophically, Spencer was called a monist because he believes the principle governs the whole cosmos. Thus, Spencer thought societies should evolve and should be free from all State intervention. He believed reform would not do any good anyway because reformers can try to nurture people, but they can never overcome the power of nature. Moreover, Spencer inverted Marx's concept that the moral order was based on the material order.

We have introduced a lot of publications in this chapter. Make sure you know the name of the authors, the title of the books, and what they are about for the exams.

Emile Durkheim (1858-1917)

FROM THE EYES OF WOMEN:

The Temperance Movement

Numerous women were involved in the temperance movement for several different reasons. The majority of women hoped if there was no alcohol available to men, that they would view women differently and even treat them better--especially when they were involved in marriages. Many temperance societies were formed throughout the 1900's. Some societies were formed through churches, which involved Christianity, while others were just independent organizations.

However, one persistent woman stands above the rest when it comes to the fight for prohibition this was "Cyclone Carry," otherwise known as Carry Nation (1946-1911). Carry was a violent activist, who was against the consumption of alcohol. She decided that the only way to stop the crazy drunkenness caused by alcohol was to take physical action, instead of making legal or political changes. At the age of 21 Carry left her husband because of his violence due to his constant drunken state. She felt there was no such thing as a temperate use of alcohol, prohibition was the only answer.

She traveled through many states such as Kansas, Illinois, Ohio, and New York; stopping at bars along the way and causing destruction. She soon acquired a group of followers who would accompany her on her smashing tantrums at bars and taverns. Carry Nation even started a biweekly newspaper in 1901, titled The Smasher's Mail.

Although, Carry's radical and destructive habits were not without severe consequences. She was arrested an amazing **41** times, and she went to trial on four occasions to determine her sanity. She was also ruthlessly attacked by bartenders and guards, and sometimes mobs would throw rotten eggs at her. Not surprisingly, "Fiery Carry" constantly kept the prisons and courts in a state of chaos!

Notable Achievements

In 1911, Marie Curie received the second Nobel prize ever awarded to a woman. She became the **first** person ever to receive two Nobel prize awards. She was awarded this second Nobel prize for chemistry--the isolation of pure radium.

In 1912, the Girl Scouts of America was founded in Savannah, Georgia.

In 1914, Kate Gleason was the first woman member of the American Society of Mechanical Engineering (ASME).

Characteristics of the four types of suicide:

	Egoistic Suicide	Altruisitic Suicide	Anomic Suicide	Fatalistic Suicide
concern with belonging	to an individual	to society	_____	_____
concern with witholding of love or recognition by others	_____	_____	from society	from an individual
intrapsychic motives	sense of loss -- not sufficiently integrated into the society	_____	_____	sense of frustration -- due to the over-regulated society
social pressure	_____	too integrated into the society	"normless" society leaves peopple with no "moral compass"	_____

Summary of Chapter 5

Emile Durkheim was conservative, sociologistic, an organicist, an equilibrium theorist, a functionalist, and a very active researcher. He asserted that societies could not exist without religious forms of some kind, and he believed that God is the apotheosis of the society.

In Durkheim's social world, everything is either sacred or profane. Indeed, Durkheim thought that things are not intrinsically sacred; they are made sacred by the collective consciousness imputing sacredness to them and surrounding them with certain rituals, thus transforming them into collective representations. Moreover, Durkheim emphasized studying social facts and deviance. His greatest contribution to sociology came in his study of suicide. He concluded that there were four different types of suicide: egoistic suicide; altruistic suicide; anomic suicide; and fatalistic suicide. Make sure you know the characteristics of each of them for the exam.

THE PROGRESSIVE ERA

1900-1930

WHAT IN THE WORLD?

To many people, the dramatic changes during the Industrial Revolution were a cause for celebration and optimism. The new "tycoons" of capitalism rejoiced in their previously unimagined financial success. This new affluence touched not only the upper class, but also the urban middle class , which grew rapidly in both size and wealth; to the working class, where a few laborers experienced slow but significant increases in their standards of living.

The late nineteenth century was also a time of new problems. There was a price to pay for the benefits of financial wealth Cities were growing so fast that public services could not keep up with demand. Roads, housing, social services, government bureaucracies, and public health systems all fell far behind, as they strained to keep up with the changes around them.

During the late 1800's and early 1900's, an intense belief in reform was making its way throughout Western Europe and The United States. Most of these reforms focused on a set of problems that the people involved thought were a result of rapid industrialization, urbanization, waves of immigration, and, especially in America, business and political corruption. The reformers wanted to reduce poverty, improve the living conditions of the poor, and regulate big business. They tried to end corruption in government, make government more responsible to the people, and accomplish other goals. Some of these reformers referred to themselves as progressives. This period of history, from about 1900 to about 1930, is often called the Progressive Era.

Two of the problems confronted by the progressives are still with us today. First, the progressives faced the dilemma of how to maintain the economic benefits of the Industrial

Revolution while, at the same time, trying to bring the powerful forces creating those benefits under democratic control and opening up economic opportunities to a greater number of people. Second, progressives faced the complicated issue of how to maintain democracy and national identity amid an increasingly diverse influx of immigrants and widespread political corruption and the concentration of political power.

One cannot fully understand the Progressive Era without looking at its limitations, along with its advantages, particularly its intense dislike of radical labor movements and indifference to the difficulties of African Americans and other minorities. Progressivism brought cures to some areas of reform while further poisoning others. Chief among those was the ongoing controversy about female equality.

Many of the issues concerning foreign policy in the twentieth century have their origins in the emergence of the United States as a major world power during the Spanish-American War at the end of the nineteenth century, and in the involvement of the United States in World War I. America's intervention in World War I then set into motion the events that would make the United States a world power for the remainder of the century.

Henry Ford (1963-1947) introduced the assembly line in 1908. Parts of an automobile would move along a line of men, each one performing the same task again and again in the correct order. In one end of the factory would go parts, and out the other end would come a finished automobile. Ford introduced the "Model-T" in 1909. It was the first automobile to be mass produced and affordable to the middle class. And so , the "Age of the Automobile" began.

Jack London (1876-1916) wrote *The Call of the Wild* in1903, and *The Sea-Wolf* in 1904. Upton Sinclair (1878-1968) wrote *The Jungle* in 1906. F. Scott Fitzgerald (1896-1940) published *The Great Gatsby* in 1925. Ernest Hemingway (1899-1961) wrote *The Sun Also Rises* in 1926 and *A Farewell to Arms* in 1929.

Many aspects of American popular culture had their start at this time. The first Rose Bowl was played in 1902, the first World Series in 1903. Also in 1903, when "The Great Train Robbery" was shown, it became the first movie to tell a story. The first crossword puzzle was published in 1913. The first radio station opened in 1920. *The Jazz Singer*, the first motion picture to feature a soundtrack, opened in 1927

Konstantin Tsiolkovsky (1857-1935) had been writing about rocketry since 1903 and was the first scientist to work out the mathematical requirements for spaceflight In 1916, Albert Einstein (1879-1955) worked out the General Theory of Relativity and founded the science of cosmology. Robert Goddard (1882-1945) launched the first rocket to be powered by liquid fuel and liquid oxygen in 1926.

The Scopes "Monkey" Trial was held in Dayton, Tennessee in July of 1925. Charles Lindbergh (1902-1974) became the first person to fly an airplane across the Atlantic non-stop and solo. He accomplished this 33 hour feat on May 20-21, 1927.

Max Weber (1864-1920)

FROM THE EYES OF WOMEN:

Prohibition

All of Carry Nation's radical antics helped to propel the Prohibition movement to succeed, unfortunately Carry was not alive to see the "fruits of her labor." The United States Congress passed the 18th Amendment, (towards the end of Max Weber's life, in 1919) which prohibited the manufacture, import, export, and sale of alcoholic beverages. However, Prohibition did not have the effect people desired; rather, it only provoked organized crime and additional acts of violence. Also, it did not change the way men viewed and treated women. During the Prohibition period, speak-easies were popular--these were underground nightclubs were alcoholic beverages were sold and consumed illegally; also, in response to Prohibition, the black market for alcoholic beverages sky-rocketed. The 18th Amendment existed from 1919-1933; nevertheless, it was repealed by the 21st Amendment in 1934.

Suffrage For All

Many women concentrated all of their efforts into the "suffragette movement," including Elizabeth Cady Stanton, Susan B. Anthony, Alice Stone Blackwell, and Lucy Stone to name a few. Finally in **1920**, all the speeches, conventions, printing of literature, and rallies paid off--**Women Received The Right To Vote.** The 19th Amendment was adopted to the Constitution in 1920, and the amendment states, "The right of citizens of the United States to vote shall not be denied or abridged by the United States or by any state on the account of sex." In the presidential election of

1920, women were actually allowed to exercise their newly obtained freedom.

After women received the right to vote, it appeared as if the women's movements had done their time in the "lime-light." Some women began to presume that there was not a need for women's movements anymore; hence, a decline of women's movements transpired. Yet, the National American Woman Suffrage Association (NAWSA) was not ready to let women give up the fight for other human rights they were entitled to such as equality. The NAWSA transformed into the League of Women Voters and began to instruct women voters about contemporary political problems and debates.

Today we are preparing ourselves to enter the 21st century; however, women are still not placed upon the same pedestal as men-- will women be struggling for gender equality **forever?

Social Categorization and Social Identification

Weber believed the people in society were influenced by threats of coercion, which manifested itself in power groups. In the following experiment, Tajfel divided subjects into groups randomly, and making sure that there is no social interaction within or between category members. Group membership is anonymous: each subject knows which group they belong to personally but not the affiliations of others. Subjects are required to decide about distributing small monetary sums any way they choose between pairs of anonymous recipients (other than themselves) identified only by group memberships.

Tajfel expected that subjects would be fair. In fact, however, he and his colleagues found that subjects tend to some significant degree to discriminate in favor of ingroup and against outgroup members. This demonstrates that social categorization produces intergroup discrimination, and social identification is defined internally by the subjects. Consequently, we can think of people in different societies as a collection of individuals of different social groups, who shared a social categorization of themselves and acted on that basis.

Summary of Chapter 6

Marx Weber was a German. In his book, <u>The Protestant Ethic and the Spirit of Capitalism</u>, he focused his attention on the effects of Calvinism on the development of capitalism. With Capitalism, there were scarcely any rituals left. Moreover, Weber believed that capitalism is much more than an economic system; it is a moral system. This leads us to the famous "Weber Thesis."

One of the leaders of the Protestant Reformation, Martin Luther, says we all have "a calling" that is special to us. Luther believed that God regarded all legitimate enterprises equally, and the only was to salvation was through faith. However, Calvin believed in predestination and that faith would not get one into heaven.

In fact, Weber made many contributions and one important one was to suffuse Sociology with the notion that, in order for a social action to have any meaning, the observer (sociologist) must interpret that action from the point of view of some value system. He thought that science has to have a conscience. Another contribution of Weber was his development of the concept of ideal typologies, and his analysis of different kinds of authority (Traditional Authority; Charismatic Authority; and Legal-Rational Authority. Make sure you have a clear understanding on the characteristics of the three types of authority and distinct stratification systems, Weber's view of history, and the Weber Thesis for the exam.

Georg Simmel (1858-1918)

FROM THE EYES OF WOMEN:

The Women's Labor Movement

The Industrial Revolution began in England in 1760 and lasted to approximately 1830. Eventually, the outcomes of the Industrial Revolution including new inventions, and factories spread throughout the world and of course to the United States. The Industrial Age allowed an opportunity for women to work outside of the home, usually in factories, to earn extra money to help their families. Numerous factories were popping up everywhere in the United States; however, they were not regulated. Consequently, these factories were basically equivalents to sweatshops, they offered employees long hours, dangerous working conditions, low wages, and no breaks. Soon, unionized organizations started to increase to protect employee rights, as a result, many women became active in the labor movement and even established their own unions.

Leonora O'Reilly (1870-1927) was one accomplished woman who was actively involved in the women's labor movement. As a child O'Reilly saw the ill effects of factory work on women and children. When she was 11 years old, she worked in a shirt collar factory in New York. O'Reilly's first attempt to become involved in unions was successful when she founded a local garment workers union in 1897. In 1903, O'Reilly helped establish the National Women's Trade Union League, which promoted laws to protect the rights of women factory employees.

However, it appeared as if forming unions to help women was not enough, and that more overt action was necessary to achieve union goals. In 1909, Leonora lead a strike in New York city with the International Ladies' Garment Workers Union (ILGWU). Numerous strikes and protests occurred; although, many people were arrested for their actions, and some people even lost their jobs. The International Ladies' Garment Workers Union announced in February of 1910 that the strike was officially over, with victorious results--339 manufacturing firms reached agreements with the union, but 13 firms did not settle. Finally, in 1919 after all of Leonora's hard work she was admitted as a delegate to the International Congress of Working Women in Washington, D.C.

One "HOOSIER" labor leader was Mary Ritter Beard (1876-1958). Beard was born in Indianapolis, Indiana, and attended DePauw University. In 1907, she started to work for the Women's Trade Union League (the same organization which Leonora O'Reilly was dedicated to), and she also worked with the Wage Earner's League between 1910-1912. In addition, Beard also took the initiative and organized women textile workers in New York City, and she published numerous books such as Woman's Work in Municipalities (1915), A Short History of the American Labor Movement (1920), and Understanding Women (1931). Mary Ritter Beard's endeavors were beneficial to women everywhere, especially women factory workers and union members.

A Historic Event

At 4:30 pm of March 25, 1911, one of the most shocking events in U.S. history occurred, which later facilitated the initiation of safety legislation, fire codes, and child-labor laws. A huge fire illuminated the Triangle Shirtwaist Company, located in

Asch Building in New York City. The fire began on the eighth floor, but it rapidly spread to the two top floors of the building. Numerous workers could not escape the massive blaze because of locked doors for anti-theft purposes. In addition, the only fire escape was overloaded and collapsed, and the two elevators in the building were not operating; therefore, many employees were forced to jump to their death.

As a result of this factory fire 146 people died, and most of the individuals were young, immigrant women ages 16-23, who were trying to build a better life for themselves in the country where "streets are paved of gold"--America. On April 11, 1911, the two owners of the Triangle Shirtwaist Company, Harris and Blanck, were indicted for manslaughter because they left the doors locked. However, they plead not guilty to 7 manslaughter indictments, and in December Harris and Blanck were found not guilty and needed a police escort to exit the courtroom because an angry crowd was impatiently waiting for the two company owners.

Unfortunately, 146 people had to die before legislation and factory safety measures could be introduced. In 1913, many bills were proposed, and passed by the New York legislature, in effort to improve factory safety and protect factory employees. Furthermore, the nation as a whole seemed to open its eyes and realize the dangerous working environments factories provide, and that protective legislation and statutes are necessary.

A Notable Business Venture

In 1903, Maggie Lena Walker (1867-1934) was the first female to become president of a bank. She became president of St. Luke

Penny Savings Bank in Richmond, Virginia.

Obedience to Authority

Following the Milgram experiment that we discussed earlier in this chapter, Milgram did further research to examine what variables affect the level of obedience to an authority figure. He discovered one variable was the "psychological distance" between subject and learner. The closer the subject was to the learner, the lower the obedience level. Subjects obeyed most when they could neither see nor hear the learner's reactions to the shocks; while they obeyed least when the subject was required to hold the learner's hand on a shock plate in order to deliver the electric shock.

Another variable that he found was the "psychological distance" between the subject and the authority figure. The greater the distance from the experimenter, the less the obedience level. Obedience was least when the experimenter delivered instructions to the subject when via a tape recorder and was never actually seen by the subject. Interestingly, in the absence of the experimenter, several subjects disobeyed orders by using only the lowest level of shock.

Personal Space

Studies have shown that people studying together preferred corner seating; while coacting pairs studying separately preferred opposite seating. Probably these preferences are acquired early in life and are carried into adulthood as facilitators or inhibitors of non-verbal communication and social interaction.

Moreover, a mere change of furniture arrangement can sometimes have a profound effect on social interaction. One study showed that the introduction of merely one conversation piece (such as abstract sculpture) greatly enhanced the amount of positive interaction among initially shy people congregated in a waiting room.

HALL (1960)
FELIPE AND SOMMER (1966)
SOMMER (1969)
SOMMER AND BECKER (1969)
AIELLO AND JONES (1971)
ALTMAN, TAYLOR, AND WHEELER (1971)
MEHRABIAN AND DIAMOND (1971)

Summary of Chapter 7

Georg Simmel was born in Berlin and studied at the University of Berlin. Simmel wrote a great deal about art, culture, women, coquetry, and other subjects of the drawing room culture of his day. His primary concerns are for the place of the individual human in society. He contributed to macro-theory and is best known for his micro-theory. The combination of micro- and macro-theory really was what brought sociological thinking into the modern era.

In Simmel's mind, there are three of the several different levels of conducting sociological inquiry. The first level was called "Pure Sociology." With "Pure Sociology," Simmel is interested in the combination of psychological variables with forms of social interaction. The most important aspect of Simmel's sociology was that he was more concerned with the form than the content of interaction. The second level was "General Sociology." This deals with the social and cultural products of human history. The third level was called "Philosophical Sociology." This concerns the basic social nature of human beings, and ultimately, the fate of humanity.

Simmel's concept of society is one built around the dualisms of human existence. He thought one of the problems that arises from the dialectical tension between objective and subjective culture is the way in which objective culture comes to have a life of his own. In addition, Simmel's dialectic is apparent in his view in the difference between dyads and triads. He believed that a stratification system and an authority structure can emerge in a triad but not in a dyad. Moreover, Simmel was also concerned with the distance of social relationships. He discusses social distance in his essay on "The Stranger."

Simmel did not really believe in utopianism. His combination of the usually radical mode of dialectical thinking with a usually conservative respect for individualism in explaining how society works is what makes Simmel difficult to categorize.

George Herbert Mead (1863-1931)

FROM THE EYES OF WOMEN:

The Birth Control Crusade

Today, the women of the 90's take for granted the convenience and availability of birth control devices, aids, and methods. Yet, birth control was not always easily accessible or even legally obtainable in the United States. During George Herbert Mead's lifetime, one of the most influential and persistent individuals lived--Margaret Higgins Sanger (1883-1966). Margaret Sanger actually **coined** the term "birth control," it was previously referred to as voluntary motherhood. Throughout the early 1900's, it was illegal to distribute birth control devices or even information pertaining to birth control. Sanger felt the only way for women to be on an equal playing field with men socially, and economically was for women to be able to avoid unwanted pregnancies.

In 1912, Sanger started her uphill battle by working as a nurse for poor women in New York City. Sanger wrote about her experiences as a nurse in her autobiography My Fight For Birth Control (1931). In one exert of her book, Margaret Sanger wrote, **"Constantly, I saw the ill effects of childbearing on women of the poor. Mothers whose physical condition was inadequate to combat disease were made pregnant, through ignorance and love, and died. Children were left motherless, fathers were left hopeless and desperate, often feeling like criminals, blaming themselves for the wife's death--all because these mothers were denied by law knowledge to prevent conception."** Soon she joined a socialist party, became a feminist, and devoted her entire life to the birth control movement.

Sanger first introduced the term birth control to the public in 1913, when she started to publish a monthly newsletter titled The Woman Rebel; which, helped Sanger gain support for her movement. However, Sanger's beginning of a successful movement was hindered when she had felony charges brought upon her for having "obscene" views on women's sexuality, Sanger fled to Europe without her children or husband. When Sanger arrived for her trial the charges were dismissed because of the abundant amount of public support she received. Sanger was the least bit discouraged and decided to open up a birth control clinic in 1916, in Brooklyn, New York. Just 10 days after the clinic was opened, a police raid closed it down, and arrested Margaret Sanger for distributing illegal information about contraception.

In 1921, Margaret Sanger was still determined as ever, even after several disappointing setbacks and imprisonments. She established the Birth Control League to promote family planning. The organization was soon known as the Birth Control Federation of America, and in 1942 it was changed to the Planned Parenthood Federation of America as we known it today. In 1921, Sanger also promoted the growth and development of the birth control clinics, and by 1930, there were 55 centers spread among the United States located in 23 cities in 12 states. In 1995, there were over 800 clinics nationwide with approximately 27,000 volunteers, and operating staff.

Finally, in 1927, Margaret Sanger decided to go international with her birth control movement, and she spoke at the first world population conference in Geneva, Switzerland. Sanger made an enormous impact on society, without her persistent efforts who knows how much longer women would have had to wait to be able to control their lives on physical, social, and economic levels.

The New Feminist Movement

One woman has made an impact on women's rights and equality, since the 1950's--Betty Friedan (1921-). Some individuals have considered Friedan to be the founder of the women's liberation movement in the United States, and "the mother of the new feminist movement." In 1963, Friedan published her best seller The Feminine Mystique which talked about the American woman's pressure to conform to the role of housewife, mother, and the apparent lack of self-expression expected of women by society. Betty Friedan described this as "the problem that has no name." It was because of her book that many women realized their feelings were shared by other women everywhere.

In 1966, Friedan put her feelings into action when she helped found the National Organization for Women (NOW), to help women fight for equality. This organization is still active today in helping women achieve their rights. In addition, Friedan helped devise the National Women's Political Caucus in 1971, which promotes women to become involved in politics and try to pursue political offices. Hence, Friedan's accomplishments have helped to persuade the women of the 20th century to continue their ongoing struggle for equality. **Will it ever end?**

Interpersonal Influence

Our interactions with others can have large influence on our behavior. Research in social psychology provides insight into the power of the group in motivating us to conform. Solomon Asch (1965) conducted conformity studies and showed that about 80% of the participants in the experiment conformed to a group decision at least once even though that decision was clearly wrong. When interviewed after the experiment, many participants indicated that they did not question the group's decision but rather wonder why they differed from the group. These participants also expressed a strong desire to conform. These kind of studies imply that the presence of others who opinions differ from our own generates within us motivation to conform. Moreover, people behave differently in different situations. For example, students take notes and ask questions in class, and they may drink alcoholic beverages and dance at a party. Thus, our behaviors are considerably influenced by both situational factors and by the presence of other people. Therefore, motivation may be analyzed not only at the physiological or individual level, but also at the level of groups. Groups can influence our motives and, in conjunction with situational variables, alter the ways in which we behave.

Imitation of Film-mediated Agggressive Models

Learning is an important factor in motivated behavior. Albert Bandura conducted a research to outline the interrelationships of learning and motivation in generating behavior. In that classic demonstration, Bandura showed a group of children a film in which the adult models punched, hitted, and kicked a life-size Bobo doll. Later, the children in the experiment showed a greater frequency of the same behaviors than did children in control conditions who had not observed the aggressive models (Bandura et al. 1963). Subsequent studies showed that children imitated such behaviors just from watching filmed sequences of models, even when the models were cartoon characters.

Bandura's research is important for understanding of motivation at the level of the individual because it strongly suggests that some motivated behaviors are learned through observation. Thus, if the models we observe show us that they are motivated to work hard, pursue excellence, and be successful, we are likely to be motivated in similar ways.

Summary of Chapter 8

Symbolic interaction (SI) is a highly interpretive form of sociological thinking. It was named by Herbert Blumer and developed by George Herbert Mead. Mead was one of the first Americans to influence major changes in sociology. He was one of the first sociologists to concentrate on the link between the individual and the society in a unique way. However, most sociologists would save the honor of being one of the first, social-psychologists for the brilliant German, Georg Simmel. Mead was said to have been an extraordinary lecturer. However, he never wrote any books himself, therefore, his students complied a number of his papers and the content of his lectures in a book called Mind, Self, and Society after his death.

The focus of the kind of interpretation that interested Mead was the symbolic order of society. Mead disagreed with Comte that the reality of society is "out there" to be discovered. He believes we are born *tabula rasa* -- a principle developed by the English philosopher John Locke which holds that our minds are like a "blank tablet or slate" when we come into the world. According to Mead, human identity was generated out of interaction. Moreover, Mead says there are two major stages to develop a self of the socialization process, they are: 1) the play stay, and 2) the game stage. Additionally, he thought the process the disclosure of self is a process of negotiation. One of the symbolic interactionists, Charles Horton Cooley developed a simple by revealing concept he called looking glass self -- seeing ourselves as we see others to be seeing us.

The effect that Mead had that was the most enduring was to combine a theory of action with the symbolic dimension of society. We will go through several studies (such as the autokinetic effect) in class to demonstrate this concept.

THE DICTIONARY OF SOCIOLOGICAL TERMS

TABLE OF WORD LIST CONTENTS

THE DICTIONARY OF SOCIOLOGICAL TERMS

TABLE OF CONTENTS

Specific Concepts:	Page

DICTIONARY OF SOCIOLOGICAL TERMS

Definitions pertaining to the "Preface" of
Elements of Sociology Through Theory --
(WORD LIST #1)

sociology: a social science concerned with the systematic study of human society, which has a special interest in the development of systematic knowledge about the phenomena arising out of the **group** relationships and collective dynamics of human beings. Its practitioners (sociologists) study the processes and patterns of individual and group interaction, the various social institutions of the society, the different ways social groups are organized, the relationships among these groups, and group influences on individual behavior.

society: Although the term is variously defined by different sociologists, most would agree that a society has the following qualities:

First, a society has a continuity from generation to generation. In other words, if you saw a society at one point in time, and then saw it 50 years later, you still could recognize it as the same society because one generation passes most of the society's essential social norms and prescriptions for interaction along to the next generation, and so on. Obviously, certain things would change drastically, and some things disappear, but you still could recognize the same society at the two time periods. Imagine yourself as a space visitor seeing American films from the 1930s and the 1990s. Presumably, after a time, you would be able to conclude that you were watching films of the same society, if by no other way, through the language.

Second, a society has relative self-sufficiency. Obviously there are societies that cannot meet all of their own needs. For example, Japanese society relies on other societies for meeting its needs for petroleum products. For the most part, however, a society will meet, or find ways to meet its essential needs, or the society will be imperiled. Of course, we are entering a period in history when we may see more and more of a trend toward a world society, just as we have seen the switch from national economies to a world economy. The sobering thought here is what happens when we see the development of "world culture?" Will this lead to a huge decline in the rich variation in different cultures? It already has in many places as culture becomes "mass culture."

Third, a society is a social unit of relatively large size. There is, of course, no precise unit of size that a society has to reach to be considered a society. Perhaps, it is best to consider the size issue by comparing it with other social units. A society is larger than a **"community,"** for most communities do not manage to meet all their own needs. A society is **much less specialized than most organizations. Indeed, one of the characteristics of most societies is the high degree to which they are structurally and functionally differentiated.** Finally, a society should not be confused with a **nation.** While it is true that some nations are societies, all societies are not nations because societies do not necessarily have specific political boundaries, as is the case with a nation. A good case in point is Canada. Although it has one set of distinct political boundaries, it has at least two very separate societies if one considers the magnitude of difference in the province of Quebec from the rest of Canada. In short, societies typically are massive, yet invisible. What does that do to your concept of the difference in appearance and reality?

liberal arts: the liberal arts are a part of a university curriculum designed mainly to provide general knowledge and to hone a student's intellectual capacities such as her or his ability to reason and make informed judgments. The liberal arts curriculum usually is different in scope and intent from the curricula of professional or vocational schools, which have very focused intellectual and practical goals in mind, such as a school of engineering, a medical school, a school of pharmacy, a nursing school, a school of agriculture, a school of education, a school of business, a school of management, a school of law, a school of social welfare, a school of architecture, etc.

The liberal arts typically consist of literature and other arts, language studies, the study of history, philosophical studies, and studies of the natural and social sciences. Because the word liberal appears, that should not be confused with the concept of **liberalism**, which will appear in a later portion of this dictionary and has a very specific political-economic meaning quite apart from the notion of liberal arts.

socialization process: the process whereby individuals learn and internalize the skills, attitudes, values, needs, affective dispositions, and behaviors that are expected of persons who wish to be participating members of their society. This process is supposed to ensure that the individual will develop an identity, including the motivations, self-image, and knowledge to perform adequately in the **social roles** (see definition) he/she is called upon to enact throughout his/her lifetime.   Moreover, the person is supposed to behave **willingly** in accordance with the prevailing standards of his/her culture.   The process of socialization is carried out by such socialization agents as the family, peer groups, schools, and the media (especially television).

Put fairly simply, socialization is the process that gives the individual a social self and which seeks to ensure the perpetuation of the continuity of the culture and the society. In its earliest form, the socialization process is the mechanism we use to domesticate our wild citizens -- which I believe we call "children." In getting unsocialized people to accept willingly the norms of the society, the society lays the groundwork for its continuation.

natural science: any of the sciences such as physics, chemistry, biology, etc. that deal with the nature of matter and energy and the transformations of, and interrelations between matter and energy. The natural sciences typically deal with forces and causative sequences that are not affected by human intelligence. For example, an electron **can** be manipulated by a human experimenter, but, in its natural state, an electron will follow rules of its own, quite apart from any concern with the desires or expectations of human intelligence.

Sometimes the natural sciences are called the "physical sciences" because they typically deal with physically measurable phenomena. Sometimes they are called the "hard" sciences, while the social and behavioral sciences are referred to as the "soft" sciences. The implication here is that the physical or natural scientists deal with much more predictable, controllable phenomena that are subject to discoverable and invariant rules, while the social and behavioral sciences deal with more interpretive circumstances that have rules which are much more difficult to discover and change with changing social contexts. Most people who have a lick of sense do not use the distinction "hard sciences" versus "soft sciences" because it really disgusts social scientists, and probably most sensitive natural scientists.

Moreover, intelligent scientists of all ilks have come to realize that most science is highly interpretive, with the discoverable rules often being "proven" rhetorically rather than by reference to some unalterable Truth. In other words, if I can convince you that "up" is "down," the crucible of what really **is** up or down will be based more upon your beliefs of up or down than the objective reality of up or down.

Personally, I think the separation of the natural sciences from the social sciences, and both of them from the arts and the humanities was one of the worst conceptual disasters in human intellectual history. They are all beautiful; they are all interesting; they are all fun. And anybody who does not take a big drink from all of these wells while in college is really "screwing up."

social science: a branch of science that deals with: **1)** the institutions of human societies and how they function; **2)** the interpersonal relationships of individuals as members of society; and **3)** the learned and shared behaviors of society, usually referred to as **culture.** The social sciences include disciplines such as **anthropology, economics, law, geography, political science, psychology, and sociology** (although you might find some economists, geographers, and jurists who would not agree with this categorization).

Some scholars will refer to the social sciences as the "**behavioral sciences.**" Typically, these individuals are persons who subscribe to a paradigm that is a component -- often times a controversial one -- of the social sciences called "**behaviorism.**" (**See the definition starting at the bottom of the page.**)

humanities: the branches of learning such as philosophy, history, languages, etc. that investigate human constructs and concerns as opposed to investigating natural processes, as the chemist, biologist, zoologist, physicist, etc. might do. For example, humans philosophize; chemical compounds probably do not, not in a human way, anyway. Humans make history; protons probably do not make history in a human way, anyway.

Not incidentally, there are some interesting parallels between the human and the natural world. For example, although humans are the only beings that can make human history, geological structures such as the Grand Canyon <u>do</u> have a history. Certainly the rocks do not grasp the changes that have occurred in the Canyon in the way humans do. But who are we to say that there is not some "rock historical consciousness?" Rocks may just communicate muuuuuuuuuuuuuuuuuch more slowly than humans do.

behaviorism: This view, popularized by the psychologist, **B.F. Skinner**, is too complex to do it justice in a short definition. The essence of it, however, is that all we can know objectively about human beings is their behavior; thus, unobservable phenomena such as "motivations" or "feelings" should not be the focus of, or even an integral element of, scientific study. So, behaviorists believe that **behavior should be the focus of scientific study**. There are different kinds of behaviorists.

Radical behaviorists do not believe in inner private mental states that are totally distinct and separate from behavior. In other words, something like "choosing" is not based on a mental event, but is seen purely in its behavioral dimension -- choosing being a behavioral response to some stimulus (usually someone else's behavior or a cue from the social or natural environment).

Another example of the way a radical behaviorist might view a human phenomenon would be in looking at speech in terms of laryngeal movements, muscular contractions, skin and eye responses. Thus, language and speech are stimulus-response activities that do not give any grounds for assuming some underlying mental states. Indeed, some behaviorists see what we construe as inner mental states as a form of covert (hidden) language activity -- thus making these states a form of behavior. The radical behaviorist sees emotions as visceral ("gut" not cognitive) reactions. I know that such an approach may be hard for some of you to believe or even to conceptualize because most of you are taught to believe that human behaviors are motivated by internal mental states such as feelings or values. But the radical behaviorist will argue (sometimes quite persuasively) that you are wrong.

There is another kind of behaviorist -- a **methodological behaviorist**. By the way, a radical behaviorist usually will be a methodological behaviorist, although a methodological behaviorist will not necessarily be a radical behaviorist. Methodological behaviorists who are not radical behaviorists are just as likely as not to believe that internal mental states such as feelings or motivations based on values do exist. These scholars just believe that such states, if they do exist, are scientifically irrelevant. Why? Well, according to them, a scientist really can't directly examine mental states such as feelings. To these scholars, there is no way to confirm the existence of "feelings" by any objective measure, or to make scientific predictions about human behavior on the basis of feelings or motivations. Instead, the methodological behaviorist believes that we can examine stimulus-response behavior, measure it, and make certain predictions on the basis of it. Methodological behaviorists could be seen as behavioristic agnostics because most of them really are not sure about the whole issue of the existence of "inner states," although many do not rule them out; in other words, they just don't know. There also are some behaviorists who believe that nonbehavioral internal mental states such as "feelings" **do exist**, but that these states have no causal influence on human behavior.

One is not likely to find many sociologists who are behaviorists, although most sociologists do observe, <u>among</u> <u>other</u> <u>things</u>, human behavior or activities. If you are interested in behaviorism, one of B.F. Skinner's most famous and accessible books is entitled, **Beyond Freedom and Dignity.**

Weltanschauung: (Velt-on-shau-ung) German word for "world view" -- the distinctive outlook of the members of a group, or a class, or the outlook that is held by people during certain historical periods, or who live in particular regions based on common experiences. Usually, when people share a world view, they share this view because they are experiencing common social conditions and a common culture.

paradigm: (pronounced pair' a dime) a collection of major assumptions, concepts, and propositions in a substantive area (biology, sociology, particle physics, for example) that provide a particular way of looking at the world or a segment of the world. This may be one of the most disagreed upon concepts in all of science. Let us look at an example: Isaac Newton was responsible for the final overthrow of old Aristotelian notions of physics. Aristotle believed that for an object to move, something else had to be pushing it; Newton proved several centuries later that an object, once set in motion, will continue to move forever unless an impediment such as friction, gravity, etc. stops it. The Aristotelian view and the Newtonian view represent two different paradigmatic views, or paradigms regarding the physics of motion because the two views have different assumptions, concepts, and propositions.

Another example would be the paradigmatic differences represented by socialist political-economic thinkers and capitalist political-economic thinkers. The problem with paradigms, as people use the term, is that we often do not have very good agreement on what is encompassed by a particular paradigm. For example, some capitalist thinkers believe in no government intervention in the economy, while others who call themselves capitalists believe in varying amounts of governmental intervention. Thus, is the noninterventionist school of thought a paradigm and the moderate interventionist school another and different capitalist paradigm, or do they just represent differences of opinion within the same paradigm, which we call capitalist philosophy? Distinctions such as this can make the term paradigm difficult to understand in its use. Because of that, probably **the best way to think of a paradigm is to view it as a fundamental way of looking at the world that substantially differs from other fundamental ways of looking at the world.**

philosophy: comes from the Greek roots *philos* meaning "love" or *philia* meaning "friendship" and *sophos* meaning "a wise person" or *sophia* meaning "wisdom," "knowledge," "skill," or "intelligence." There are many definitions of philosophy. Most of the definitions, however, give "philosophy" the following qualities: **1)** an attempt to present a systematic view of reality; **2)** a concern for the ultimate nature of reality; **3)** an effort to try to determine the limits and scope of human knowledge; **4)** a procedure for investigating the sources and standards of validity of knowledge; and **5)** a search for a general understanding of values.

ideology: the totality of subjective ideas, beliefs, knowledge, modes of thinking in terms of which groups or social movements explain relevant aspects of life which usually are geared to maintaining various political, social, and class interests.

Marx and Engels, in The German Ideology (1846), were among the first to use the concept in its sociological context. Marx and Engels held that ideology reflects class interests and is characterized primarily by its effort to maintain the existing class structure. Thus, they argued that the social knowledge (such as philosophies, ideas and laws) which is implicit (or explicit) in an ideology is linked to the material conditions and class interests of those who produce such knowledge. According to Marx, if there is a dominant ideology in a particular society, it will determine the major social institutions of that society. So, if monopoly capitalism has the power and wealth to manufacture an ideology for a culture, the capitalistic version of that culture's politics, family institutions, religion, education, medicine, etc. will be the version of those institutions that will be portrayed as normal and desirable.

In an important book called, **Ideology and Utopia (1929)**, a social thinker named **Karl Mannheim** refined and extended the earlier notions of ideology. Mannheim argued for a distinction between two categories of thought: **1) ideologies**, ideas that functioned to maintain the existing social order; and **2) utopian ideas**, which contained visions of a different social order and a critique of the existing social order.

Mannheim argued that ideological thinking was not limited to the ruling class, but that all social classes had a particular material existence, social perspective, and set of interests that led them to have their own ideologies.

empiricism: the idea that experience rather than reason is the source of knowledge; therefore, knowledge depends ultimately on the **use of the senses** and on what is discovered through them. Proof of the existence of a phenomenon is validated through seeing, hearing, touching, tasting, etc., or, by our ability to measure in some tangible manner the extent of the existence of the phenomenon. Clichés that could be seen to be empiricist-type statements are: "The proof of the pudding is in the eating"; "Don't count your chickens until they have hatched"; "If I hadn't seen it, I wouldn't have believed it"; "Show me."

nihilism: The word can be pronounced either nihilism (long "i" after the "n") or kneehilism. It comes from the Latin *nihil* meaning "nothing." This viewpoint holds that all knowledge is worthless, meaningless, and insignificant. Thus, no knowledge is possible because all the stuff people call "knowledge" is pointless. Of course, if one looks at the world in that way, existence is senseless and there can be no objective basis for truth of any kind, especially moral truths.

The nihilist denies the value of all distinctions such as real/unreal, illusion/truth, accuracy/error. Put bluntly, a nihilist just doesn't give a damn about any values whatsoever because they are seen to be pointless. Nothing can be proven; nothing denied. Everything is nothing.

paradox: There are several dictionary definitions of paradox; but the way I use it is twofold. **First,** a paradox is a situation in which two statements that are contrary or opposite of each other both appear to be true. A classic example of this is the old trick of writing the following:

"The statement below is true."

_____

"The statement above is false."

Second, there is the kind of paradox sometimes referred to as the Megarian Paradox, or Eubulides' paradox. In this form of paradox, if a statement is regarded as true, it leads to it being false; or, if it is regarded as being false, it leads to it being true. For example, if I say, "I am lying," the statement is true if it is false, or false if it is true. Or, if I were to say, "What I am now saying is false," this leads to the same paradoxical conundrum.

We will examine several paradoxes in the text, but the first context in which it was raised had to do with the nihilist's statement that the, "world is meaningless," which, of course is a meaningless statement, thereby making it possible that the world has meaning. Another paradoxical situation would be one in which a person tried to stop all change in their lives. One aspect of such a decision would be to hold one's breath, as breathing causes change. But, of course, if one held his/her breath long enough, the person would either faint or die, which is a rather profound change.

relativism: a belief that there can be no absolute standards of knowledge by which to measure or judge the rightness of another society's values because absolute, commonly held norms do not exist that are applicable at all times and in all places. Thus, if we wish to talk about **cultural relativism**, no one culture should be used as a standard against which to judge the moral values of another culture. Can you think of any examples of practices that are considered perfectly moral and obligatory in one culture, but are considered immoral, deviant, and punishable in another culture? If you are at a loss for examples, have a librarian teach you how to use **The Human Relations Area Files.**

logic: the branch of philosophy that studies the formal rules of exact reasoning. Another way of saying this is: "Logic studies the forms that are taken by valid patterns of thought." The utilization of logic in reaching a **logical inference** (a conclusion we reach based upon certain premises and/or evidence) does not necessarily mean we have discovered Truth. What logic does for us is gives us certain ground rules of thought which, if we break, will lead us to illogical conclusions. Now, an illogical conclusion is not necessarily false (it is a very strange world, as you all know); however, an illogical conclusion is going to force us to have to confront certain "flaws" in our thinking, such as contradictions, that greatly erode the possibility that our inferences are valid.

abstract: Something is abstract when the fundamental principle that is being represented or discussed is seen apart from reference to any particular (or **concrete**) object, event, or activity that would give that principle a pictorial or narrative content. For example, when we think about the notion of "peace" or "friendship," or "courtesy," or "patriotism," or "redness," or "roughness," all of us may get very different concrete pictures of the meanings of those kinds of words in our minds. That is because we are trying to take an abstract principle (one apart from a specific instance) and concretize it. Remember when you were a little kid in arithmetic class, how you or some of your classmates used your fingers to count the numbers you were supposed to add up? That is because the concept of "five" or "fiveness" is very abstract. But if we apply it to a specific instance such as five fingers, it is much easier to visualize and understand.

One of the things some people find difficult about understanding sociology is that we deal with many abstract concepts. Even fairly simple ideas such as "norms" or "social roles" or "social status" can be pretty abstract if one is dealing with them for the first time in a systematic way.

7

Definitions pertaining to CHAPTER ONE:
"Sociology: Why?" of Elements of Sociology Through Theory --
(WORD LIST #2)

metaphysics: In effect, there is little agreement on the precise definition of metaphysics because it often is used to encompass other subcategories of philosophy such as: cosmology, ontology, epistemology (all of which will be defined in a later part of this word list). Probably the best way to define metaphysics is as **speculative philosophy.** The reason metaphysics would be called "speculative philosophy" is that experimental or scientific methods are not essential in obtaining metaphysical knowledge. In other words, you can just let your mind roam freely. For example, have you ever sat under a starry sky and speculated with a friend on what it is all about? You can get a pretty good laugh about that sometimes because the whole situation is such a cliché.

Metaphysics typically is concerned with the ultimate nature of reality, and, of course, it is difficult to be anything other than speculative about something that massive even if you have spiritual or religious beliefs that explain part or most of it. Of course, if you think your belief system explains everything, then you probably would not need to engage in metaphysical speculations. That is completely up to you; but one wonders, if everything is already explained to you, what in heaven's name are you doing in college?

social stratification: a system of social inequality based upon hierarchical ordering of individuals or groups according to the share they receive of societal rewards such as wealth, power, opportunity, or status. (See the next definition below which explains **hierarchy.**) In other words, social stratification is the division of society into a series of levels or strata (such as the multi-colored bands of rock in The Grand Canyon.). Persons from one stratum usually are ranked above or below persons from strata different than their own. Once a person is consigned to a particular stratum or **social class** -- usually on the basis of where they are economically in the hierarchy (See the definition below which explains **social class.**) -- the membership in that class can be used to justify an unequal distribution of the society's rewards to them and keep them from having full participation in the opportunity structure of the society. For example, you probably are not going to get the opportunity to go to Harvard if you are poor, no matter how smart you are.

In any event, social stratification sets up inferiority-superiority relationships and a status hierarchy. Movement from one stratum to another is called **vertical social mobility**, and one can move vertically either **up** the status hierarchy (as one would see with a poor person who obtains an education and betters his/her status), or there can be **downward** vertical social mobility (as one would see with an old person who made a great deal of money during his or her life, but gets sick, and spends so much of that wealth on the health care system that his/her status is lowered in the status hierarchy).

Social stratification takes three fundamental forms: **1)** **social class** -- a form of stratification typically based upon one's economic position in the status hierarchy (See definitions of "social class," "socioeconomic status," and "social caste" below.); 2) social caste; and 3) estate -- a somewhat antiquated form of stratification similar to that which existed in feudal times, when a person's position in society was based upon the circumstances of his/her birth; i.e., the status of his/her family (you know, being the son of a Duke or the daughter of a landed aristocrat or the like).

Do you know the social stratum to which you belong? Are there particular viewpoints about the world that go along with belonging to that stratum? What are these? ("Strata" is plural; "stratum" is singular.)

social class: a totality of persons having one or more common characteristics. The term most frequently refers to **people who have life chances in common** as determined by their power to dispose of goods and skills for the sake of income; i.e., **socioeconomic class.** (See the next definition.) Social class is related to the notion of social stratification; that is, a social class is a stratum on a hierarchically stratified social structure.

It sometimes is argued that members of social classes ought to have a clear understanding of their position in the social hierarchy and, as a result of this, an identification with the values and needs of other members of their class. This common identification is called "class consciousness."

Although there are many definitions of social class (some of which we will examine when we study Marx), the most common usage of class implies a definition framed in terms of persons who are in the same categories because they share relatively equal amounts of economic resources, prestige, and political-power. Even though sociologists often have disagreed over the precise meaning of social class, the many studies based on these differing definitions have shown that, under most of the definitions used, there is a marked relationship between one's social class and one's life chances. For example, there are correlations between social class and: 1) mortality rates (death rates), 2) morbidity rates (sickness rates), 3) educational and occupational success, 4) mental illness rates, 5) work satisfaction, and 6) general life satisfaction (to name only a few).

As you will see, some of the most important concepts in sociology -- such as social class -- are also some of the most controversial. Sociology is complex and it is not nearly as easy in sociology as in some other social or natural sciences to obtain consensus over what constitutes basic principles or categories such as social class. The complexity of sociology not only can make it frustrating, but such complexity also can make it a great deal of fun.

socioeconomic status (SES): a general designation of social standing or social class, as measured by **income** or **wealth.** Some sociologists take a much broader approach to their meaning of SES, including factors such as place of residence, education, and other status indicators. That is why it is very important that you find out exactly how SES has been defined when you are reading an article about SES or listening to someone speak on subjects related to SES.

You probably are thinking: "Wouldn't it be nice if these sociologists would agree on exactly what they mean when they define concepts such as SES." Well, maybe that wasn't exactly what you were thinking, but it would be convenient if sociologists could have more agreement on what central concepts mean to us. The problem is that science is meant to be contentious (argumentative). One finds that, whether it is a natural science or a social science, there is going to be a lot less consensus (agreement) on concepts than most non-scientists think there will be. Of course, you could think of this tension and disagreement among scientists this way: "Sometimes, it takes a little friction under the wings to get the aircraft of thought aloft."

hierarchy: a set of persons or groups ranked in terms of the degree to which the persons or groups: **1)** have power, **2)** exercise control over persons, **3)** have control over or possess resources, and **4)** enjoy privileges that others do not enjoy because of their **social status**. (See the next definition, which explores "social status.") The power structure is usually triangular, with one or only a few people at the top and many at the bottom of the hierarchy. For example, in a university there are Chancellors, Vice-Chancellors, Deans, Associate Deans, Assistant Deans, Distinguished Professors, Full Professors, Associate Professors, Assistant Professors, Lecturers, etc. That configuration represents a status hierarchy; some would call it a "pecking order" or a "chain of command." Any time we become part of a group, we assume a position in the **status hierarchy** of that group.

Just as **individuals** are part of the status hierarchy of each group to which they belong, different **groups** usually have a place in **group hierarchies.** For example, in hospitals, physicians typically have higher status than members of other groups that make up the health care team. For example, doctors usually have higher status than nurses, even though nurses do work that is just as important as doctors do.

Is it possible to imagine a society in which there is such an emphasis on the equality of individuals and groups that there would be no hierarchy? Imagine yourself marooned on a beautiful island from which you could never be rescued, but which provided all the resources needed to sustain life. Imagine that you are marooned with 99 other people of roughly equal intelligence, skill, talent, etc. Imagine that everybody would like to create a society without a status hierarchy. Do you suppose you could do it? If so, what would it look like? What kind of rules would it have? How would social decisions be made? If you could not create such an egalitarian society, what would be factors that could militate against the establishment of this society without hierarchy?

social status: in the most general terms, **a position** in a socially stratified hierarchy. More specifically, status is defined as a position in a socially stratified hierarchy based on: **1)** wealth, **2)** prestige and/or, **3)** life style. If we were to key on the word "wealth" in the preceding sentence, we would be talking about a particular type of status called socioeconomic status. (See definition below.)

When wealth is not the primary determinant of status, something else such as prestige or life style might be the primary determinant -- or something else altogether such as skill. For example, Michael Jordan, perhaps the greatest basketball player to have ever played, enjoys a very high status based largely because of his remarkable skills. He also has high socioeconomic status owing to his huge income. Conversely, in a status hierarchy based upon political legitimacy, he probably has a modest status compared to someone such as Jessie Jackson. So, just remember, there are different kinds of status that depend upon what it is that is being used to define the concept of status..

Of course, most status positions have an array of socially expected behaviors that go along with them. These behaviors, taken as a whole, provide the person occupying the status with a **social role.** Put more simply, **social status is your position in a status hierarchy; social role is what you are supposed to do** (how you are supposed to act) if you occupy that status. Thus, **social role is really the dynamic (acted out) component of status.** Not incidentally, if you have one status and try to play a role not socially prescribed by that status, you might run into some problems. Unless you can convince the members of society that you are expanding the scope of the role associated with your particular status, you might very well loose your place in the status hierarchy. For example, college professors are not supposed to be "pimps" as a sideline to their teaching and research. "Knowing one's place" is just another way of saying, "knowing one's status," and playing the role associated with that status.

It is also important to remember that most people have several different kinds of status (for example, your professional or occupational status in addition to your status as an athlete, or an artist, or social companion, or a politician, or a parent, etc.). Because every status carries certain roles with it, we also are expected to play many different roles. It is not surprising, then, that some of our social roles conflict with each other, which, as we will see, is called, **role conflict.**

social role: the expected behavior; i.e., rights and obligations of a person with a particular status or status set. Role delineates the part one is expected to play in certain social situations by virtue of having a particular status. Thus, as we have seen, role could be defined as the dynamic (acted out) aspect of status. Status usually is defined by the society, while the role a person plays in that status may have **some** room for interpretation, even though most of our roles and the way we are supposed to play them are determined for us by "the script" society writes for us. For example, if you become a teacher, there are certain things that the society expects you to do; however, different teachers are allowed by society to have a certain amount of variation in the way they play that role. Some people look for roles to play that give them a lot of latitude, while other people look for roles to play that are fairly narrowly prescribed by society.

Some people invent their own roles, which can be very confusing to society when it attempts to provide those people with a status commensurate with the role, since status usually come before role. Think about it for a minute: people who create roles for which there are not existing statuses often are the creators, the artists, the geniuses of the society. For example, the Beatles created a role for which the society had no real status . . . Yet! By the same token, people who create roles for which there are no statuses can be the real outcasts of the society. Try to create something unique -- a new role -- and you may be socially defined as a genius, a madperson, a saint, a savior, a paria, or any number of other statuses; or you may just be ignored.

It is possible to play several roles as part of the dynamic of having a single status. For instance, think of the many roles you play in your status as students. Do these ever have built-in role conflicts?

role conflict: a term typically used to mean two related things; **role conflict** means either: **1) competing demands** made on a person who, because of his or her relationships with others, is forced to engage in contradictory behaviors -- for example, the school superintendent who is expected by a school board to lower costs, while he/she is expected by teachers to improve educational facilities and ensure hefty raises; or **2) the role strain** experienced by an individual because of the behavior required by one or more of his other roles -- for example, the quandary of a policeman who arrests his son while the boy is committing a crime.

caste system: a traditional, closed system of social stratification once prevalent in India. In a caste system, a person's social status usually is **ascribed**; i.e., based on the circumstances of what one **"is"** (age, gender, disability) or **"is born into,"** rather than **achieved**; i.e., based on the status one **earns**. The term caste often is generalized to apply to any stratification system that is highly rigid and in which there is **little or no upward social mobility** -- that is, a system that does not allow persons to move from one status to another higher social status. Is it possible to have both a caste system and a class system in the same society?

conservatism: a social philosophy that tends to resist rapid or radical social change, and adheres to and supports the established or traditional social arrangements, particularly the distribution of power, privilege, and wealth. Conservatives are part of the political right (right wing). On the continuum of right wing philosophies, the most conservative individuals frequently are referred to as **reactionaries.** Reactionaries are not content merely with maintaining the established order of the present (the *status quo*); **they wish to restore some ideas and/or practices of the past.** This can be very confusing. For example, most environmentalists tend not to be conservative; most are liberal or radical. Yet, in their wish to conserve natural resources, much of the rhetoric these people use lauds the unsullied natural environment of the past -- with an implied or stated sense that it would be desirable to return to that past. So, how can a person be both a liberal or radical and a reactionary at the same time, when radicalism and reactionary ideas are at opposite ends of the political spectrum? You figure.

Conservatism is opposed to liberalism and radicalism. Philosophically, it could be argued fairly persuasively that, without conservatism, there could be no social institutions at all. However, with a too wide-ranging and rigid conservatism, social institutions themselves become rigid and produce a static (unchanging) society. Conversely, it is often held by conservatives that the social realization of complete radicalism (the far left political wing) could produce chaos. What kind of balance between social fixity and social change can produce the best society? And, if you have an answer for that, ask, "the best society for whom?"

liberalism: a political philosophy typically aimed at social reform through embracing social change. The term can be somewhat confusing because a much earlier form of **L**iberalism (note the "l" is in upper case) was actually a conservative philosophy. Modern liberalism, however, usually is portrayed by liberals as seeking greater social equality for all of the populace and much more political participation in governance for all citizens. Liberalism is sometimes called classical liberalism, whereas liberalism is often called progressive liberalism so as not to confuse people.

Whereas conservatism is a political philosophy that attempts to preserve the *status quo*, (or, at least a high degree of social equilibrium of venerable social institutions), liberalism endorses moderately rapid social changes, assuming these changes lead to needed social reforms. As a rule, while modern conservatives seek to minimize the role of the State in daily life -- especially in that of the economy -- modern liberals advocate the use of State power to aid disadvantaged individuals and groups.

Liberalism of the moderate left can be contrasted with radicalism of the extreme left. Conservatism of the moderate right can be contrasted with ultra-conservatives, who want virtually no change, or reactionary groups of the extreme right, who, as we see, want change that reverts to the past.

radicalism: Radicalism means to get to the root of the matter and comes from the Latin word *radix,* or root. Sociologically, radicalism usually is used to denote philosophies (ideologies) and people (radicals) who have extreme differences with the ideology and actions of those in power. Implied in the concept of radicalism is the necessity for fundamental change in the institutions of the society -- thus, solving social problems by getting at the **root** of them. In other words, theories of extreme and fundamental change advanced by the left (the left-wing) are called radical.

Usually, **theories of extreme and fundamental change** advanced by the right-wing are called reactionary rather than radical because there is often an element in them that seeks to return to an historically previous social period because of some political-economic characteristics of that period -- for example, a longing for the "good old days." Thus, even though reactionary viewpoints may be "radical," they are not called radical in terms of seeking a new, never before implemented, social change; they are an extreme longing for elements of the past.

culture: the learned and shared behaviors of a society and the cultural artifacts produced by that society. **Culture** is just a way of referring to socially acquired behavior patterns that are socially transmitted to members of the culture through the use of **symbols.** A culture usually has unique forms of: **1)** language, **2)** industry, **3)** art, **4)** architecture, **5)** science, **6)** law, **7)** government, **8)** morals, **9)** religion, etc. The **artifacts** referred to above would be things such as: **1)** buildings, **2)** tools, **3)** art objects, **4)** communication devices, **5)** machines, and so forth.

One way to look at the difference in **culture** and **society** is to think of a pitcher and what is poured into it. **Society** is like the pitcher; it is the structure that is the container for culture. **Society** is comprised of the building blocks -- the infrastructure of the collective sense -- such as the social institutions. The **culture** -- the particular cultural manifestations of those institutions -- such as particular forms of art, religion, polity, economics, science, etc. are contained within the structure of the society. For example, every society has religious institutions, but the specific forms of religion the society has and the "things" associated with those religions are part of the **culture** of the society.

eschatology: comes from the Greek roots *eschatos*, meaning "the last," "the furthest," "the outermost," or "the last time," and *logos*, meaning "the study of." The branch of philosophy dealing with **final things** such as death, the apocalypse, the Judgment Day and the Second Coming of Christ in the Christian religion, the last moment of history, and the relationship of human beings to these phenomena. When an atheist says, "when it's over, it's over; there is nothing after death and I will be impervious to my nonexistence," that is an eschatological statement. When a Christian says, after the death of a loved one, "He is in a better place now," that is an eschatological statement. When Christ said he would rise again at the day of reckoning, that was an eschatological statement.

teleology: comes from the Greek roots *telos*, meaning "end," "purpose," or "completed state," and *logos*, meaning "the study of." The branch of philosophy dealing with the idea that nature or natural processes are directed by movement toward some end and shaped by some purpose. Don't confuse teleology with eschatology. Eschatology has to do with "the end" itself, whereas teleology has to do with a certain order in nature that propels it towards certain "ends," "goals," "purposes." **Teleology has to do with the process of getting to "the end." Eschatology has to do with what "the end" will be.**

If a flood victim is trying to comfort another flood victim by saying, "God works in mysterious ways; there is a purpose for everything including our suffering," that is a teleological statement. Or when Yogi Berra said, "It ain't over till it's over" (referring to the ultimate outcome of a baseball game), that was a teleological statement. Or when Marx expressed his belief that there were certain contradictions in capitalism that would almost surely lead to its downfall, that was a teleological statement. All these statements have to do with process.

aesthetics: a branch of philosophy dealing with the nature of the beautiful and judgments concerning beauty.

ethics: a branch of philosophy dealing with what is good or bad or right or wrong, and with moral duties and obligations. **Ethical absolutism** stresses the idea that there are certain ethical standards which are so important that they apply to all persons regardless of time during which they live and/or the culture with which they identify. **Ethical relativity** (also referred to as **"situational ethics"**) stresses the idea that there is no known ethical standard that is equally applicable to all persons at all times and in all cultures. In other words, **the ethical relativist** would say that what is considered morally and ethically correct in one culture may be seen as morally and ethically deviant in other cultures -- that there are no absolute standards or norms of ethical behavior. Thus, ethical absolutists and ethical relativists often are at odds.

epistemology: a branch of philosophy which deals with: **1)** what knowledge is; **2)** how and where we derive knowledge; and **3)** the limits and validity (accuracy) of information we possess which we call knowledge. As you think about epistemology, ask yourself, "What is the difference in knowledge and other concepts such as belief, opinion, fact, reality, imagination,

14

truth, and possibility?" Also think about how you know things and how you know when you know something.

ontology: comes from the Greek roots *onta* meaning "the really existing things" or "true reality," and *logos*, meaning "the study of." The branch of philosophy which asks the question, "What does "to be" or "to exist" really mean? Ontology, which is a kind of sub-set of metaphysics and epistemology, focuses on the reality of things. So, for example, when I got into the discussion of the nature of reality early in the text, that was metaphysical speculation on my part, but the subject matter -- reality (or Reality) versus illusion -- was ontological in nature. When, in the song, Strawberry Fields Forever, the Beatles said, "Nothing is real," that was an ontological statement. When Descartes said, "I think; therefore I am," that was an ontological statement.

thanatology: comes from the Greek roots, *thanatos* meaning "death" and *logos*, meaning (you guessed it), "the study of." This one is easy. The branch of philosophy dealing with all aspects of death and dying. Thanatology is a cousin of eschatology because, as we have seen, one of the foci of eschatology is the study of final things such as death. Thanatology, however, is focused exclusively on the study of death. The famous studies of Elizabeth Kubler-Ross are concerned with thanatology. She is the scientist who has traced the stages she believes people go through when they find out they are dying of a disease. Of course, she uses evidence obtained from patients. A thanatologist might just as easily speculate or theorize about death by using formal logic or metaphysics, rather than talking to actual people. Which approach would you trust most?

cosmology: comes from the Greek roots, *kosmos*, meaning "world" or "universe," and *logos*, meaning "the study of." The branch of philosophy dealing with the universe as a rational and ordered system. In other words, cosmology seeks to look at the universe as something that follows certain consistent rules. Under those circumstances, it is not surprising that cosmologists (which we all probably are to some extent) are interested in basic physical concepts such as space, time, matter, motion, force, causality, etc.

Cosmology is that branch of philosophy which probably has maintained the closest relationships with the natural sciences. For example, many astronomers and astrophysicists still focus their efforts on phenomena such as the origin of the universe, its structures (stars, planets, black holes, etc.), its characteristics (the effects of gravitational and electromagnetic forces on moving bodies, for example), and the development of the physical universe (such as the "Big Bang" theory). So remember, there is a branch of cosmology based largely upon metaphysical speculation about the universe and another major branch more interested in the physical properties of the universe that can be studied through careful scientific observation and experimentation.

Where do **you** think the cosmos came from? How did it get started? Will it stop or "run down?" Is there anybody out there? Is there anybody out there? These are **cosmological** questions.

science: a procedure for developing reliable and valid information or knowledge about the world, usually based upon the probability that, under specified conditions, particular relationships exist between given empirical (measurable) phenomena (things or events), resulting in bodies of knowledge each of which is organized into a coherent system of general propositions.

religion: a unified system of beliefs and practices relative to sacred things which unite into single moral communities called **Churches**, all of those persons who adhere to the beliefs and practices of the particular religion in question. This definition is essentially that of the sociologist, **Emile Durkheim**, and appears in a major work of his called, **The Elementary Forms of Religious Life.**

Religions typically are characterized by three factors: **1)** specific portrayals of the nature and character of the deity (God) or deities (gods) being worshipped; **2)** a covenant outlining the reciprocal duties and obligations between the deity or deities being worshipped and the humans doing the worshipping; and **3)** a set of rewards and punishments associated with the human worshiper's behavior. As you will see, when we study **Durkheim**, he would add a fourth and, probably to him, most important, factor to the definition of **religion: 4) social rules that regulate behavior among human beings.** As you will see, **Durkheim did this because he believed that religious rules are really social rules** and that "God is society apotheosized" (God is the perfect example of society and the perfect citizen of the society) -- that society is the real God. We will discuss this very perplexing statement in much greater depth in the Durkheim chapter.

Definitions pertaining to CHAPTER TWO:
"The Mad Prophet" of Elements of Sociology Through Theory --
(WORD LIST #3)

methodology: the branch of logic concerned with the principles, rules, and methods involved in scientific inquiry.   Among other things, a method typically considers the general grounds for the **validity** (Defined below) and **reliability** (Defined below) of scientific procedures.

Methodologies are ways we go about conducting scientific inquiries.   There are many different methods to study any social question and usually, different methodologies are used with different theoretical approaches.   This is because a particular theoretical perspective typically will limit both the options of research design and the kinds of data appropriate to a study.   For example, a **Spencerian** (a Social Darwinistic follower of Herbert Spencer, who we will soon study) will approach a scientific inquiry much differently than a **Marxist.**   An **experimentalist** would conduct research very differently than a **survey researcher**, who would conduct research differently than a scientist who undertook **case study** investigations.   A person who did analysis of census data would approach a problem much differently than a person who did **participant observation** (went out and lived and worked with the people being studied).   A scientist who conducted **quantitative analysis** (analysis based on statistics) would conduct research differently than a scientist who did **qualitative analysis** (based on stories told by the people being studied).

As already suggested, there are differences of opinion between scholars regarding whether the methods used in the **natural sciences** are appropriate to the study of human societies, or whether other methods must be used when we are looking at people in society rather than when we are looking at amoebae in a laboratory.   In other words, there is no one "scientific method" any more than there is only one theory to explain the social world.

Although methods of inquiry vary, three phases tend to characterize most methods.   There is the phase of **research design.**   There is the phase when **data are collected.**   There is the phase when **data are analyzed.**   ("Datum" is singular; "data" are plural.)

It is possible to apply more than one kind of methodological approach to a single scientific inquiry.   That way, one set of methods can be used to check the validity and reliability of other methods.   If several methods are used and they all come up with the same answer, there probably is a greater sense of accuracy to the researchers' scientific conclusions -- although, if one's fundamental perspectives (theories) about a social phenomenon are wrong, that researcher could apply every method known to science and still come up with an absolutely air-headed conclusion.   That is one important thing you have to understand about science.   It is not like religion.   Just because you have faith in a particular method or view of the world, that is not going to ensure that, if you use it, your answers will be right.   And, believe me, there are many scientists who treat their methods like religions.   Very sad; very dumb.   (And that is no reflection on religion which, at least, has the dignity of accepting faith without pretension.)

scientific explanation: A **scientific explanation** typically is based on the application of methods of empirical research and deductive or inductive inference (comes from the verb "to infer"). The two major purposes of most scientific explanations are: **1)** to explain causal factors (what causes certain things to happen) in the relationships between phenomena, and **2)** to specify how the **causal** relationship works in probabilistic terms (for example, the **probability** that thing A causes thing B). Of course, Comte was not sophisticated enough to have applied probability theory to his brand of science.

The causal emphasis of scientific explanation is designed to permit the scientist to move beyond simple description of phenomena. In other words, it is one thing to describe a social phenomenon; it is quite another to explain how it works and what its relationship is to other social phenomena.

Scientists frequently make predictions about the relationship -- especially the probability of a causal relationship -- between two or more social phenomena. One of the major reasons scientists are concerned about reliability is that reliable statements possess a high degree of likelihood that what is predicted will be observed.

Meaningful scientific explanations tend to rely upon the successful combination of theory (a cluster of ideas that purport to explain how certain phenomena work) and research designed to test the theory (See **deductive reasoning** below). It is important to test theory because, if we just have a theory without testing it, it remains an unproven (or unfalsified) theory, and, if we attempt to conduct research without any theoretical sense, there is nothing to guide the research (something to act as a basis for the hypotheses we might like to test). Conversely, if we do inductive studies (See **inductive reasoning** below) that, in some cases, tend to be less dependent upon pre-existing theory, there is no guarantee that a theory which explains the phenomena being studied will emerge automatically from the facts we collect. Thus, theory is related in one way or another to scientific knowledge.

What is scientific knowledge? **Scientific knowledge** about the natural and social world is knowledge that has been collected using systematic scientific methods that have sought **scientific explanation.** Social scientific knowledge usually helps to uncover the underlying regularities and relationships between and among social phenomena.

Scientists are supposed to try to be as **objective** as it is possible to be; i.e., not to be unduly swayed in their conduct of inquiry by their own **biases.** (See **bias** below.) Because biases are so deeply ingrained in people, it generally is recognized that true objectivity may be unattainable in both the natural and social sciences. That notwithstanding, adherence to rigorous scientific methods and the exposure of scientific findings to critical appraisal by the scientific community limit somewhat the possibility of severe distortion of reality that can result from subjective bias. Of course, the price we pay for this is that scientists argue a lot. What do you think; do we profit from scientific disagreement; and, if you believe that premise, by extension, do societies need to have a lot of friction to make them work, or to make them interesting?

utopia: an imaginary, idealized and perhaps unrealizable state of society, free from human imperfections. The best of all possible worlds. The word is derived from the Greek *ou topos,* meaning "no place." The word itself was coined by **Sir Thomas More** in his book, **Utopia**

(1516). By a play on the word _ou,_ in which More changed it to _eu,_ meaning "best," the concept of _ou topos_ (no place) became _eu topos,_ or "best place." Do you believe in the possibility of the human realization of a utopia? What would your utopia be like?

The Renaissance: a huge transformational movement that began in Europe roughly during the mid-13th century and reached a high degree of momentum by the early 14th century that marked the change from **medieval** or feudal times (the so-called **Middle Ages** or Dark Ages) to modern times. The term "renaissance" literally means "rebirth." The Renaissance **was** a rebirth of the great humanistic interests of the Age of Greece, when the arts and humanities in general flourished and science made important strides.

feudalism: the prevalent form of social, political, and economic organization in Europe during the Middle Ages, sometimes called the medieval period (c. 500 A.D. to 1450 A.D.). At one time, the Roman Empire had conquered and governed much of Europe. However, as the Roman Empire disintegrated, powerful military leaders (feudal lords) began to conquer much of what had been the Roman Empire. These feudal lords would distribute portions of conquered land to their followers, usually called vassals, who served in the lord's armies. In turn, the particularly powerful vassals would become lords in their own right, maintaining armies by further dividing land they had been given or conquered and "giving" it to **their** followers.

Unlike the Roman Empire, in which cities had flourished, during the Medieval Period, social life centered on the feudal lords' manors (the large agricultural estates held by the lords and their vassals). The feudal manor was usually an economically and politically self-sufficient unit. Thus, one aspect of feudalism was a decentralization (fragmentation) of power.

Also living on the feudal manors were the most exploited class -- peasants (usually called serfs). The serfs were expected to stay on a particular manor and were compelled to work the land and give up a sizable portion of what they produced to the feudal lord. Indeed, the feudal lords had such domination over the lives of the serfs that the latter might just as well have been slaves.

In feudal society, there was no such thing as the State. Feudal society was too decentralized for there to be anything resembling a State -- at least until the most powerful feudal lords consolidated their control over vast territories by force, thereby concentrating power in a few hands.

The feudal system broke down for a host of reasons. One major reason for this breakdown was the way that new technologies created a surplus of labor on the manors. For example, a more efficient horsecollar and/or a plow with a metal plowshare would reduce the human labor needed to create deeper, cleaner furrows than had been made by the old wooden plows pulled by people or by horses wearing horsecollars that choked the horses. As a result of the labor surplus (the people didn't have anything to do to earn a living), many people began to move to population centers that eventually became cities. It was in these cities that the earliest economic forms that were the precursors of capitalism developed.

19

amelioration: to make things better. One ameliorates a situation by making it better; e.g., to ameliorate the condition of homeless people by helping them find a place to live. Of course, one person's idea of ameliorating a situation may be another person's idea of making the situation worse.

The Enlightenment: a philosophic movement of the **18th century** characterized by a rejection of traditional social, religious, and political ideas. The **major characteristic** of the Enlightenment was its emphasis on **Reason**. (See **Reason** in the next definition.)

Reason: A cluster of ideas popular during the **Seventeenth and Eighteenth Centuries** that saw Nature and humans to be good, rather than couched in sin, and which suggested that, if we can discover the natural laws that govern the world, and put society in accordance with them, we can create better societies. It emphasizes the idea of **progress.**

You should distinguish between **R**eason and **r**eason, as they mean different things to most authors. To be able to **r**eason means to have the mental capacity to abstract, comprehend, relate, reflect, infer, discern differences and similarities. In other words, when reason is referred to with the "r" in lower case, it is concerned primarily with human intellectual capacities. Most philosophers do not believe that "lower" forms of animals have the ability to reason the way humans do, if at all. Reason frequently is contrasted with concepts such as emotion, intuition, faith, sensations, perceptions, or experiences.

Industrial Revolution: this was a period characterized by fundamental changes in the system of the production of goods in Western societies that occurred **at the end of the 18th century.** The revolution in methods of production was brought about by the introduction of mechanical power to do operations that had been accomplished by animal or human power before the introduction of machines, or, that simply could not have been done at all without machine power.

The Industrial Revolution was marked by certain basic changes in production: **1)** the development of the factory system (which would eventually evolve into "production line" methods of manufacturing goods such as cars); **2)** the application of industrial technology to agriculture (where early versions of the tractor began to replace the horse, and harvesting machines replaced human labor); **3)** greatly improved and faster modes of transportation and communication; and **4)** an increase in consumer goods (before the Industrial Revolution, commodities could not be produced in great enough numbers to make them widely available to portions of the general population). **Capitalism** expanded enormously during the Industrial Revolution, moving from its primitive, small scale beginnings to become huge industrial capital.

social equilibrium: the state of a society in which its social institutions are balanced in such a manner that internal and external social forces have great difficulty changing the society. In other words, all parts of the society are functioning harmoniously.

Some sociologists (usually conflict theorists) see the kind of society that is in a state of equilibrium as static and undesirable because social change is difficult to bring about and because the *status quo* may be unfair to certain groups in the society, particularly in the distribution of material goods. Even the most committed **equilibrium theorists (the opposite of conflict theorists)** are reluctant to posit a society of no change. Most of these equilibrium theorists believe that the appropriate degree of equilibrium cannot be maintained unless some changes occur to repel or absorb forces that might alter the basic pattern of the society -- necessary change that forestalls undesirable change. In any event, there is usually a good deal of controversy (and conflict) between persons who believe that equilibrium promotes stability and abiding values, and those conflict theorists who believe that equilibrium promotes stagnation and perpetuates the human inequities of the past. What are your views on social change and the extent to which social change ought to be permitted to affect social equilibrium?

positivism: Auguste Comte's philosophy based on his conclusion that sociology progresses only to the degree that it is grounded in facts and experience about which one can make positive (unequivocal) statements. Like empiricism, positivism rejects all explanations that do not depend on sense data. Positivism is, however, a more extreme form of empiricism. For example, if I am a positivist, and I see a spotted cow standing on a hill with her side to me, is it a positivistic statement to say, "Look, a spotted cow!"? Not really; because the only thing I am positive about is that I perceive one side of a cow which appears to be spotted. The cow may be orange or some other color on its other side. I cannot be positive the cow is spotted until I have seen the spots on the other side. Indeed, I can only surmise that the cow even **has** another side until I have positively verified that it does.

Another way of looking at positivism is to view it as a philosophical position that rejects metaphysics in favor of scientific explanations of reality based on observation and experimentation. Of course, the positivists' extreme reliance on empirical data raises an important issue that always is problematic for empiricists: **"Is there a difference in the world we perceive with our senses and the reality of the world -- a difference in appearance and reality?"** This is both an epistemological and ontological question that most scientists still grapple with every day.

social structure(s): the established pattern of internal organization of any social group or society. The elements of social structure include patterns of kinship, descent, and affiliation, forms of family, residence practices, marriage patterns, inheritance rules, and a host of other social institutions.

One way of visualizing society and social structure is to see society like a huge building. The building has to have steel girders to hold it up -- a skeletal structure. The most fundamental building blocks that make up the skeletal structure of a society are its **social institutions.** (Defined below) Of course, societies are different than buildings because buildings stay in one place (they are static) while societies change (they are dynamic). So maybe a better metaphor for social structure would be to see it as a living organism, which has a skeletal structure, but which also changes. (See **organicism**, which is the next word defined.)

The problem with the organicistic metaphor is that it still is not dynamic enough for some people because the implication of the organic metaphor is that, if any part of the organism is

21

radically changed (such as, if the heart dies), the whole organism dies -- which, when applied to societies, leads to a very conservative attitude regarding change in social structures.

In any event, you see how we can go on making up metaphors that give us the blueprints of a society's structure (so far, a spiderweb, a pitcher[in the text], a building, and a human body, here). You doubtless also can see how different people will find varying reasons to agree or disagree with social implications of the various metaphors. The important thing for you to think about is the various ways that social structures can be described and the way that different views of social structure usually carry with them fundamentally different ways of looking at the world. Think about it; what kind of social structure does our society have? What are the implications of your particular view on this matter for the way you act?

organicism: the social view that societies are like biological bodies or organisms. Like a body, society grows, experiences **structural differentiation** (various parts of the whole become different from each other), and **functional differentiation** (different parts do different things), and threatening one organ is a threat to the whole body. Any social philosophy based upon organicism tends to be a fairly conservative philosophy because of the view that upsetting the equilibrium of any part of the society can threaten the whole society. Therefore, it is not surprising that organicists believe that we should not let changes occur (or, at least, occur too rapidly) that can upset the equilibrium of any part of society. Organicism, thus, is closely tied to the notion of **equilibrium theories** as opposed to **conflict theories.**

social institutions: enduring, complex, integrated, systematized, organized aspects of collective life controlled by customs, rituals, norms or laws and by means of which fundamental social desires or needs are met. When it is said that social institutions are **enduring,** it means that they are stable over time and do not depend upon a particular individual or group for their existence; they just **are.** For example, all societies have some form of family structures and always have. When it is said that social institutions are **integrated,** it means that the various parts of the institution (whether in the form of processes that occur, or structures through which processes are enacted) are related to each other in a holistic way; a change in one thing usually means a change in everything. When it is said that social institutions are **systematized,** it means that there is careful specification of what can and should be done by those involved in the institution. You have a social role (or maybe several related to the institution) and you should play it. When it is said that social institutions are **organized**, it means that social roles and role relationships associated with those who participate in the institution are specified. In other words, you know what you are supposed to be doing. **Social institutions are one of the most important concepts in sociology** because they are the basic building blocks out of which **social structure** is forged.

Another way of looking at social institutions is to see them as prevalent ways of thinking and acting that are centered around **such basic social functions as marriage, the family, government, religion, the military, economic forms, education, medicine,** and a host of other crucial social functions. All societies have such basic social institutions, even though they may be quite different in the way they play themselves out in different societies. For example, some societies' marital social institutions are centered around **multiple partner marriages** rather than **monogamy.**

Another way of defining **culture** (in addition to "the learned and shared behavior of people in a society," as we did earlier) is to see **culture as a synthesis of social institutions,** each of which establishes social norms that direct social behavior. Social institutions are particularly important to the formation of cultures if we consider the **synergy** that comes from the interaction of all of the society's various institutions.

Make sure not to confuse a social institution such as marriage with a specific place such as a mental institution! *Mui Impotante!* Mental institutions may, in fact, be part of a society's social institutions regarding mental health and deviance, but they are not, in themselves, social institutions. In fact, places such as mental institutions, hospitals, convents, boarding schools, military posts, prisons, etc. are called **"total institutions"** because, in a total institution, virtually all of the activities of all persons living there occur within the confines of a geographically localized area. In other words, **"total institutions" are self-contained. Social institutions are an abstract concept; total institutions are concrete examples of places where activities take place.**

conflict versus equilibrium theories: **Conflict theory** focuses on the way opposing forces in societies engage in open struggle over **values** (democracy vs. autocracy, for example) or **resources** (such as competition for, property, income, power, etc.). In other words, societies, nation states, tribes, clans, families, political parties, and other groupings are not always in a state of equilibrium (a condition of balanced order). (Big surprise, huh?) **Conflict theorists** typically advance arguments that examine the reasons which lead to the disequilibria **between** and **within** the social groupings that make up society, and the conflicts between different societies.

Despite the ancient nature of human attempts to understand conflict, that understanding took a quantum leap sociologically with the writings of **Karl Marx** -- who we will study in some depth. **Marx** is seen as a **conflict theorist** because he viewed conflict as a characteristic of all societies -- the source of the conflict usually emanating from the struggle between **social classes** of **"haves"** and **"have nots."** Marx's appeal as a theorist was that he looked at conflict in a very systematic fashion and attempted to relate his theory of class conflict to **all** previous societies. Moreover, Marx made global predictions for humanity's future based upon his conflict theory. Because of the robustness and complex integration of his theories everything fits and can be applied to almost any social phenomenon in the world, most conflict theories, as well as equilibrium theories since Marx, have been reactions to Marx's statements.

A basic generalization that applies in most discussions of **conflict theories versus equilibrium theories** is the notion that **radical thinkers** tend to view **conflict** as inevitable (and sometimes good), while **conservative thinkers** tend to be organicists who view **equilibrium** as desirable or **essential** for the survival of the society. Why do you suppose that would be the case?

polytheism: the belief that there are **many gods.** As opposed to monotheism.

23

monotheism: the belief that there is **only one God.** As opposed to polytheism.

totemism: a very early form of religion. As typically used, denotes a society in which kindred people (kin) or clan members believe they have a special relationship with some animal, plant, or other inanimate object, the name of which is applied to the clan (example, the bear clan). In cases where the totem is a plant or animal, there are taboos against harming the totem, although that taboo may be relaxed during certain ritual ceremonies.

Freud believed the totem to be a representation (Freud called it a sublimation) of the primal father, who was killed by the sons of the primal horde (because he was usurping the sexual favors of all the females of the horde), and that worshipping the father's sublimated form through worship of the totem is a way of expiating the guilt members of the society felt for that primal crime of killing the father. Freud always takes us to the edge.

animism: a situation in which life is attributed to **natural phenomena** (such as clouds, the wind, lightening) or **inanimate objects** (such as rocks). Frequently, these natural phenomena or inanimate objects are merely seen as sensate spirits who can become involved in human life for good or for ill. Occasionally, the natural phenomena or inanimate objects are given the status of divinity; that is, they are viewed as gods and worshipped as such. Animism is a very early form of religion.

clan: Originally, the term came from a group of Celtic households, especially in the highlands of Scotland, whose heads traced their lineage from a common ancestor. (Not incidentally, even though the term comes from a relatively recent historical time, that does not mean that clans are a recent historical development; they have been around for thousands of years; the word is just relatively new.)

In modern times, the word "clan" is used in a much more general way than its initial Scottish usage. It refers generically to a group of people who see themselves to have descended from a common ancestor or ancestoress (actual or mythical) and who think of themselves as kinfolk who have special rights and responsibilities relative to each other.

To anthropologists, the word "clan" has very specific meanings. **First,** there is what is known as the **totemic clan.** In the simplest terms, the totemic clan is a group whose social organization is associated with totemic practices in which the group believes that the members of the clan are protected by and have a special relationship with a plant or animal. **Second,** there is the clan type that traces its lineage through women only. This is known as a **sib.** **Third,** there is the clan type that traces its lineage through men only. This is known as a **gens** or **patrilineal sib.**

anthropomorphism: the ascription of **human characteristics** to nonhuman phenomena. More specifically, anthropomorphism is used in religions where supernatural beings such as gods have human traits. For example, the Judeo-Christian God can be angry, compassionate, condemn people, etc.

24

theocracy: literally, the rule of God in society. Historically, theocracy has been characterized by a State and/or society ruled by the representatives of God, usually a priesthood -- somewhat like we have seen in Iran during the last two decades.

absolutism: the belief that there is only one, unchanging, correct, true, objective explanation of reality. Obviously, this is the **opposite of relativism.**

group: two or more people between whom there is an established pattern of social interaction and reciprocal communication of some kind which is recognized as existing by the members of the group, and usually by others who are not members of the group because of the particular behavior which characterizes the group. **A group of only two members is called a dyad.** The concept of the group is probably one of the most important concepts in sociology. If you stop to think about it, **a crowd usually would not be a group.** Why not?

norms: a standard of behavior developed by members of a group to which they conform and with which they are encouraged to comply by positive or negative sanctions. **Folkways, mores, and laws are all forms of social norms.** Thus, a social norm is a shared expectation of a social group or society.

Much human behavior is influenced by the normative content of an individual's culture; norms are one very important way the social group affects the life of the individual. Just as certain people have argued for the existence of cultural relativism or ethical relativism, some very important sociologists (Durkheim, for example) have posited the notion of normative relativism; i.e., the way in which some very different norms regulating the same phenomena are developed in different societies, different cultures, different subcultures within the same society, and even different groups within particular subcultures. Think about how something that is considered normatively correct in one segment of our society might be considered completely incorrect (even deviant) in another segment. This kind of relativism obviously is most prevalent in societies with a great deal of **cultural diversity** -- as in our own society.

folkways: a type of norm that is customary, but is not insisted upon and, therefore, does not involve severe negative sanctions (punishment, for example) for those who deviate from the socially expected pattern of behavior. That notwithstanding, people who deviate from folkways usually are sanctioned by exclusion from the social group (never getting into the group in the first place even though the person might want to), through avoidance by the group's members (the "cold shoulder" or "silent treatment"), or ostracism from the group (being thrown out of the group).

Folkways are the popular habits and traditions of a culture. Phenomena such as fashion, etiquette, or storytelling traditions are examples of folkways. **Folkways** are distinguished from **mores** (pronounced **more-a's**) in that mores are a kind of norm that is insisted upon and is severely negatively sanctioned by the social group when someone breaks the rule (more).

mores: (pronounced **more-a's**) a type of norm in any given society that the society's members, in general, believe to be essential to the society's welfare and continued existence.

25

Mores are not as powerfully sanctioned as laws in a formal sense (although they can sure be heavily sanctioned in an informal sense, which may make the transgressor feel worse than if he/she had broken a law), nor are the sanctions as formally codified as laws, but mores are the "must" behaviors and **contain the elementary morals of the society.** Mores are more powerfully sanctioned than folkways.

laws: commands (do this) or prohibitions (don't do this) emanating from the authorized agencies of the State and backed up by the authority that provides for punishment of violators. In other words, a law is a **norm** that provides specific commands (this form of norm is sometimes called a **prescriptive law**) or prohibitions, and for which there are specific or codified (written down) negative sanctions (punishments) if people break the law.

Folkways or mores are sometimes thought of as a kind of "law" that is referred to as **common law** -- that is, they are laws based upon custom rather than statute. As soon as a folkway or a more is written down, given special penalties that go along with breaking them, and backed by the force of the State, they become **statutory law.** A statutory law obviously is a stronger social statement than a folkway or more **(more-a)**. Try to imagine circumstances in which people in a society are much more compliant with certain folkways or mores than with certain laws even though the law is supposed to be the strongest of the three forms of norm. Many people are more inclined to break a law than a more. Why is that?

sanctions: any provision for regulating a norm. More specifically, a sanction is a penalty for disapproved social behavior, or a reward for approved social behavior. **Rewards are called positive sanctions** and **penalties are called negative sanctions. Diffuse** sanctions are **informal** means of social control (ridicule or gossip, for example) that can be used by anyone, while **organized** sanctions are **formal** methods of social control that can be used only by the proper officials (imprisonment, for example). Think about whether sanctions or the threat of them are very pervasive in your own lives? What kinds of sanctions are most effective in dictating or altering your behavior? Can you think of reasons other than sanctions that people comply with social norms?

tribe: a social group consisting of smaller social units such as clans (or sibs), bands, lineages, villages, and other sub-groups, all of whom occupy a common territory. These units also share a common and distinctive culture, including such things as a unique language or dialect. A tribe also typically has: **1)** a shared name (the name of the tribe); **2)** a shared descent (the tribal members can trace their descendence to the same "family tree," although it may be a very big and complex tree); **3)** a common ideology or unified political organization (having a chief or chiefs who most members of the tribe recognize as leaders); **4)** a common sense of mutual solidarity (**a sense of community**); and **5)** a sense of common solidarity and protection from threatening outsiders (a banding together for organized violence or war when any part of the tribe is threatened).

Tribes either can be very small or very large. Obviously, the earliest tribes were probably pretty small at their outset. In the modern world there are, of course, tribes -- some of the largest of which live in Africa -- that may have millions of members. These very large tribes often are difficult to discern from a nation; hence, we get phrases such as "Zulu Nation."

Gemeinschaft and *Gesellschaft*: two concepts formulated by the sociologist, **Ferdinand Toennies (1855-1936)**. *Gemeinschaft* means "**community**" and describes relationships that are traditional, intimate, face-to-face, and informal -- such as might be found in a tribal village. The intimate, face-to-face relationships just described typically are called **primary relationships** or **primary groups** by sociologists.

Gesellschaft means "**association**" or "**society**" and refers to relationships that are contractual, impersonal, voluntary, and usually limited in scope or duration. Such contractual, impersonal relationships typically are called **secondary relationships** or **secondary groups** by sociologists.

The main thing for you to remember about these two concepts is that the long-term historical trend has been away from social relationships typified by *Gemeinschaft* and toward those that are characterized by *Gesellschaft*. In other words, our society is moving away from a predominance of primary relationships to a predominance of secondary relationships, which may explain how, with so many people in the world to be friends with, there is still so much loneliness. I suppose one should expect such loneliness in societies in which people treat each other merely as means to other ends (such as consumers) rather than as ends in themselves.

homogeneity: **of the same or similar nature.** For example, most basketballs are homogeneous in some important respects.

heterogeneity: **consisting of dissimilar ingredients.** Differentness. Apples and cement mixers are heterogeneous.

continuous versus discrete: principles associated with the quantification of any phenomenon. For purposes of helping us understand the principles, let us think of data we might collect that would be of a continuous nature versus that we might be able to collect that would be of a discrete nature.

Continuous data are phenomena for which any values can be obtained so that no number or amount or degree is ruled out. For example, if we had sensitive enough instrumentation to measure it, today's temperature could be 72.5699304 . . . degrees. In other words, our measuring device might be only sensitive enough to calculate that it is 72 or 73 degrees, but the real temperature moves along a continuum that allows it to fluctuate by matters of fractions of degrees.

Discrete data are quite different than continuous data. If, for example, someone were to ask how many people were registered for this class, we could not say "493.665439 . . . ." People can only be counted as a single unit; there are either 493 people or 494 people. I suppose we could cut somebody up and then say we have 493 and one-third person, but, if we cut somebody up, they would no longer be a live person. Thus, discrete data are phenomena for which only certain values can be obtained.

Another way to think about these phenomena is to recognize that **continuous data are called continuous because they are on a continuum,** which is a coherent whole characterized by a progression of values varying by minute degrees. Another example: we know the Renaissance began, but we don't know the exact minute or day because it was a progression along a continuum of minute degrees of progress. The same holds true for Comte's "Law of Three Stages." We may be able to tell when we are approaching movement from the theological to the metaphysical stage (if we even believe in his theory). Or, we may know when we are in one of the stages; but we can only arbitrarily say that on a certain day at a certain time we passed from one stage to another. Obviously, history **does not always work that way.**

For example, we know that on December 7, 1941, at a certain time, the United States declared war on Japan. We also know the day and time that war ended. Thus, we were able to calculate by specific events **discrete changes** along that temporal continuum.

If someone who is in a position to know, tells you that you are **"really smart"** relative to your classmates, that is a **continuous bit of data.** If someone tells you that you have a **specific "IQ"** relative to you classmates, that is a **discrete bit of data.**

social contract: like any contract insofar as it has binding agreements on all parties to the contractual relationship. A **social contract,** though, is agreement among members of a group that they will be bound by conditions that afford them rights if they meet certain responsibilities within an institutionalized system of political rule.

It is interesting to see the very different ways that the concept of social contract has been interpreted by different social theorists. For example, **the Frenchman, Rousseau,** believed that total individual freedom prevailed among humans until they contracted with other humans to create government, which limited everyone's freedom. Conversely, **the Englishman, Hobbes,** believed that, before the social contract was set up, humans were in a perpetual state of war, with everybody fighting everybody and no one having property or any other rights. To Hobbes, the social contract provided the freedom to be protected in this once warlike environment. Needless to say, Hobbes viewed the state that resulted from the social contract in a somewhat brighter light than did Rousseau, who longed for the freedoms enjoyed by "the noble savage."

In American Society, the fulcrum of the social contract is really based on **representative democracy.** Although there are certainly many elements to the social contract, the most pivotal one is that the general populace will allow certain elected officials to conduct matters of state if these politicians agree to represent the interests of the electorate. You win some; you lose some.

reciprocal: to reciprocate is to return in kind or degree. In other words, "If you'll scratch my back, I'll scratch yours."

democracy: a social system based on a commitment to equalitarianism (all people being equal), especially in the political sense. Democracies typically rely on rule by the majority, but usually have specific protections for the rights of minorities insofar as it is possible in a system of majority rule for the majority to tyrannize the minority. Ostensibly, in a democracy, the supreme power is held by the societal members in general who are supposed to want to exercise that power in periodic free elections. Yup, folks, that's how it's supposed to work -- you know, elected officials representing the interests of the polity, everybody voting, everybody's vote being equal.

differentiation: a process whereby persons or groups acquire characteristics that tend to make them unique or different in **function or form.** A classic example of differentiation is the way specialization occurred in societies as they became more complex. Look at it this way: the earliest people probably took care of most of their individual needs themselves. Then, it started to make sense to "divide the labor." So, for example, if it was a hunting and gathering culture, it might make sense for some people who were particularly good hunters to be responsible for most or all of the hunting, and for others who were particularly good at making clothes or pottery or tanning hides to stay at the encampment and make clothes and pottery, tan hides, or do other specialized duties. And then, there were the gatherers who went foraging for seeds, medicinal plants, etc. In short, the roles people played became more focused or specialized.

The more complex the society gets, the more complex the division of labor becomes until we have, as in modern societies, people whose primary social task may be to do one thing -- deliver the mail, wash the windows, paint cars, preach to their flocks, deliver medical care, etc. Thus, the more complex a society becomes, the more "different" kinds of things there are to do; hence, the more differentiated the society becomes, especially in its division of labor. (We will see later in the text that norms also tend to become more differentiated as a society becomes more complex.)

inductive reasoning: the opposite of deductive reasoning. In inductive reasoning, we reason **from the particular to the general.** To take a rather simplistic example, if we observe that 49 out of 50 of all dogs prefer the taste of meat to that of cucumbers, we might be prepared to generalize that most dogs prefer meat to cucumbers. Of course, we could have arrived at a similar conclusion deductively, based on the general notion that dogs tend to be more carnivorous than herbivorous, and thus, we could have predicted their preference for meat over cucumbers by using logic. There also is a more abstract definition of inductive reasoning than that above.

Induction is a form of logical inference that generalizes characteristics of a sample taken from a larger population to the whole population (at least those cases in the population that are similar to the sample population). Thus, a generalization is made about the whole population on the basis of observation of part of the population. Induction is based upon the notion that, if we can assume uniformity and relative permanence in nature, careful observation of representative samples of natural phenomena permits reliable generalizations from them to the larger populations from which they are drawn.

The quality of induction depends on the representativeness of the sample that is taken from the whole population. If the sample is typical of every other possible instance of the phenomenon being studied, then the generalized traits derived from the sample have a high probability of being true for the whole. **For example, when you go to the physician to have your blood tested, he/she does not take all of your blood; the physician assumes that a little bit of it will be representative of the rest of your blood.** One problem associated with conducting social research is obtaining a sample that is truly representative of the whole population of persons being studied. Many scientific procedures have been developed for the purpose of obtaining representative samples, although, in almost any inductively-based social research, critics will accuse the researchers of some kind of sampling error (unrepresentativeness).

deductive reasoning: the type of logical and scientific reasoning and method **that proceeds from the general to the specific.** Deductive reasoning is used in the scientific method when specific hypotheses or particular predictions are derived from broader theoretical principles. To put it another way, deductive reasoning is a form of logical inference in which particular or specific conclusions are drawn from general principles. For example, if, like Karl Marx, we were to believe that differences in **social class** position are both inevitable and the basis of most human conflict, and we wanted to have a better understanding of racial conflict, we would attempt to study how social class differences affect **racial** conflicts. Thus, we might **deduce from the general principle a hypothesis** which said that people of different races do not fight with each other primarily because of racial hatred. Rather, racial hatred is based on social class differences or threats to social class position -- that, for instance, poor white people become racist, not because they inherently dislike Black or Latino people, but because the white people view Blacks and Latinos as threats to their jobs in the labor market, therefore representing threats to their social class position.

The classic deductive argument is the **syllogism, which consists of three parts: 1) a major premise, 2) a minor premise, and 3) a conclusion.** For example: 1) All men are mortal; 2) Socrates is a man; therefore, 3) Socrates is mortal. As you can imagine, a syllogism can be factually false, even though it may be deductively logical. For instance, if one of the premises is incorrect, the factual nature of the deductive process will yield factually incorrect information. Consider, for example, the medieval belief that the earth was the center of the universe. It might be deductively logical to say: All planets circle the earth; Mars is a planet; therefore, Mars circles the earth. Obviously, the logic is correct, but the incorrect premise -- that Earth is the center of the universe -- makes the conclusion false.

The issue discussed in the preceding paragraph is one of the real problems with deductive reasoning as it relates to the research of sociologists. If one's guiding theory has a factually incorrect premise, then the phenomena we try to investigate on the basis of that theory may adhere to the logic of the theory, but yield factually incorrect conclusions. Let us look at another example. Some people believe that evolution is based solely on the "survival of the fittest." For purposes of this discussion, let that be our **major premise.** Our **minor premise** then could be that people born with certain disabilities are not "as fit" as people born without those disabilities. (It is always helpful if it is specified what those likely to survive are "fit" for; but let's assume that "fittest for what?" has been answered to our satisfaction.) The **conclusion** might be that people with disabilities, through the evolutionary process of natural selection, will cease to survive.

Thus, if we accept the theory of survival of the fittest, we might decide to test a hypothesis based upon our acceptance of that theory. We might, for example, hypothesize that people with certain disabilities will die out because of their inability to earn a living. So we have based our hypothesis on a theoretical premise that may be incorrect. **First,** it does not account for the fact that many people with disabilities are quite capable, and cannot be considered to be "unfit for survival" just because able-bodied people may find such a disability undesirable. **Second,** the theoretical premise does not account for the fact that, in many societies, able-bodied people have shown a great deal of compassion and a helping attitude toward people with disabilities, and that such compassion (and the survival of people with disabilities) may be the surest sign that a society **is** evolving.

The point of the last paragraph is not to assert that deductive reasoning is bad, or that science cannot advance as long as it uses deduction to formulate testable hypotheses; in fact, most of the natural sciences' greatest discoveries have come about as a result of tests of hypotheses based on deductive reasoning. The point of the last paragraph is, that like all forms of thinking or reasoning, deductive reasoning is vulnerable to certain common errors, and, just because something is "logical" within a certain system of thinking, that does not necessarily make it true. Sorry, Mr. Spock.

If you were developing a project of social research, do you think you would be more likely to proceed deductively or inductively? Why would you choose one approach over another?

bias: emotional or intellectual preconceptions or prejudices of individuals or groups that may lead to certain subjective interpretations which are partially or completely different from "objective" reality (what really is happening). When we have biases, they usually are based on conditioned tendencies to support a certain point of view or conclusion despite the absence of adequate evidence to support that point of view or conclusion. Indeed, a highly biased person (we all have some biases) often will reject evidence that does not agree with his/her preconceived notion of the issue. ("Don't confuse me with the facts; I already know how I feel and what I think.")

The establishment of the **"value-free"** (that is, trying to be without bias) position of sociology was an attempt to eliminate intellectual bias. Some persons claim that this position is itself a bias which prevents sociologists from taking professional stands on controversial social issues. In other words, if a sociologist tries to be completely unbiased, he/she may give up all sense of moral and ethical conviction relating to the things being studied. Probably the best approach to dealing with bias is: **1)** to attempt to identify one's own biases, **2)** to be aware of how these biases might affect our objectivity, and **3)** not permit them to have too great an effect on our observations and conclusions.

Do you have any biases? How hard have you worked to identify what they are? What effect do they have on your worldview? What would a completely unbiased person be like?

rationalism: a theory that **Reason itself is a source of knowledge** that is superior to sensory impressions (remember **empiricism**) in ascertaining truth, understanding the world, or solving problems. The main characteristic of rationalism that tends to make it controversial is that its adherents believe that some "truths" about the world are knowable quite independently of observation or any kind of empirical methods. Indeed, a rationalist would believe that there are truths that come prior to experience, that there is a rational method that can be applied to any subject matter to give us adequate explanations, and that, once rational logic is mastered, everything in the whole universe can be deduced from these rational laws.

variable: a trait or characteristic that can vary in value or magnitude from case to case. The term is used in contradistinction to **constant**, which is an unchanging characteristic.

As you look through some of our definitions, you will see the term variable come up periodically. The reason sociologists are so interested in studying variables is precisely because they change or vary. And, in our attempt to understand social reality, if we can isolate particular variables and then see precisely how and why they change as the result of the effects of, or changes in, other variables and constants, we can begin to obtain a picture of how social phenomena occur -- how society works.

Let us look at an example. Let us assume that we are curious about what has caused a change in enrollments at Purdue in the last few years. In other words, enrollment figures are one factor that have varied -- a variable. Now, let's assume that I believe in a **social theory** that holds that intercollegiate athletics are very important factors in American society, and that one of the assumptions I make based upon that theory is that students will tend to increase their enrollments at places with successful athletic programs. Based upon that assumption, I am going to attempt to test the hypothesis that part of the variability (change) in our enrollments at Purdue are attributable to the fact that Purdue has had a successful basketball program. Thus, the varying degrees of success of the basketball program represent another variable. But it is a slightly different kind of variable than the first, because, according to my theory, the variation in enrollments depends (**dependent variable**), in part, upon the basketball program (**the independent variable**).

Next, I have to find a way to develop a **valid** (**that tests what I say it is going to test**) and **reliable** (**consistent over several similar trials with a single group or with similar groups**) instrument or procedure to test my hypothesis. (See **validity** and **reliability** -- next two definitions after this one is completed.) Of course, because I only hypothesize that **part** of the variance in enrollments is attributable to the success of the basketball program, I have to attempt to isolate other variables that might affect enrollments (for example, variations in people's wish to have an education so they can find a better job). Then, after I isolate the variables I want to study, I have to control the study in such a way that the effects of other variables are isolated -- don't get mixed up with the success of the quality basketball program = changes in enrollment connection.

Once I have the necessary variables isolated and controlled for, I can test my hypothesis, assuming I can obtain a representative sample of students who recently have decided to enroll at Purdue. It has to be representative of all newly enrolled students because, if I only talked with students in the athletic department or students who attend basketball games, my results would suffer from "sampling error" -- or a failure to obtain a fair or representative sampling from the total population of new students -- thereby biasing my results.

If, after I have done all the aforementioned (and many other) things, I can show that a certain part of the upward variation in enrollments at Purdue was indeed a result of the success of the basketball program -- that the dependent variable does, in fact, vary as a result of the fortunes of the basketball program (the independent variable) in the manner I have predicted in my hypothesis -- then it would be considered appropriate to say that I have demonstrated, if not proven, **something . . . .**

Another thing I have to do is to specify **the degree to which I was able to ascertain there to be variance in the dependent variable as a result of the independent variable.** After all, the degree of variance might be so small as to be inconsequential.

What remains to be done then is for the study to be **replicated.** (See **replication** in the definition that follows **reliability** below.) If the experiment is repeated in several different places with the same results, then we might actually have discovered something of social consequence.

Finally, I have to make my findings available to the scientific community so that the interested members of that community can criticize any shortcomings in my methods of investigation, or my interpretation of the results. Then, other members of the scientific community and I can try to decide whether college athletic programs of the type described here do cause college enrollments to vary. If that variance turns out to be true in every situation in which the hypothesis is put to a rigorous test, scientists may feel more comfortable in adding that piece of information to "the scientific body of knowledge."

And, folks, what we just went through here is only the tiniest tip of the iceberg as it relates to social research, if for no reason other than that the aforementioned study is only one of hundreds of different ways of doing research. Now do you see why social science can be so challenging, and for some of us, so much fun, especially if a person is curious about people and enjoys a challenge? Ok; so it bored you. I like it, but, then again, some people kiss cows.

validity: the degree to which a research instrument (a questionnaire, for example) actually measures the things (variables) that are supposedly being studied -- or the degree to which the instrument measures what it purports to measure. In other words, you may make up a questionnaire by which you think you are measuring people's generosity towards persons less fortunate than themselves, when, in fact, you may be measuring only people's willingness **to report** their generosity to a researcher. Thus, if you look at what people say, and conclude that they are very generous to less fortunate persons, when all they have really told you is that they like to have researchers think they are generous, you haven't measured what you said you were going to measure, which invalidates your findings.

Moreover, if you have reported data gathered with an invalid instrument, your report of those data confuses the issue of generosity rather than sheds light on it. By the way, the reason I used the example I did in this case is because we know that there are often major contradictions between what people say they do and what they really do when placed in the role of research subjects who are permitted to make self-reports.

If one wants to become more specific about **validity,** there are actually several different kinds of validity. **First,** there is **apparent validity.** Here, the measuring instrument is so closely linked to the phenomenon under investigation that it "obviously" is providing valid data. For example, the place at the carnival where one strikes a lever with a large hammer to try to ring a bell is supposedly a measure of a person's strength. If the hammer, lever, and bell are not "rigged" to cheat the striker, then one has apparent validity between the measuring device and what it is supposed to measure (strength).

Second, there is **instrumental validity.** A measurement procedure is said to have instrumental validity (also referred to as **"pragmatic"** or **"criterion"** validity) if it can be shown that observations match those generated by an alternative procedure that is accepted widely as being valid. For example, if your SAT scores correlate precisely with your performance in college, there is reason to believe that the measures by which your college performance is assessed are valid measures, and the SAT scores are valid predictors.

Third, there is **theoretical or construct validity** in which there is substantial evidence that the theoretical perspective used as the basis of the observations corresponds with the observations themselves (provided you haven't let your biases get the best of you while making or interpreting the observations), then the inquiry can be said to have **construct validity.** For example, if you believe the source of virtually all human conflict is social inequality and you do a fair and unbiased piece of research relating to conflict -- which discovers that social inequality does lead to human conflict -- then there is a likelihood that your study has construct validity. Of course, this one can be very problematic because scientists may only look at the factors that validate their world view. As Paul Simon said: "Man sees what he wants to see and disregards the rest."

Now look at the definition of reliability because most social research is relatively useless unless the methods used to conduct the research **are both reliable and valid.**

reliability: As you will find in your statistics courses, the statistical sense of reliability is a very precise measure that can be learned easily with the help of a good statistics teacher. For purposes of this dictionary, the concept will be defined somewhat more simplistically than it should be, but it will give you an elementary sense of what reliability is. Now to that explanation of reliability.

If you were a social scientist who was going to use a particular instrument (let's say a questionnaire) to measure a specific group's attitudes (let's say surgeons' attitudes) about a particular variable (let's say surgeon's fears of contracting AIDS while operating on patients), the instrument you use ought to produce similar results when being used with similar groups of surgeons. Moreover, if you were to go back to a single group of surgeons and administer the questionnaire to them two weeks after they filled it out the first time, the results ought to be similar the second time they fill it out to what the results were the first time. In other words, if there is a consistency within groups regarding their views on certain variables, or, if there is a consistency across groups, the instrument you are using to ascertain these views is probably a reliable instrument to measure the variables. **Thus, reliability is the tendency of a measurement procedure to obtain the same results each time it is applied under similar circumstances.**

Validity and reliability are bound up with each other in important ways. In very simple terms, validity is the extent to which a measurement procedure gives a correct answer. It is easy to obtain perfect reliability with no validity at all. Take, for example, a broken thermometer that is stuck at a particular temperature. The thermometer is very reliable because it gives exactly the same temperature every time you look at it. However, the thermometer is not at all valid in the temperature readings it gives if there are actual temperature fluctuations in the environment.

replication: the duplication of the procedures followed in a particular study in order to determine whether or not the same findings are discovered using the same procedures. Thus, to replicate a study is to repeat it. If scientists can repeat an experiment with the same results as were predicted by the earlier experiment -- whether it is conducted by a different team of scientists in the same locale and at the same time as the first study, or in different locales at different times -- there is reason to believe that the conclusions regarding the first study were valid and may generalize to all situations identical to the experimental situation. Thus, the more times an experiment is replicated with identical results, the more valid are the conclusions.

By the way, you probably can see why the **reliability** of scientific instruments and procedures is important when we replicate scientific experiments. To wit, if we replicate the same experiment with very different outcomes, and we do not know if our research instruments and procedures are reliable, we don't know whether the difference in outcomes is attributable to unreliable instruments and procedures, or to invalid hypotheses. If, on the other hand, we know our instruments and procedures are reliable, and the outcomes of a replicated experiment are different, we usually can conclude that our original hypotheses are not valid.

All of this is very complex, but you can figure it out quite easily, and, if you stop to think about it, I'll bet you use many of the same principles that scientists use in their experiments in your daily decision-making and reality testing; you just don't give them "highfalutin" names and you may not be quite as rigorous in your employment of sampling, control, reliability, validity, and other procedures. Think about instances in which you act much like a scientist in your everyday life.

social control: the techniques and strategies for regulating human behavior in any society, either by conditioning or limiting the actions of individuals or groups. A few generalizations can be made about social control.

Social control is sometimes at work as coercion, sometimes as persuasion. Coercive control usually emanates from the agencies of law and government and is accompanied by force or the threat of force. Raw physical force has never been a long-term deterrent to social deviation because, eventually, people will feel they have nothing to lose by revolting.

Social control as persuasion is probably the most prevalent form of social control. All of us doubtless can think of many ways in which suggestions are made to us to which we respond (such as advertising). Further, we come to be controlled by our wish to imitate certain people (such as the "star" system in the arts), or we come to be controlled by our wish for praise, reward, or recognition (such as we see in systems of promotion in bureaucracies).

Often times, social values internalized in a person through persuasion are more powerful social controls than force. For example, a common religion and a concern for an afterlife have been very powerful forces in many societies to encourage conformity. Moreover, as we have seen with informal sanctions, gossip and ridicule directed at persons who fail to conform to community norms can be very effective means of social control, especially when the person being sanctioned interacts frequently, and on a face-to-face basis with members of his/her community, and with little privacy from the scrutiny of the group. Not incidentally, such informal norms tend to break down in the privacy or impersonal anonymity of urban life.

As you will see, especially when you turn your attention to the critical theorists, some social thinkers believe that much social control in American society relies increasingly on manipulation and technological controls. For example, our behavior often is controlled when we are induced to internalize "new needs" to consume the latest consumer products.

As for technological means of social control, we see the expenditure of huge amounts of money to improve surveillance of suspected nonconformists, further breaching individuals' rights to privacy. The development of certain drugs ("chemical straitjackets") also has been quite effective in controlling potentially deviant behavior. The list of technological controls could go on, but the point is that the power structure of a society (as well as large portions of the citizenry) expect compliance with certain norms and often will go to great lengths to ensure that compliance. The questions you ought to keep in mind about social control are: Who really sets social norms in modern societies? How do we distinguish legitimate from repressive social controls? Is it possible for people to believe in the utilization of social controls that are not necessarily in their best interests or the interests of the society? Are there social controls of which we are unaware that determine our behavior? And so on. Big questions.

reductionism: In the simplest terms, reductionism means that the explanation of a highly complex, multi-faceted phenomenon is reduced to a single and oversimplified facet of that complex phenomenon. A slightly broader definition of reductionism is subscribing to the notion that the principles explaining one range of phenomena are adequate for explaining a completely different range of phenomena. For example, if a person believes that **all** human behavior -- both individual and group -- can be explained by genetic factors, that person would be ignoring the effect of symbols, environment, psychological factors, etc. on human behavior. Another example of reductionism would be the attribution of all human motivation to economic factors. In other words, we can reduce the explanation of all manner of complex issues to single factors that are seen to be "most important" or "all important."

Typically, reductionism is seen to be a negative approach to trying to understand aspects of the world because the implication is that the reductionist is very "narrow-minded" -- ignoring important aspects of life for a highly simplified view of a highly complex world. But, if you really stop to think about it, most scholars tend to be at least somewhat reductionistic. I am a sociologist; naturally, if someone asks me to explain an event, I'm likely to attribute the factors responsible for that event to social or sociological phenomena. Sociological reductionism is called sociologism. And many sociologists, even those who see the remarkable complexity of the world, will tend to be sociologistic. That being said, does it mean that sociological reductionism or any other kind of reductionism is necessarily "bad?" Good or bad really isn't the question though; a critical assessment of reductionism is not an "either bad/or good" question so much as it is a matter of assessing the degree to which a person is reductionistic.

Let's face it: people are going to explain the world in terms of what they know best. The world is becoming increasingly specialized; so individuals are going to come to know more and more about a very narrow "band of reality." One can't be faulted for taking refuge in what one knows best to explain things. Some people just take reductionism to such an extreme degree, their arguments become preposterous. If, just because I am a sociologist, I believe that sociological factors are the most important in explaining human activities, that is to be expected. If, just because I am a sociologist, I say that biological factors, psychological factors, cultural factors, and so forth are completely unimportant -- indeed irrelevant -- in explaining human activities, then I am just being a fool.

In life, we are all, from time to time, going to get "backed into a corner" in which we will be expected to take a stand or express a preference on "what makes the world tick." The major issue with regard to how to respond is the degree to which we can demonstrate with facts why our position or preference is important without being reductionistically intolerant. Sometimes that is a tough task. By the way, what do you think is the most important factor in accounting for human activities?

sociocracy: the kind of society Auguste Comte had in mind, in which sociologists would be the high scientific priests of society who would discover, through the employment of positivistic methods of observation, experimentation, and cultural comparison, all of the invariant natural laws that governed human behavior in societies. With the discovery of these laws, the sociologists then could create societies in accord with these natural laws, providing the society with a high level of predictability of human behavior, in large measure because, once the invariant natural laws were discovered, citizens of the society would have responsibilities to obey them. One wonders if, in Comte's sociocracy, there would have been many more responsibilities than rights. The sociological "priesthood" would control society, not only by being the discoverers of its invariant natural laws, but by being in charge of education of the young.

humanism: the doctrine, and the related social movement, based on the idea that humankind itself is the supreme value in the universe and that humans, therefore, should be concerned primarily with human interests rather than, as in the past, with the assumed interests of a deity (God) or deities (gods, in polytheistic societies).

Basically, humanism is a secular religion that places the kingdom of "heaven" here on earth. If there is an essential feature of humanism, it is the belief in the unity of humankind, coupled with the belief in the perfectibility of humankind through human beings' own efforts.

Think about humanism; why do you suppose people with certain religious beliefs find humanism so reprehensible? Do you think that having a deep respect for humans and humanity is a bad thing? And, if you don't, how far do you believe it is permissible to go in making humanity the supreme value in the society?

Definitions pertaining to **CHAPTER THREE:**
"The Radical" of <u>Elements</u> of <u>Sociology</u> <u>Through</u> <u>Theory</u> --
(<u>WORD</u> <u>LIST</u> #4)

<u>stereotype</u>: a simplified and preconceived image of what all members of a certain group are like, regardless of their individual characteristics, or the realities of their lives. Usually, a stereotype carries negative connotations with it. Typically, a stereotype is an exaggerated belief associated with some particular human characteristic, especially as it relates to a national, ethnic, or racial group.

Stereotypes are a characteristic feature of prejudiced thinking. **<u>Stereotypes</u> <u>are</u> <u>based</u> <u>on</u> <u>a</u> <u>fixed</u> <u>mental</u> <u>image</u> <u>of</u> <u>a</u> <u>group</u> <u>or</u> <u>category</u> <u>of</u> <u>persons</u> <u>and</u> <u>are</u> <u>applied</u> <u>to</u> <u>all</u> <u>members</u> <u>of</u> <u>that</u> <u>group</u> <u>or</u> <u>category,</u> <u>with</u> <u>no</u> <u>attempt</u> <u>to</u> <u>test</u> <u>the</u> <u>preconceptions</u> <u>against</u> <u>reality</u>.** Stereotyping often is associated with bigotry, although we all probably harbor certain stereotypes. Ethnic or racial jokes take a stereotypical look at the groups about which they are "humorizing." Think of the most prevalent stereotypes in our society. Can you think of any new stereotypes that might be developing?

<u>totalitarianism</u>: **<u>total</u> <u>control</u> <u>exercised</u> <u>over</u> <u>all</u> <u>activities</u> <u>of</u> <u>all</u> <u>groups</u> <u>comprising</u> <u>the</u> <u>body</u> <u>politic</u>.** Typically, totalitarian regimes -- usually characterized by a dictatorship or a committee of all-powerful political functionaries -- do not allow opposition, criticism of the regime, or representation of divergent group viewpoints. Totalitarian regimes not only seek to control the political process, but seek control over all social institutions and agencies, **<u>including</u> <u>the</u> <u>most</u> <u>private</u> <u>spheres</u> <u>of</u> <u>individual</u> <u>life.</u>** Indeed, there are supposed to be no spheres of individual privacy.

Governmental surveillance of all citizens characterizes the totalitarian state. **<u>Compliance</u> <u>with</u> <u>the</u> <u>activities</u> <u>and</u> <u>goals</u> <u>of</u> <u>the</u> <u>totalitarian</u> <u>state</u> <u>usually</u> <u>are</u> <u>achieved</u> <u>through</u>: 1) <u>mass</u> <u>movements</u>** (as we saw in the huge rallies in Nazi Germany), **2) <u>terror</u>** (as we see in many parts of the world today -- e.g., Iraq -- which discourage nonconformity), and **3) <u>technology</u>** (which facilitates surveillance and goads citizens into activities that can be monitored easily). In a totalitarian world, even your innermost thoughts are not supposed to be private and you are not only supposed to fear "Big Brother" but love him as well, and protect him from any hint of nonconformity to the totalitarian ideology, should your neighbor deviate from the totalitarian ideology.

<u>idealism</u>: a basic philosophical view, put forth by such thinkers as **<u>Plato</u> <u>and</u> <u>Hegel,</u>** that the world (reality) is the expression of the mind -- that everything we perceive is basically "mind stuff." In other words, idealism suggests that humans understand the external world by living in our heads, that is, through our ideas about the external world. Indeed, to many idealists, the external world is not a physical world; it just doesn't exist. Thus, reality is dependent for its existence upon the mind and its activities. Ideas are the ultimate reality. Insofar as idealists believe that the qualities we experience in objects are the sensations of our minds, they tend to believe that reality is understood through Reason.

An extended definition of idealism would posit the view that we can transform our ideas into social realities, that the ultimate social reality resides in ideas, and that the ultimate social good can be achieved by striving toward the ideals associated with these ideas. This concept, called **social idealism,** usually is accompanied with an attitude centering on the unattained welfare of humanity -- the "have nots." As you study further, note how **idealism** and **social idealism** relate to **altruism, liberalism, and utopianism.**

socialism: **an economic system in which the means of production (the things used to make or grow other things) are collectively or publicly owned and controlled, and are used in the interests of society as a whole, rather than being privately owned and controlled for private profit.** There are several variations of socialism; however, the term usually is used to mean ownership of the means of production by the State, with control in the hands of State-appointed boards.

Many early theories of socialism specified ownership by communities or by workers themselves, which, of course, makes these forms of socialism much closer to **communism** than the form of socialism in which the State is a central feature. **Indeed, one of the major differences in communism and socialism, as Marx defined them, was the withering away of the State in communism, whereas the State persists in socialism.**

In addition to public ownership of the means of production in socialism, as opposed to private ownership as in **capitalism, socialism typically involves large scale central planning rather than reliance on market mechanisms** (such as the laws of supply and demand in capitalism) for determining production and distribution of goods.

materialism: another way of describing something **very unlike idealism.** The materialist viewpoint holds that society does not change primarily because of the prevalent political, religious, familial, or societal institutions (to name but a few), or through the influence of prevalent ideas, or through the actions of great individuals. **Rather, a materialist philosophy holds that society changes (is transformed into newer forms) primarily because of the economic institutions of society -- especially such things as the relations of production, and alterations in technology, and the products of technology.**

One of the great misconceptions about materialism comes from its confusion with materialistic values. For example, one might hear that a rich kid from the "burbs" is so materialistic that he doesn't care about anything else other than the stuff and money he can accumulate. To a degree, that is a manifestation of materialistic values. However, the political materialist has a very different emphasis.

The political materialist is characterized by the fact that he or she thinks that people's fundamental material needs for food, clothing, shelter, etc. have to be taken care of before any other needs can be met. Thus, **one form of materialism** has more to do with greed and a bankruptcy of crucial values, **and the other,** more to do with human survival that permits other activities. Maybe the best way to think about the two senses in which materialism is used is to consider that **one form deals with wants, while the other deals with needs. The unifying principle of all forms of materialism, however, is that economic factors and institutions are epicentral in constituting human social activities.**

    grand theories: social theory that is articulated at a very high level of abstraction and usually is generalized to the whole of society. Typically, there are three levels of social theory. **First,** there are **empirical generalizations,** which usually are based on a few observations of a single population or a sample drawn from that population (although the sample may be small or quite large). **Second,** there are what are called **middle-range theories;** middle-range theories usually interrelate two or more empirical generalizations. **Third, there are grand theories, into which all concepts, empirical generalizations, and middle-range theories can be fitted.** Most of the large-scale theories of social life such as those of **Marx, Weber, Durkheim, and Mead, are grand theories. In other words, they aim to explain, in a systematic way, virtually every aspect of the social life of a society.** Be very careful not to confuse this concept of grand theory with the specific functionalist "Grand Theory" developed by a sociologist named **Talcott Parsons.**

    scientific socialism: another name given to Marxism. This came about because Marx's brand of socialism was based not only upon ideas (the logical appeal of socialism), but because **Marx gathered a great deal of empirical data to substantiate his claims,** and was thus considered scientific in this regard by some persons.

    dialectical materialism: the **materialistic** aspect of Marx's thinking is apparent in his belief that human consciousness is determined by the material conditions of our existence. For example, Marx believed that the flow of history could be understood as being moved forward by the economic (material, as opposed to philosophical) struggles and victories of opposing social classes. His theory is materialistic because membership in one or the other of the opposing classes is based on the relations of production between the classes; i.e., some classes are workers, some are owners -- the workers only having one thing they can sell, which is their labor.

    To put it another way, the materialist believes economic (or material) realities determine the human consciousness people experience as historical reality. This view contrasts with Hegel's idealism (see earlier definition) which sees consciousness as determining material existence, or, at least, the history associated with material existence. (The reader will remember that idealism has a very specific view of the material world -- essentially seeing it purely as "mind stuff.")

    The **dialectical** aspect of dialectical materialism is based on Marx's adaptation of Hegel's notion of dialectical thinking, **which Hegel applied only to the realm of ideas,** while Marx applied dialectical thinking to the material realm of societal formation and transformation. (We have not studied dialectics in any depth yet if you are reading this definition in sequence; so don't be concerned that you don't understand.) For now, let's just say that Marx sees each epoch in history as containing the conditions of its own opposition; i.e., circumstances that will arise to challenge the *status quo.* Remember: Marx was a conflict theorist. Because society -- especially capitalist society -- contains contradictions in the way it is structured (which we will discuss in detail, especially when we get to "the Law of The Rate Of Falling Profit"), Marx believed that capitalism would pass through certain stages of history evoked by those contradictions which finally would destroy capitalism and result in the formation of a classless society.

So, when you think of dialectical materialism, think of economic circumstances that lead certain economically unequal groups to have conflicts that must be resolved if society of any kind is to continue. We'll talk about the rest in the text.

communism: a political-economic philosophy based upon a mode of social organization that perceives **the ideal society to be one in which there is no social stratification,** and in which the economic system favors **public ownership of the means of production.** In other words, **communism opposes the private ownership of the land, factories, and machinery (examples of the "means of production")** that are used to produce the goods and services a society consumes.

According to early communist theory, in a communist society, wealth and power would be shared in harmony by the whole community. Today, the term communism refers mainly to the materialist-based conflict theory of Karl Marx, although there have been many different types of governments that claimed to be implementing Marx's principles. (This, by the way, is in opposition to Marxist theory, which views communism as having to be an international system, rather than a multiplicity of systems, all somewhat like Marxism, being implemented in many different nation states. **In other words, Marx believed communism could exist only on an international basis.**)

According to Marx, the moving force of history is the struggle of exploited social classes against their exploiters, leading to the eventual overthrow of the latter by the former, or the collapse of the exploiters' economic systems because of inherent contradictions in the logic of the systems. **Marx believed that the social class which owned the means of production under capitalism -- the bourgeoisie -- derived their wealth from the work of laborers (a social class he called the proletariat).**

Further, Marx believed that the accumulated wealth of the bourgeoisie gave them the power to exploit more and more ruthlessly the labor of the proletariat, resulting in a concentration of the wealth of the society in fewer and fewer hands, and a greater and greater impoverishment of the proletariat. Marx held that as more wealth was concentrated in fewer hands through the exploitation of labor, the proletariat would become fully conscious of how it was being exploited by the bourgeoisie and would rise up in a violent revolution against the bourgeoisie and seize the means of production from them.

Marx argued that society would, after the revolution, pass through a period of socialism and State-ownership of the means of production. (Indeed, the primary difference in a communist and a socialist society is that there is still a state in socialist societies.) Marx contended that history would demonstrate that the State is merely a vehicle of class domination, and therefore, even the socialist State would wither away and be replaced by a communist society. **Marx maintained that the end of capitalism and the withering away of the socialist state would spell the end of social classes -- that communism would lead to a classless society.**

Under communism, Marx asserted that all people would be free to realize and maximize their human potential, and that the economy would be planned by the people, rather than be based on market economies ostensibly responding to the laws of supply and demand, as is the case in capitalist economies. Moreover, the economy in communist societies would be planned in such a manner that there would be enough of what people really require for survival being produced to meet everyone's fundamental needs.

The process of capital investment also occurs in communist/socialist systems. But the view of communists and socialists (most of them) is that labor produces the surplus ("profit," in capitalist jargon) that pays for new equipment. Hence, communists and socialists feel that wealth should not accumulate in the hands of a private individual (as capitalists do) who can own and control the means of production. Conversely, socialists believe that the means of production should be held collectively and used for the benefit of all persons in the society, and, that laborers ought to decide whether to produce a surplus, and, if so, what to do with it.

Just as there are many different manifestations of capitalist economies, so are there many different types of **socialist** economies -- **no fully communis**t economic form ever having been realized that has proven enduring so far. **When you try to think about capitalism and communism, probably the most important distinction to remember is who owns the means of production and who gains from the labor of the workers in the society.**

shibboleth: a test of membership, a watchword or password employed without regard to the intrinsic validity of the word itself; i.e., the conceptual content of the word is unimportant. As a matter of fact, in its use as a shibboleth, the word's only content emanates from its use as a password. The word received its meaning as a password from the biblical story of when the Israelites of Gilead wished to detect the Ephraimites (with whom they were at odds). Because of their language, the Ephraimites could not make the sound "sh" very effectively; thus, when they were asked to pronounce the word "shibboleth" (meaning "river"), they gave themselves away as spies.

Think of passwords that identify you as members of groups, irrespective of the conceptual content of the word itself. If, for example, a person says something is "awesome, dude!," that jargon may function more as a password identifying the speaker as having certain values he believes to be similar to those values held by the person with whom he is talking, rather than saying anything about the object or event that is being described as awesome.

political Left: typically those elements in the political spectrum that seek significant, often radical, change in society. Socialism is a leftist movement. Communism is a leftist movement. Liberalism is somewhat left of center. And so on. The term "Left" comes from the seating arrangements in European legislative and parliamentary bodies in which the radical members sat on the presiding officer's left. An example would be in the French National Assembly of 1789, where the conservative nobles took their seats to the right of the President -- given that etiquette of the time held that the place of honor in any formal meeting was at the host's right. Because the room was shaped like an amphitheater, the moderates took seats at the center of the room -- giving us the notion of centrists. And, of course, the radicals ended up on the left side of the room.

operationalization: When we operationalize a term, we enter an agreement with all other persons with whom we will be using the term that the term has a very specific meaning (usually arrived at by using prespecified procedures). This kind of agreement to define a thing in a particular way typically is referred to as "operationalizing a definition." Everyone may not agree with how we should operationalize the term; some persons or groups may believe that the term's real meaning should be operationalized a different way; but, when we operationalize the term, at least other persons know what **we mean by it when we use it** -- "where we are coming from," so to speak. For example,   intelligence often is operationalized as: "how a person scores on an intelligence test." Of course, there are many people who believe that such tests do not measure real intelligence and that these tests are culturally and racially biased. No matter how one feels, though, if we know that people will be using the "IQ. test score = intelligence" as their operationalized definition when they talk about intelligence, we know what **they** mean.

As you can imagine, there are some terms it might be impossible to operationalize if we expect to obtain a consensus on what it means, no matter how hard everyone is trying to optimize communication. For example, ideas such as "freedom" or "patriotism" would mean very different things to different persons. However, if we can convince others to recognize that, right or wrong, our operationalization of the term is what we mean by it when we use it, this can save us a lot of trouble and miscommunication when we are trying to talk about a particular concept. In most societies, there is supposed to be an informal standard of normative consensus on what words and concepts mean. Obviously, it doesn't always work that way. "Peace."

capitalism: **a form of economic organization characterized by private ownership of land and capital resources -- what were characterized earlier as the means (or tools) of economic production. Initiative for economic decisions is private rather than public; the system is dedicated to the task of earning private profit for the owners of the means of production.**

Remember: private property in the form of regular **consumer goods** such as houses, cars, clothes, etc. are not considered to be the "means of production." To repeat, the means of production are the property and other capital goods such as land and factories and large-scale manufacturing machinery that are used to produce consumer goods.

You will find that some persons (especially **capitalists**), in discussing communism, erroneously hold that there is no private property allowed in communist systems as there is in capitalist systems; that is not so. That would be like saying you had to use a communal toothbrush; a toothbrush **is** private property. **What is not allowed in communist systems of any kind is the private ownership of the means of production. Conversely, in capitalist economies, it is the rule rather than the exception that private individuals or companies own the means of production.**

44

Although there is some controversy over what motivates capitalists to want to accumulate evermore capital (wealth), there is little doubt that capitalists do try to accumulate capital in the form of profits. (**You will find that what capitalists call "profit" is referred to as "surplus" or "capital" by socialists or communists.**) The language can be a bit confusing, but you usually can identify a person's political leanings on the basis of whether he/she calls the difference in what it costs to produce something and what the product sells for, "profit" or "surplus." Most modern industrial capitalists argue that by investing profits in such things as technologically more advanced equipment, they are able to increase the productivity of their workers -- the amount the workers can produce at a given cost -- and thus, that the capitalist can increase profits and total wealth either for savings, consumption, or further investment.

Traditionally, capitalism has had an emphasis on private wealth, individual (as opposed to collective) decisions about production, and "free" competition (as opposed to an economy in which production decisions are planned for by the whole society, or representatives of the whole society). Thus, capitalism has tended to be associated with the notion of minimizing governmental intervention in economic affairs.

Despite rhetoric about keeping the government out of the free marketplace, it should be pointed out that capitalism has occurred in very diverse political systems (e.g., Nazi Germany, on the one hand, and Sweden's "welfare state," on the other). And even at the height of nineteenth century "*laissez faire*" capitalism (completely unregulated capitalism), capitalist-friendly governments were quite strong in their intervention in economic affairs **for the protection of the system of private property and contracts.**

Moreover, the need for increased profits and economic growth has caused most capitalist-friendly governments to pursue active foreign and military policies designed to expand markets, protect investments, and assure the orderly flow of raw materials for capitalist production from around the world. Thus, in spite of all the talk about "free markets guided by the laws of supply and demand," **there is a great deal of governmental intervention,** even in what is supposed to be these self-regulating market economies. Put simply, when it is to the advantage of the capitalist and the capitalist can exert control over the political process and the government, we rarely see unplanned, competitive, freewheeling market economies free of governmental intervention.

Of course, in modern capitalism, governments intervene in many ways in the society. For example, because the only way most people have of earning a living is selling their labor, poverty often exists among those whose labor brings little return, such as portions of: **1)** the aged population; **2)** persons with certain disabilities; **3)** the population of dependent children; **4)** the unskilled laborers of the society; **5)** displaced entrepreneurs such as farmers who have lost their farms through bankruptcy; and **6)** certain groups who are the objects of discrimination.

Additionally, many people are thrown out of work when the economy goes through periods of stagnation, recession, or depression (which capitalists associate with fluctuations in the "business cycle," while Marxists view these economic dislocations as the inevitable by-products of capitalism's overproductivity and call them "crises of capitalism"). In any event, to soften fluctuations of the business cycle or the crises of capitalism (whatever you choose to call them), modern capitalist governments frequently have programs of: **1)** social welfare and/or compulsory social insurance (such as Social Security); and **2)** fiscal policy (such as taxation programs, spending programs, and programs of manipulation of the currency supply and/or interest rates).

There is another reason for government (public) intervention in an economic system such as capitalism that is supposed to be free of governmental intervention is imperfect competition. For example, instead of many small businesses competing for laborers and for consumer dollars, a few companies **(oligopoly)** may control large areas of the economy. **When a single corporation controls a whole portion of the economic system, this is called a monopoly.** The anti-trust component of the government occasionally intervenes in these cases so that consumers will not be completely at the mercy of these mega-corporations. After all, a monopoly can charge pretty much what it wants to, since it is the only producer making a particular product and controlling a particular portion of the economy, including the labor force associated with that portion of the economy.

Despite government intervention designed to prevent monopoly, the overwhelming trend in the leading capitalist economies has been a greater and greater concentration of wealth and industrial and political power in the largest corporations. In other words, there has been a trend towards oligopoly or monopoly, or, to put it another way, a concentration of greater wealth in fewer hands. This is why modern capitalism frequently is referred to as "monopoly capital," especially by leftists.

dialectical method: a method of thinking brought to a philosophical pinnacle in the work of Hegel. Dialectical thinking juxtaposes the tensions or contradictions that exist within ideas. Sometimes it is explained this way: there is a prevalent idea (the **thesis**), then, there is another idea that challenges the prevalent idea (the **antithesis**), and, finally, after the two ideas conflict with each other there is a resolution of the tensions between the two forms of the idea called (the **synthesis**). Hegel believed that the history of the transformation of ideas proceeds through this process of the creation and resolution of the tension between opposites. The historically dynamic aspect of dialectical thought comes from the fact that a synthesis eventually becomes the new thesis and then is challenged by a new antithesis, and so on. Hegel believed that dialectical processes brought our ideas to higher and higher planes -- levels that moved toward ideational perfection. The major importance of the Hegelian dialectic to sociologists is in Marx's adoption of dialectical principles and his adaptation of them to the social (material, rather than just ideational) world.

value(s): any phenomenon that has some degree of worth to an individual or group and which possesses the capacity to satisfy human needs, wishes, or desires. It is important to distinguish the concept of value from that of utility (usefulness) because value's reality is in the human mind (if you look at it psychologically) and/or the collective consciousness (if you look at it sociologically), not in an external object itself as is the case with utility. **Value per se is strictly a matter of belief.** Thus, an object may have absolutely no apparent utility, but be very valuable to people. Of course, items that have great utility typically have value attached to them as well.

Many sociologists are interested in values because values influence the selection of the means and ends of human actions, and values serve as criteria by which objects or actions are appraised. What are the major values of American society? Are any of your values different than the major social values? If your values and those of the society are nearly identical, to what extent is it accurate to describe you as a socially determined creature? And if you are such a creature, how do you feel about that?

objectivity: a person's ability to examine and interpret phenomena without having his/her views and interpretations **unduly** distorted by personal feelings, prejudices, preconceptions, or any other forms of **bias.** It sometimes is said that objectivity can be equated with relying on evidence and reason rather than emotion. To be objective does not mean to be without emotion (since that is impossible); it only means that one should identify one's emotions and not let them hold sway over one's perceptions and the interpretations of those perceptions.

A **solipsist** (definitely a word worth looking up) would argue that there is no such thing as objectivity as it relates to our perceptions of the world **because we only can know ourselves.** To state solipsistic premises another way, the solipsist would say: "We only can perceive reality through the filters of our personal feelings, biases, prejudices, or preconceptions."

Do you think objectivity is possible? Do you think objectivity is desirable? Would you rather see objectivity in artists, politicians, religious leaders, and "scientists" than in the other persons with whom you communicate? In other words, are there realms of human experience and expression where objectivity would have great value and others where it is not of much worth or downright undesirable? And, if that **is** the case, which realms of experience, thought, and inquiry should be very objective, and which realms would objectivity ruin?

subjectivity: relating to internal mental states such as emotions or attitudes. When a person is being subjective, that means that he or she is interpreting his or her experiences in terms of emotions or attitudes without sufficient regard for reality as determined by rigorous activities such as experiment or other means of careful investigation. Why do we talk so much about objectivity in science? Would it be possible to learn to use elements of our subjectivity to be better scientists?

historicism: the view that history is so constitutive of making things the way they are that giving a descriptive account of a phenomenon's history is a sufficient analytic explanation of the cause of the phenomenon. **Historicism is based upon the fundamental view that there are inexorable laws that determine all historical events.** A case in point of an historicist viewpoint would be Comte's "Law of Three Stages." It is a nearly perfect example of the idea that there "are inexorable laws that determine all historical events."

Marx was an historicist because he believed the "inexorable laws that determine all historical events" are the laws of dialectical materialism -- the view that, at each stage of a society's development, there were contained within that stage the conditions of that stage's own opposition -- that capitalism, for example (as thesis) had contradictions within its fundamental philosophy that would evoke antithetical or opposing ideas. These ideas, in turn, would lead to conflict that would have to be resolved by some new philosophical and **material** synthesis, and so on.

A major difficulty associated with trying to define the notion of historicism is to distinguish it from the concept of **determinism.** (See the next definition.)   Remember, even though the historicist believes there are certain unalterable laws that govern the unfolding of history, **those laws have the capacity to evoke very different outcomes in a given historical situation.** A good case in point would be Marx's philosophy.

Even though Marx believed that capitalism had contradictions within it that would lead to its own destruction, he allowed as how capitalism might (probably would) fall as a result of a class war between the workers and the owners, **but that there also was a possibility** that capitalism might just collapse of its own contradictions without so much as a shot being fired. **A purely deterministic view would not have allowed the "either"/"or" possibility; a purely deterministic view would have shown us exactly what would happen and how it would happen and why it had to happen that way.**

determinism: **the philosophical doctrine that any phenomenon at any given moment must be as it is at that moment because of a necessary chain of causation.** An example would be the Genesis story in the Christian Bible. Adam and Eve did have the free will either to commit or not to commit the original sin. However, once that sin was committed, it unleashed a series of historical events -- including Christ's crucifixion and the Second Coming -- that, in Christian theology, had to occur; i.e., were determined in advance.

Almost any way of thinking has an element of determinism embedded in it somewhere, especially if it has causal models that make predictions. Can you think of any deterministic models of thought that are prevalent in our society?

praxis: Marx used the term to refer to what humans do in the realm of revolutionary activity. It is really his term for "practice." Marx uses a different term than "practice" because he was opposed to the dichotomy (separation) between theory and practice he perceived in bourgeoisie thought (e.g., "the man of thought" vs. "the man of action").

For Marx, theory gives rise to praxis because theory provides an objective understanding of the way the contradictions of capitalism make the transition to socialism possible, and thereby, theory compels workers to assume their role in the class conflict, which is to destroy bourgeoisie's domination of the proletariat. By the same token, theory is tested by praxis (one finds out if the theory was accurate based upon the outcome of the actions predicted by the theory), and, to a certain extent, one uses praxis to develop theory (one changes one's theory if history as revealed in actions does not validate the theory).

economic reductionism (materialism):   in its most extreme form, the view that economic or material factors are the only causes of social patterns. In a less extreme form, the view that economic or material factors may not be the only factors causing social patterns, but that economic factors are dominant, over other factors such as biology, psychology, politics, and culture. A parallel interpretation is that consciousness is determined by economic realities because economic realities are the most fundamental element of human existence and, therefore, represent the most fundamental needs.

Critics of economic reductionism have stressed the idea that the economically reductionistic view pays too little attention to the other factors that are at work simultaneously with economic factors. For example, **Max Weber believed culture had significant impact on economic behavior,** although Weber did not try to downplay the huge importance economic factors have on social life. If you stop to think about it, Marx (the materialist) has an arguable position; for although "we do not live by bread alone," it is very difficult to stay physically or emotionally healthy enough to be very formative in the creation of society if we are starving.

mode of production: the prevalent productive techniques of a particular economy at a particular period in history. Some undeveloped societies have a mode of production that could best be described as primitive handwork, while other highly developed societies have fully automated modes of production. A society or an historical period may be characterized by making reference to the customary techniques or modes of production of the time, such as "the machine age," or "the age of robotics."

Marx inspired the term "mode of production" and put great emphasis on it in his political economic philosophy. He believed that the mode of production of a society determined the character of the major institutions of the society and often had great influence on the relations of production (the relations between workers and owners and between workers and other workers). Indeed, you will remember that Marx believed that what an individual is coincides with her/his relation to production, both in terms of **what they produce and how they produce.**

social class (The Marxist Version): For Marx, social class position is determined by the relationship of members of particular classes (the two primary classes of Marx's time being the bourgeoisie and the proletariat) to the means of production. **For Marx, the most basic relationship a person can have to the means of production is either to own capital or not to own capital. The owners are, to Marx, the bourgeoisie; the workers who own no capital, are the proletariat.** Marx also believed that social factors such as differential prestige, style of life, and interaction patterns came solely from social/economic class.

A sociologist named Max Weber disputed this notion and argued that there were independent groups of people who were members of classlike clusters as a result of sharing similar life styles (example: yuppies), or because they were part of a special subculture (example: the country club set), or because they had similar levels of prestige. Weber labeled these categories, **status groups** in order to distinguish them from classes. Some sociologists tend to look at status groups as being the same thing as social classes. So you need to know what people mean when they talk about social class because they may be interpreting it as Marx did (primarily economically) or interpreting it as some of Weber's followers have (differential prestige, differential life styles, differential subcultures, or predisposition to interact frequently with only certain other kinds of people).

There is a third way besides the ways Marx and some of the Weberians defined class to define the concept. **Gaetano Mosca** and **Vilfredo Pareto** disputed Marx's interpretation of social class by basing their definition of class membership on a person's relationship to the means of force or the person's relationship to the government. In other words, unlike Marx, they did not believe that political control was based only on economic control. Mosca and Pareto's was instead a power-based conception of social class. Modern theorists such as **Gerhard Lenski** have taken the power-based conception of social class to its logical conclusion; he believes that social classes are various aggregates of people who are in similar power positions. Some people like this approach because it allows the same theory to be applied to discussions of social class in both capitalist and communist social systems.

social class consciousness: as Marx would define it, the awareness of people in the same social class (particularly among the working class) of their common social, economic, and political conditions and class interests. Marx noted that workers tended to lack a common realization that they were being exploited by the ruling class, and may even have accepted the ideology of the bourgeoisie.

Marx held that until workers could see they shared common conditions of life with other members of their class, including common goals and common enemies, these persons could not have a fully developed class consciousness. Marx believed that the development of the class consciousness of the proletariat would lead these class conscious persons to work in a unified manner to overthrow the capitalist political economic system that oppressed and exploited them. It sometimes is argued that members of social classes ought to have a clear understanding of their position in the social hierarchy and some sort of identification with other members of their class -- a class consciousness.

Many studies by sociologists have shown that class consciousness is not highly developed among workers in the United States and other industrial societies of the west. Some sociologists believe that workers do not have the kind of class consciousness envisioned by Marx because the workers believe that the society offers them enough social mobility (the ability to move from one class to another) to belong to the middle class (and maybe even the upper classes), which many of these working class people wish to do.

Moreover, the society offers even working class people enough inexpensive consumer goods, expensive goods bought on easy credit, and a homogeneous access to the middle class ideology via the media, that they may feel they belong to the middle class even if they do not by economic standards. **This lack of consciousness of their own class and its conditions is what Marx and others (notably Gabel) called false consciousness.**

reification: to regard something that is abstract or theoretical as a material or real thing. So, for example, if, like **Freud,** we decide there are things such as **the id, the ego, or the superego** that are part of the human personality and treat the concepts as if they were "real" in the material sense, we are reifying the concepts. (Find me an id and bring it to class.)

Another definition and example might help you to understand reification. Think of it as a circumstance in which a concept is confused with the real phenomenon it is supposed to represent. In **the study of urban sociology,** for example, there is a concept called **"concentric zone theory."** This just means that there are a series of zones -- starting with a core zone in the center -- and moving with concentric circles (each representing a different zone) out from the center. Each zone is seen to have different populations, normative structures, subcultures, etc. Now, if you go to any city in America, you might see "zones" that are adjacent to each other pretty much as concentric zone theory predicts. But you are not going to see lines of demarcation painted in pink, green, yellow, or any other colors to form nice well-divided concentric circles in the city. Thus, the abstract notion of concentric zones may reflect, to a certain limited degree, social reality; but it is not material social reality, and, if we begin to treat it as though it were -- as though those concentric lines are painted -- **then we have reified the idea** of concentric zone theory.

The word reification comes from the Latin *res*, meaning "thing." **Thus, we reify something when we treat as a real or concrete thing, something that is an abstraction. Try to think about reification when we look at Comte's "Law of Three Stages," Durkheim's typology of suicide, or Weber's types of authority, or Mead's concepts of the "I" and the "me."**

laissez faire: a French word meaning "to let alone," or, more precisely, "to let them do." Denotes a socio-economic doctrine whose advocates assert that government should not interfere with an individual's freedom to follow his or her own interests, particularly in economic relationships, and especially that there should be no government intervention in the productive sphere. This belief was incorporated into the writing of **Adam Smith's, The Wealth of Nations.** Smith believed that the market mechanism in a free-enterprise competitive economy has a self-adjusting factor (what Smith called an "invisible hand") that harmonizes the productive process so that the appropriate amount of goods are produced, income is distributed optimally, and full employment is achieved without any intervention of the government in the economy.

You probably can see how a "market economy" operated by "the invisible hand" of the laws of supply and demand would differ significantly from a so-called "planned economy," in which the government or the people, through the apparatus of the State, plan very specifically for what goods are needed and which of these needs will be supplied. Of course, modern capitalistic economies are actually "mixed economies" insofar as the market mechanism operates to a limited degree without interference of the State. However, the State does interfere in many aspects of the market (for example, there are anti-trust laws which do not permit monopolies to form). In short, there really are no *laissez faire* capitalist economies, even though many capitalists probably wish there were much less governmental regulation of capitalist economies that do exist.

bourgeoisie: During the French Revolution, the term designated the newly developing middle class, which was between the working class and the nobility. In a more general sense, the bourgeoisie was the class that would displace the feudal landed aristocracy as the ruling class through the power of the bourgeoisie's control of the newly dominant industrial system of production called capitalism.

With the rise of modern industrial capitalism, the meaning of the term bourgeoisie broadened and it came to designate collectively all those whose interests that were allied with the owners of the means of production (agricultural land, factories, machines used in large-scale manufacturing, etc.) -- such ownership causing the bourgeoisie to be viewed as the ruling class in capitalist societies.

Marx distinguished between the ***haute bourgeoisie*** (captains of industry, such as Rockefeller) and the ***petite bourgeoisie*** (the small scale entrepreneurs who operated small businesses). The bourgeoisie thus represents a class of people which is at the opposite end of the economic spectrum from the proletariat or working class, who do not own any of the means of production, and whose only source of "wealth" is the sale of their labor.

The term bourgeoisie has come to have a different meaning in modern times than the original Marxist meaning -- the new meaning sometimes being used synonymously with the term "middle-class." So, when someone uses the term bourgeoisie, it probably would be useful to your understanding of their position if you can find out exactly what they mean by it.

proletariat: industrial and agricultural workers who sell their labor to live because they own no capital; that is, they are not in possession of any of the means of production, nor are they in alliance with the owners of the means of production as managers are.

lumpenproletariat: a term used by Marx to denote the lowest stratum of society. The lumpenproletariat (or "reserve army of the unemployed" or "reserve industrial army") is comprised of unemployed or periodically unemployed individuals who live at the edge of existence, economically. Because of the instability of economic life for the lumpenproletariat, Marx did not see the lumpenproletariat as having much of a revolutionary spirit, especially in their willingness to help break labor actions (strikes) which were being conducted by the proletariat. In other words, if people are poor enough, they will not care if they cross a picket line or work as a "scab," even if it means that they work for subsistence wages and their actions may keep labor movements from gaining any power. Who do you think would most benefit from the existence of a lumpenproletariat and why do you think that?

exploitation: the use of a subordinate group by a group in a superordinate (higher) position for its own selfish purposes. There are many ways in which people are exploited, but the common factor is that they always are used like a tool or means to some end by the exploiter. Typically, the superordinate (dominant) group uses the subordinate (exploited) group to acquire a valued commodity. For example, workers have been exploited for their labor so they can create a surplus of capital or money for a dominant group. Women (and sometimes men) have been exploited for their sexual favors in sexist societies. Nation states, governments, or corporations have exploited less powerful, usually undeveloped, countries for their natural resources.

monopoly: a situation in which an organization (or, in rare instances, an individual), acting as a seller, controls the market for a commodity or service because that organization has exclusive possession of that commodity or exclusive capacity to provide that service. A monopoly turns a market exclusively into a seller's market; thus, if you want to buy the commodity, you must pay the monopoly price or find an alternative to consumption of that commodity, or make it yourself. Obviously, if an individual or organization gains a monopoly, the purported initiative to excel in the production of goods or delivery of services that comes from competition is gone and the consumers are totally at the mercy of the monopolist. Can you think of any benevolent monopolies? Can you imagine a capitalist who would not like to have a monopoly if his or her company could have it?

labor theory of value: the Marxist notion that laborers create the surplus (profit margin) between what it actually costs to produce something (wages, material, overhead of other kinds) and the exchange value (the price for which the product is sold). Marx held that capital (money) cannot create that surplus (profit) because money cannot produce (work), and thus any surplus that is created should go to laborers because it is the laborers who create this surplus.

Marx did not believe that capitalists ought to receive a profit for their investment of capital because it was surplus that was squeezed from some other laborers at some earlier historical period of the exploitation of labor by capital. In other words, it really should not have been the capitalists' money to invest in the first place. Moreover, capital oftentimes was inherited, which made it twice removed from the process of creating the surplus represented by the difference between the cost of production and the exchange value.

Labor theory of value is one of the most controversial aspects of Marx's system of economics; many Marxists do not even believe in it. Do you think Marx believed that **capitalists** should receive a fair wage for their labor in organizing the production of goods? Trick question. He did not believe there should be capitalists.

affluence: Usually used in the economic sense, where it refers to an abundance of wealth. American society is considered one of the most affluent societies on earth because the vast majority of its citizens have many material goods, and an unusually high number of individuals have great wealth. Obviously, with poverty and homelessness, not all Americans can be considered affluent. What are the signs you use to determine if a person is not affluent? Would many of the nonaffluent of our society be considered quite well-to-do in many other cultures of the world?

alienation (Marx's Definition): term used by Marx, who believed that industrial workers would be alienated by their lack of control over the labor process because these workers would have little say about what is produced, how it is produced, and what their relationship would be to other producers. Marx also suggested that when we are alienated from our labor, from a meaningful voice in the process of what will be produced and how it will be produced, and from fellow producers, we become self-estranged or separated from our essence as human beings (or, as Marx called it, from our "species life" or "species being"). This separation prevents us from becoming all we can become as human beings; thus, although the labor process should broaden laborers' perspectives as human beings, according to Marx, labor under capitalism mainly worked to put limitations on workers' growth. Scholars since the time of Marx have broadened the applicability of the concept of alienation, which is defined in its more generic usage in the next few paragraphs..

alienation (**generic** **as** **opposed** **to** **Marxist** **meaning**): The reason this dictionary has two definitions of alienation -- a "generic" definition, and the one developed by Marx -- is that Marx's meaning of alienation is very specific and restricted almost totally to the alienating effects of capitalism to any persons connected with the economic productive process.   The more generic term is much broader in its meaning.

In the broadest sense, alienation means that the alienated person becomes estranged from his/her society. This estrangement can be for any number of reasons. Maybe the person just doesn't "fit in." Maybe the person subscribes to an alternative set of values from the primary values of the society. Maybe the person comes from a group against which the society or groups within it discriminate. For instance, consider persons who come from the ranks of the poor, unemployed, disabled, or certain minority groups. Throughout history, persons from these kinds of groups have felt estranged from their societies because they have confronted obstacles -- usually economic -- that made their lives so difficult that they were unable to feel part of the larger social group. Today, many of these same groups still feel left out (like beings from another planet.)

Of course, economic or social "comfort" or "success" do not guarantee that a person will not be alienated. Think of all the people who are economically affluent who cannot find a meaningful social and/or personal life. For instance, think of the numbers of rich people who are alcoholics, drug addicts, or who commit suicide. If you get a chance, see the movie, "Reversal of Fortune"; that says it all.

Another example of the way alienation is discussed by some writers has to do with the effects of rapid social changes on the creation of at least three different types of alienated behavior. The **first** type has to do with human beings' inability to adapt to rapid social change. The **second** is related to the first, in that social change has produced a trend toward urban living, and this trend has resulted in depersonalized living relationships and interactions (what been defined as **secondary** **relationships**).   **Third,** rapid social changes often are accompanied by social upheavals that introduce doubts and/or serious disagreements about what appropriate behavioral standards are. In other words, when there is social upheaval, the rules break down, and, without familiar rules, we feel alienated.

If you stop and think about these three kinds of alienation, you will notice that they are based upon the idea that alienation in the forms of unadaptability, depersonalization, isolation, and anomie (a state of normlessness) comes from rapid social change. Conversely, when we examine Marx's view of alienation, you will note that it is based upon the view that the only way we can avoid alienation is to change society (particularly the relations of production) in a radical way. Thus, depending upon one's political view, alienation either can come from too much social change, or from too little of it.

So, not "fitting in," having value conflicts with the society, coming from an economically disadvantaged or a stigmatized group, encountering difficulties associated with social change that is too rapid or too infrequent are just a few of the many ways that a person can come to feel alienated in the broadest sense. It is this broad swathe that is used to paint alienation that is the problem with the concept. The term "alienation" has been so overused and applied to so many states of human consciousness that it has become a "catch-all" word that almost has lost all of its meaning. I think the best way to conceptualize alienation is to go back to the Latin root **alien**, which means "foreign." If you feel like a foreigner in your own environment, or, as **Heinlein** said, a **Stranger** **in** **a** **Strange** **Land**, and you feel that way chronically, you probably are experiencing what has been called alienation.

stigma: (**Special** **Note:** The following definition is going to be much less associated with Marx and political economy than any other in this section of the **DST**. But **stigma** is a very important principle and, as we have seen throughout the chapter, in which the bourgeoisie stigmatize the proletariat, the proletariat sometimes stigmatize the bourgeoisie, Marx stigmatizes the bourgeoisie, the proletariat stigmatizes the lumpenproletariat, etc., stigma is a very big part of many social interactions.) **Stigma** is any defect, undesirable differentness, or component of a person's history (such as a prison record) which has a serious negative effect on the stigmatized individual's social acceptance.

The sociologist, **Erving** **Goffman,** was one of the primary theorizers about stigma. Because of his dramaturgical view (he believed our interactions in life were like little plays or dramas we put on for each other), Goffman tended to view stigma from the standpoint of how it could disrupt the person's performance and, thereby, discredit the identity the person is attempting to portray.

Some stigmas are obvious to observers, such as a severe facial deformity. In such cases, the person with the stigma would find it difficult to play the role of an individual who does not have such a deformity. Thus, the person may adopt certain techniques designed to neutralize the effect of the stigma when he or she is interacting with others. Joking about one's stigma is a standard neutralization technique designed to relax other persons who do not know how to respond to visible stigmas, which tends to normalize interactions between the stigmatized person and the other.

Where stigmas are not obvious to other persons -- say a person has a prison record -- the stigmatized person often will attempt to "pass"; i.e., to act out their role as though they do not have a stigma. For example, they might talk as though they have contempt for criminals or people with criminal records. Another example of "passing" behavior occurs when a person carries symbols of "normalcy" to feel unstigmatized and/or to mislead other persons. For instance, some mentally retarded people wear watches, even though they may not be able to tell time. Any such symbol is called a "disidentifier."

Because all people probably have or will have some concealable stigma that potentially could discredit their role performances as "normal" persons, Goffman defined two sorts of identity ~t everyone has. First, we all have a "virtual identity," which is the self a person claims to be.

Second, we all have an "actual identity," which is the self we could become known to be, if discrediting information which we have concealed were revealed.

Goffman believed, given the range of stigmas that can be discrediting in our society, that most of us have an actual identity that is quite different (and much more discreditable) than the virtual identity with which we usually present ourselves in playing our various roles. When you ponder your own life, do you think he was right? Moreover, consider the various things about which a person can be stigmatized in our culture. What do you suppose is the main reason we have stigma in our society?

egalitarianism: the view that all humans are equal and should share the same liberties, rights, access to opportunity, chances to develop their capacities, fulfill their needs, etc. **Egalitarianism** and **equalitarianism** frequently are used interchangeably.

power: the ability to get other people to do what we want them to do whether they want to do it or not. In more dramatic terms, the ability to dominate people, to coerce and control them, obtain their obedience, interfere with their freedom, and compel their action. The variety of power described above is called **coercive power** because it is enforced by reward or punishment. There is another type of powerlike entity that is called **authority.**

authority: a form of "power" based on the acceptance of the authority's legitimate right to exercise power by those persons over whom the power is exercised. For example, we often do what physicians tell us to do because we believe they have a legitimate right to exercise expert authority in the area of medicine. However, if we do not do what they say, typically they cannot force us to comply with their directives; i.e., they cannot, or are not supposed to, use coercive power. Authority is distinguished from coercion -- a form of power based on the capacity to reward or punish. A good way to think about the difference in coercive power and authority is to recognize that when coercive power is exercised, it usually is because legitimate authority has broken down.

false consciousness: an attitude toward one's social class position in the social world that is out of touch with the actual material conditions of one's existence. Marx used the concept of false consciousness to explain why oppressed classes sometimes not only accepted as true, but attempted to adopt themselves, the very ideology used by the ruling class as a rationale for exploiting the oppressed classes. It seems unimaginable that oppressed people would embrace the ideology used to oppress them. However, many contemporary Marxists use the idea of false consciousness to account for the lack of political radicalism among the Western world's working class. These Marxists say, if the workers had a working class consciousness, the workers would see that many of the ideological tenets they currently embrace are in opposition to their (and their class's) best interests.

The concept of false consciousness does raise some interesting questions. For example, why would the average factory worker favor the notion of individual enterprise when most of them never would have the resources to start a business of his/her own? Why would the average citizen favor liberal democracy when he or she knows that money can buy influence, giving wealthy people more than the power of a single vote?

The issues of false consciousness are very controversial, not only because they call into question some of our most revered social institutions, but because the concept seems patronizing to people who do not like to be told that they are too thickheaded to act in their own interests -- this especially in an era when people often are accused of being too concerned about themselves. Do you think there can be such a thing as false consciousness? Can you think of examples? Is the concept just a cop-out by Marx because his belief in the formation of class consciousness didn't and doesn't work?

social mobility: the upward or downward movement of individuals or groups into different positions in a social status hierarchy. Social mobility can be based on changes in wealth, income, occupation, education, power, or any other scarce social resource. Societies with high rates of social mobility generally are regarded as more "open" societies, while those with low rates of social mobility are seen to be more "closed" societies, such as one would see with a caste system.

Social mobility can be **horizontal,** as when one changes jobs with no gain or loss in status. Social mobility also can be **vertical,** with upward mobility representing a gain in status, and downward mobility representing a loss in status. An example of upward social mobility would be seen when the daughter of uneducated parents who do menial labor becomes a brain surgeon. An example of downward social mobility would be seen when the son of a prominent lawyer, drops out, joins a criminal subculture, and ends up spending life in prison.

mass culture: usually describes the way of life produced in advanced industrial societies. Mass culture involves the standardization of most aspects of culture. For example, there is mass production of material goods (everyone in America can buy a pair of 501 Levi jeans). There is standardization of art (example, nearly everyone in America can rent a video of the newest movie or buy a print of the newest work of graphic art). There is standardization of styles (example, new fashions that are very much the same in appearance to each other can be purchased at K-mart or Bloomingdale's). In short, there tends to be a standardization of ideas, values, tastes, objects, etc. This homogenization of culture is attributed to the mass media.

In one sense, mass culture is the ultimate democratization of our consuming patterns, and an attack on all forms of ideational and aesthetic elitism, or, pluralism. For example, critics of mass culture decry the way in which mass culture arrests the development of "high culture" by absorbing and debasing it. In other words, a work of art of which there was only one copy in high culture will appear on lunch boxes and t-shirts in mass culture. The critics of mass culture do not believe that this is undesirable in and of itself, but that it is undesirable because it exerts pressure on serious artists to produce for uncritical mass markets, which may undermine the artists' artistic vision -- especially the revolutionary aspects of their art. A good example of the debasement of high art would be the use of the Beatles' song "Revolution" to sell Nike running shoes. It was a good ad, but it really cheapened the whole concept of the song and the artistry that went into its creation. It may have been written to sell records, but it was not written to sell shoes. (To their credit, Nike discontinued the ad.)

Another criticism of mass culture is that every aspect of the culture is commercialized. Things to which a price should not be attached are mass-marketed (for a price). There also is the concern that mass culture vulgarizes our consumption patterns with a plethora of mediocre ideas and products, and a profusion of gimmickry. In 1995, there were ads showing marbles running down the "cracks" of cars. One company does an ad showing this -- which has absolutely nothing to do with the "drivability" of the car; so another car company makes an equally vacuous ad responding to the first one. Are you going to go trickle marbles along the place where the hood meets the fender to decide whether you are going to buy a car?

People who defend mass culture hold that it actually raises the quality of cultural appreciation of the masses and leads to aesthetic democratization through the wider consumption of "high art." One of the questions we have to ask ourselves is, "What is high culture?" Is it elitist? In order for art to be art, does it have to portray illusive realities that challenge our taken-for-granted view of the world? Or is a good day-glo Elvis on black velvet just as aesthetically important as a Gauguin?

acquisitive: strongly inclined to seek riches; greedy. Of course, people can be acquisitive about many different things. Some seek to acquire prestigious positions, some press clippings, some power, and so on.

imperialism: when nation-states engage in policies that result in an effort to expand either their boundaries or their spheres of influence in such a fashion that they attempt to dominate or have sovereignty over another nation-state, society, culture, or political community, it is said that the powerful nation is engaged in imperialism.

Marxist theories view imperialism as a necessary development of capitalism. According to Marxists, capitalists need to have new markets for their goods (because capitalism is overproductive), and the cheap labor to produce these goods that can be extracted from the population of dominated societies. (Remember: Marxists have pointed out that the proletariat of a particular capitalist country need not live within the boundaries of that country.) Moreover, say the Marxists, capitalists need cheap and constantly new sources of raw materials and land (another way capitalists come to control increasing portions of the means of production). These and other needs associated with capitalism require that advanced capitalist countries expand beyond their boundaries and spheres of influence into less-developed countries.

Furthermore, Marxist theorists predict, as expanding imperialist powers confront each other in the limited geographical space of the globe, war is inevitable. Of course, the Marxist critique of capitalist imperialism raises issues of imperialistic tendencies of Marxist countries -- such imperialism not being surprising, insofar as Marx believed that communism had to be an international system.

Obviously, not everyone agrees with the Marxist viewpoint as an explanation for imperialism. Other reasons given for imperialism (some of which certain Marxists have gone along with) are: **1)** assertive nationalism by certain nation states (such as was seen in Nazi Germany); **2)** hatreds based on historical enmities between certain nation-states for each other or hatred of one group in a nation-state for another group in another nation-state (such as one sees between Israel and much of the Moslem world in the Middle East, and, currently, in parts of Eastern Europe, and Africa); **3)** major changes in international relations as a result of such things as technological changes in weapons systems (for example, a country expands its geographical sphere to counter the effect of another country obtaining a missile system that can hit targets which have never before been able to be hit in the expansionist country); **4)** a sense of a civilizing mission (although this traditionally manifested itself as colonialism -- the civilizing mission often being an attempt to bring a certain religion to another people who have a religion that is seen to be "primitive"); **5)** a nation-state's desire for greater power and prestige (expansionism to gain international status); **6)** feelings of ethnic or racial superiority (the belief that another race or ethnic group are so inferior as not to be able to govern themselves or use their resources in their or anyone else's best interests); **7)** the effort to deflect attention from domestic difficulties (for example, starting a war to keep the citizenry's minds off a disastrously flagging economy); and **8)** a sense of insecurity (expand and crush other nation-states before they do it to you). Can you think of other examples of reasons that imperialism might develop?

pluralism: a state of society in which members of diverse ethnic, racial, religious and other such social groupings maintain autonomous participation in, and development of, their traditional culture or special interest within the confines of the larger society. A pluralistic society is a society in which there is a lot of opportunity for ethnic, racial, religious, cultural, and social **diversity**.

Pluralist theory argues that resources -- wealth, education, prestige, skill, votes -- should be divided equally, and that no group has, or should have, a monopoly over any such resources. A pluralist should be tolerant and not have elitist tendencies. Can you think of a more pluralist society than ours? Or, is the pluralism of our society only an illusion perpetuated by mass culture, which actually is controlled by certain elites?

middle class: the diffuse social stratum between the working class and the upper class in the stratification hierarchy of most industrialized countries. Membership in the middle class is determined by a whole array of factors, such as: income, prestige, power, and life style. Persons who do nonmanual labor (so-called "white collar workers") also are frequently referred to as middle class. Actual membership in the middle class depends upon how we wish to operationalize the term, although it usually includes income and some combination of other factors.

Most sociologists recognize that there is stratification even within the middle class. For example, there are upper and lower middle classes identified in some typologies, old (entrepreneurial) and new (bureaucratic) middle classes in others. Whereas the sociologists who divide the middle class up into categories focus upon the diversity or heterogeneity within the middle class, other sociologists use the term **middle mass** to insinuate an increasing homogenization of life styles between persons who belong to the middle class and working class.

polarization: a situation in which opposing and competing ideas, interests, and antagonisms in a total group situation are becoming clearly contrasted and two conflicting subgroups or rallying-points are observable. **As people choose up sides in a situation, polarization increases; i.e., they are at opposing poles.**

Malthusianism: An economic perspective developed by **Thomas Malthus (1766-1834)**, which held that the population would outgrow the capacity to produce food supplies to feed that population. Malthus was highly critical of the doctrine held by many persons of his time which recognized the possibility of the "perfectibility of man" -- the notion that human societies were evolving toward some carefree, utopian existence. Indeed, in a book called, **An Essay on the Principle of Population,** Malthus argued that population would increase in a geometric progression (2, 4, 8, 16, 32, etc.), whereas food production would increase at an arithmetic progression (2, 4, 6, 8, 10). He believed that the population would always tend to increase to the limits of subsistence, at which point there would be a dramatic reduction in living standards, resulting in mass starvation. There were some "positive checks" on population growth -- war, famine, pestilence (epidemics) -- but Malthus also stressed there were checks that could be set on population growth by "moral restraints" such as sexual abstinence and marriage later in life.

The massive increase in productive capacity in the late nineteenth century tended to undermine Malthus' predictions. In light of this revolution in productive capacity, Malthus' predictions were seen as unwarrantedly gloomy (in fact, it was Malthus who was responsible for economics sometimes being called the "dismal science.")

Even though the productive capacity of the modern day world could feed (and provide most other essentials for) the entire population of the planet today, Malthusian principles are beginning to be taken a bit more seriously in light of predictions that planetary overpopulation will result in the death of millions through starvation in the late twentieth century and early twenty-first century..

dictatorship of the proletariat: Marx believed that, after the successful revolution of the proletariat, the working class would establish a period of temporary rule. During this period, the proletariat would expropriate (take away) the means of production from the defeated bourgeoisie. The period of the dictatorship of the proletariat would be a socialist period, during which the means of production would be held (at least in its initial phases) on behalf of all of the citizens by the State.

Because Marx believed the State to be a political structure that promoted class domination, or, at the very least, political oppression of the underclasses, he believed that during the dictatorship of the proletariat, there would commence a period of the "withering away of the state." Thus, one can see the period of the dictatorship of the proletariat as a time when the proletariat becomes the ruling class and, in the interest of the masses, institutes programs that result in movement toward a classless society.

As most of you will have noted by now, in some societies which fancied themselves as Marxist societies, the dictatorship was not always that of the proletariat, and a classless society has never been the outcome. This ought to provoke us to ask whether any society ever conforms in reality to its theoretical formulation. And if there never is such a correspondence between theory and practice, why not?

primitive capitalism: At the end of the feudal period, as the cities or "burgs" began to develop, the earliest form of capitalism as we know it developed. Two things are important to note about this: **1)** early capitalism was not industrial capitalism as we came to know it in the late nineteenth century; it was instead a system of many small scale entrepreneurs; and **2)** capitalism was, in its beginning stages, a very radical system, responsible to a large extent for significant scientific, political, technological, and social experiments that would complete the overthrow of the feudal (medieval) way of life. In other words, if one looks at early capitalism in dialectical terms, it was antithetical (the antithesis) to feudalism.

anarchism (anarchy): This is a definition that is really an anti-definition. Let me explain: When I used the word **anarchy** in the text, many readers interpreted what I meant as, "a state of complete chaos." That **is** what I meant. **But that is not what anarchy really is.** So now you have a chance to learn how not to misuse the word -- like practically everybody does. So let's define **anarchy:** **a social philosophy or a form of social organization that advocates the abolition of the State and formal government.** Anarchists believe in this abolition because they hold that structures such as the State corrupt people who are basically good, and who can better operate their societies without structures and institutions that tend to corrupt that goodness.

One of the features of the anarchist's concept of the State that is most maligned by anarchists is the way (they say) the State prevents people from really being equal and free. The anarchist says that, by using force (or the threat of it) both to bolster an unfair system of private property, and to demand compliance with the State's many repressive laws, there can never be equality and freedom.

Anarchism rests upon the doctrine that people are inherently communal and sharing, and that, without structures such as the State working to ensure unequal systems of private property, people naturally would share equally in the wealth of the society. Indeed, anarchism may be the ultimate form of utopian thinking and have the most optimistic view of human beings of any social philosophy. In the anarchist utopia, the society would never need to use force or coercion to administer its affairs. Thus, there would be no need for social control agents officially authorized and equipped to use force (such as the police or the national guard).

Because anarchists believe that voluntary cooperation and mutual aid between humans is the natural tendency of people, they think that political authority, in whatever guise, is unnecessary and undesirable. Anarchists believe that all vestiges of governmental authority ought to be abolished. If you wanted to describe anarchism in a single sentence, it would be, "The best government is no government."

It is interesting that, even though anarchists believe in a classless, stateless society, anarchism is essentially just the opposite of communism, insofar as communism is a conflict theory based upon dialectical thinking, while anarchism is a theory of innate human cooperation. But this raises the issue of how a classless, stateless communist society would differ from anarchy.

Needless to say, anarchism is a highly controversial theory of society. Yet, we have to ask ourselves what there is about it that makes it seem so unrealistic to most of us. Don't we believe that humans are inherently cooperative and good? And, if not, why not? Are we still dogged by the notion of original sin? Or, is it in the best interests of some people to make us think that about ourselves?

propaganda: the use of familiar cultural symbols to convey ideas very quickly to the masses -- usually through the use of the mass media. These ideas typically are designed to arouse strong, often emotional, reactions for or against some project, person, or idea. Propagandists often try to create news by staging special events. Can you think of specific examples of the use of propaganda in our society?

critical theory: fundamentally a configuration of sociological theories centered around a dialogue relating to the works of Marx and other theorists who followed in Marx's footsteps. Like Marx's work, critical theory provides a critique of capitalist societies; however, critical theory has updated the critique to account for the remarkable changes that have occurred in capitalism since Marx's time. Critical theorists tend to be activistic in terms of their scholarship, that is, conducting research and presenting their ideas in ways that are designed to bring about social change, rather than just to report upon it.

Much of the work in critical theory has been a response to the way in which history has demonstrated the failure of some of Marx's predictions. For example, the proletariat has not become polarized from the owners of the means of production, developed a class consciousness, and organized themselves to fight a class war designed to expropriate the wealth of the capitalists. Indeed, the proletariat has had great difficulty in organizing around any issue. As a matter of fact, there has been a regression of many of the gains made in earlier decades by the labor union movement, and workers are, for the most part, unorganized, atomized (separated from each other in terms of a common class consciousness), and prone to try to improve their personal economic and social circumstances, rather than those of their social class.

Another of the failed predictions of Marx that interests critical theorists is seen in the fact that when there have been socialist revolutions, they have not occurred in advanced industrial societies, but in developing, often agrarian, societies.

And yet another of Marx's failed predictions that interests the critical theorists has been the fact that capitalism has not failed as an economic system -- or been destroyed by the internal contradictions of capitalist modes and relations of economic production. Indeed, capitalism has proven to be a very adaptable and robust system, in part, by borrowing some socialist doctrines associated with the welfare state.

Obviously, there are many different views expressed as to why Marx's predictions have not come to pass. And, there have been a few proponents of critical theory who have been influential in attempting to critique Marx's theories. **One very influential critical theorist was Antonio Gramsci.**

One of Gramsci's major contributions to critical theory was his view that the proletariat was unlikely to form a class consciousness because capitalism had been very effective in getting the working class to accept the ideology of the ruling class. The ruling class, according to Gramsci, did not have to use direct coercive power on the proletariat to dominate them if the ruling class simply could convince the proletariat, through acceptance of the ruling class ideology, to accept the premise that economic **inequality** and the **hegemony (dominance)** of one class over another are legitimate.

Gramsci was particularly interesting in his views because, although he is a Marxist, he believed that too much emphasis was put on economic issues as they related to the creation of the proletariat's false consciousness. Gramsci believed that it was very important to look at the role of culture in convincing the proletariat to accept capitalist ideology. Hence, according to Gramsci, scholars must look at the role of cultural institutions such as the mass media, education, law, and religion in creating the "ideological hegemony" of the ruling class. Indeed, critical theory is critical insofar as it questions and departs from this ruling ideology.

Another interesting facet of Gramsci's thought, especially if you consider that he was a Marxist, was that he believed revolution springs from a transformation of people's consciousness -- a consciousness critical of the dominant ideology. As you will remember, Marx believed that revolution was an outcome of the material conditions in which workers find themselves, which then leads to a change in consciousness, and then a revolution. Gramsci believed that critical consciousness of ideological hegemony, rather than economic necessity, may really be the new starting point of revolutions.

The other major force in critical theory has been the social theorists from the so-called Frankfurt School of Social Research, which was founded in Germany in the early twenties. **Some of the best known of these theorists are: Max Horkheimer, Theodor Adorno, Erich Fromm, Herbert Marcuse, and Jurgen Habermas.**

The **Frankfurt School** did many extraordinary studies. For example, some of its members investigated how it could have been possible for the economic depression of the 1930s to give rise to fascism in Germany and Italy instead of creating a revolutionary working class consciousness, since the depression was one of those "crises in capitalism" that Marx predicted would lead to a workers' revolt and socialist society. **In explaining how fascism could have developed, one of the most important Frankfurters, Adorno, theorized the "authoritarian personality."** In positing the authoritarian personality, Adorno arrived at the rather sobering conclusion that such a personality type actually identifies with his/her oppressors and wants to be like them. With this rather depressing insight, it became much easier to understand how an oppressive philosophy such as fascism could flourish -- why workers would become oppressors themselves rather than revolutionaries.

In terms of addressing the question of how repressive ideologies can create false consciousness, the Frankfurt School (especially Marcuse and Fromm) probably made its greatest contribution in joining the social theories of Marx and Freud, resulting in an offshoot of critical theory that is sometimes referred to as "the Freudian Left." Marcuse was particularly effective in examining the connection between repressive ideologies and popular culture, especially art. In essence, Marcuse recognized that whoever controlled popular culture probably controlled what would be the dominant ideology of the time. He saw art as having the most revolutionary possibility in creating critical consciousness. But he also recognized that much of the art world was controlled by capitalist patrons who sought the celebration of the *status quo* in art, rather than the portrayal of illusive realities and a revolutionary spirit. Is most art in the United States revolutionary, or celebratory of the prevailing ideology? How do we distinguish between art and propaganda? Are recent efforts at censorship of artistic expression in the U.S. an affirmation of the revolutionary power of art?

Definitions pertaining to CHAPTER FOUR:
"Evolutionary Theory and Social Darwinism"
of Elements of Sociology Through Theory --
(WORD LIST #5)

Social Darwinism: **the theory advanced by Herbert Spencer (among others) that said the strongest race of humans could develop if we just let evolution, via natural selection, take its course.** Although he recognized that the "weak" or "unfit" would perish if they did not receive the help of their society, Spencer believed this to be in the best interests of society.

According to Social Darwinists, "natural" (unplanned) change was considered to be infinitely preferable to social interventions on behalf of "social progress," "humanitarianism," or "altruism." The rationale for this view was that certain classes, races, or other stigmatized categories of people were in subordinate positions in relation to other groups of people because the stigmatized individuals and groups were less well-adapted to the conditions of their life, usually because of biological inferiority. In other words, they had inborn flaws that caused them to experience difficulties in life.

In essence, the view of the Social Darwinists was that the material order (the access to the opportunity structure of a society, especially its economic advantages) was dependent on the moral order -- just the opposite of Marx's view. So, "weak" or "unfit" people were poor or sick (or had other deficiencies often associated with poverty) because **they deserved to be that way.** This is based on their supposed inborn flaws. Social Darwinism eventually evolved into the **eugenics movement,** which reached its zenith with Hitler's murder of millions of supposedly "unfit" people. As you will later see, this association of Social Darwinism with eugenics was not fair to the pioneers of Social Darwinism, as most of them would have disagreed totally with the logic of eugenics.

demography: **the scientific (usually statistical) study of population. Demographers would be interested in such things as birth rates, mortality (death) rates, morbidity (sickness) rates, migration rates, etc.** The field is divided into: 1) **descriptive demography,** in which the geographical distribution of certain cohorts of the population are described; 2) **formal demography,** also called **"demographic analysis,"** in which the statistics of population change are studied in a very abstract manner; that is, without reference to social factors that might be responsible for such changes; and 3) **population studies, the branch of demography that deals with the interaction between social factors and population changes.** Some of the earliest sociological studies by the recognized founders of sociology were based on demographic work; e.g., Durkheim's research on suicide, and the work on the economic productivity done by Weber (pronounced Vay-ber).

altruism: **the condition in which an individual freely sacrifices his or her rightful interests in favor of the well-being of another person or group of persons. Altruism also implies helping others in ways not demanded by law. Selflessness.**

Altruism is the opposite of demagogy, which means that a person (a demagogue) takes a completely self-serving approach to social issues, and considers only the selfish consequences of his/her actions. Many times, people tend to confuse the idea of altruism with that of idealism. Remember: Hegel was an idealist, which means that he had a particular philosophical point of view. Why do you suppose people talk about such things as "youthful idealism" when they probably mean to be talking about altruism? Re-examine the concept of **idealism** and try to see if there is a relationship between it and **altruism**.

utilitarianism: **a political philosophy championed by Jeremy Bentham, the primary doctrine of which was that concern for the greatest happiness, pleasure, or well-being of the greatest number of people in the society should be the aim of all social action, particularly social policy.** As you think about this, consider the issue of balancing democratic principles with the idea of avoiding a tyranny of the majority over the minority.

natural selection: a natural process tending to cause the survival of individuals or groups best adjusted to the conditions under which they live. According to natural selection, the beings or species best adjusted to their environment tend to survive and perpetuate themselves, while the "unfit" perish. Natural selection thus perpetuates desirable genetic qualities and leads to the elimination of genetically undesirable qualities. This process occurs by the recombination or mutation of genes. When you read the part of the definition that goes: "a natural process tending to cause the survival of individuals or groups best adjusted to the conditions under which they live . . . . ," does it make you think about the definition of a tautology? (See **tautology** in the following definition.)

sociobiology: **a genetically deterministic view championed by Edward O. Wilson, which he defines as the systematic study of the biological basis of all social behavior.** You will find that most sociologists seem to turn their noses up at sociobiology for a whole spate of reasons. However, in the next few decades there might well be a unifying spirit that brings the social and natural sciences together with the arts and humanities.

eugenics: a theory developed by **Francis Galton,** which he defined as "the science which deals with influences that improve the inborn qualities of the human race." Initially, eugenics was concerned with breeding perfect people (positive eugenics); then it focused on isolating, stopping the procreation of, or killing (Galton did not want to kill anybody), weak, disabled, mentally ill, deviant, old, poor, or other stigmatized groups of people (negative eugenics). It is a logical extension of the view that the fittest ought to survive that some people will begin to think they know who <u>should</u> <u>not</u> survive. **Eugenics is the opposite of <u>euthenics</u>,** which is the idea that we can improve humans biologically by improving their social surroundings. If a eugenics philosophy were suddenly to become pervasive in our society, which groups of people do you think would be "done away with first"?

fascism: a political-economic system that is most closely identified with Mussolini's Italian Fascist Party and Hitler's Germany. There are several characteristics of fascist political-economic forms. **First**, under fascism, there is a corporate state or state capitalism. In other words, as in socialism, many of the means of production are controlled by the State (for example, industry and financial institutions are brought under state control). But, unlike socialism, the means of production are not controlled by the State on behalf of the people; they are controlled by the State for the financial benefit of the State -- seemingly a reification of a reification. **Second,** under fascism, there typically is only a single political party. Other political parties are outlawed or harassed. **Third,** under fascism, trade unions are centrally organized and controlled. Obviously, under such circumstances, the trade unions are not going to go on strike against the State -- which, you will remember, owns many of the means of production. **Fourth,** under fascism any dissent is crushed violently. Extremism is encouraged, but only extremism that celebrates the ideology of the State. **Fifth,** under fascism, there is usually a dictator who is mythologized and revered. **Sixth,** under fascism, mass politics (such as we saw in Hitler's huge political rallies) are encouraged. This helps whip the people up into frenzies of nationalistic spirit and reverence for the leader. **Seventh,** under fascism, totalitarianism (governmental surveillance and control over all aspects of the public and private social life) is established. **As a rule, fascism develops in circumstances where the middle classes have fears of the power of the aristocracy, the unions, and the policies of the welfare state.**

tautology: a statement which is true by virtue of its logical form alone. A logical truth or conclusion deduced from the premise because the premise logically implies the conclusion -- there being a repetition of the statement as its own reason. For example, "the reason there are so many poor people is that so few people have enough money."   "That sound was audible to the ear." "That bachelor is unmarried." "Today is tomorrow's yesterday, and today is yesterday's tomorrow." I have found that, as a person develops a better sense of the way ideas are used in academic settings, it is astonishing how much tautological thinking occurs. Of course, that is not great discovery to those of you who already have discovered it.

Definitions pertaining to CHAPTER FIVE:
"Sociology Hits Full Stride" of <u>Elements</u> <u>of</u> <u>Sociology</u> <u>Through</u> <u>Theory</u> -- (<u>WORD</u> <u>LIST</u> <u>#6</u>)

<u>agnosticism</u>: the idea that there is not sufficient evidence to conclude anything, one way or another, about the existence or nature of God. Agnosticism is distinguished from **<u>atheism</u>** because atheism implies total rejection of belief in a deity.

<u>functionalism</u>: one of the major social theoretical paradigms. Functionalism views society as a web of interdependent social institutions, each of which makes some contribution to overall social equilibrium or stability. Functionalist theory often uses an organic metaphor (see organicism) as a rationale for its emphasis on both the study of, and desirability of social equilibrium.

In effect, to the functionalist scholar, a social structure (such as a social institution) is considered "functional" in terms of how effectively it maintains the social system. As an equilibrium theory, one would expect functionalism to be focused on the ways that equilibrium is maintained.

Functionalist theorists are locked in an ongoing clash with conflict theorists (such as Marxists), who focus their studies on social change rather than social equilibrium, and who see such change as desirable, especially if it is a manifestation of an oppressed group or class asserting its rights. Obviously, a balanced approach to sociology requires that we have both equilibrium theories that investigate social statics and conflict theories that examine social dynamics.

<u>sociological</u> <u>reductionism</u> -- <u>also</u> <u>known</u> <u>as</u> <u>sociologism</u>: a form of reasoning or explanation in which complex social phenomena are **<u>reduced</u>** to a number of basic **<u>social propositions.</u>** An assumption underlying sociological reductionism is that, because individuals are a product (completely a result) of society or the social system, all statements about the behavior of individual social actors can be reduced to propositions about how social systems affect or determine individual behavior.

As we have seen, in the logic of science, reductionism is a fallacy in reasoning in that it ignores the importance of the way in which the component parts of any social phenomenon are interrelated. Thus, the sociological reductionist discounts the role of biology (genetic heritage, biological drives) and psychology (individual as opposed to social factors) in the explanation of human behavior. In other words, the sociological reductionist can't see the trees for the forest.

Even though, as we saw earlier, reductionism does not sound like an attitude appropriate to a science, most sociologists are somewhat reductionistic. Indeed, when most people are pushed to give explanations of why things work as they do in the world, they become reductionistic.

ritual: a procedure or ceremony involving a regularly repeated, traditional, and very specifically prescribed set of behaviors intended to symbolize or celebrate a belief or a value, and/or to manipulate or entreat either a god, a humanlike supernatural entity, a human, or a natural phenomenon (like doing a rain dance). Rituals usually are prescribed by custom, rule, regulation, or law. And the nature of the ritual activities are usually very carefully described; indeed, deviations from the exact prescribed ritual activities often are punished, even if the person(s) inappropriately engaging in the ritual activity may have the best of intentions.

sacred: **in its broadest meaning,** the "sacred" traditionally has been seen as that which is holy in the religious sense, and therefore, that which is sacred is that which is sanctified and protected against violation, intrusion, or defilement. **In Durkheim's sociological view,** things are not intrinsically sacred; they are made sacred by the **collective consciousness** imputing sacredness to them and surrounding them with certain rituals, thus transforming them into **collective representations.** Therefore, we could decide to make **anything** sacred in the social sense in which Durkheim uses the term. As a matter of fact, can you think of any objects, persons, ideas, etc. that have been profane (secular) in the past which our society is beginning to treat as sacred?

collective consciousness: when we live in society or particular groups in society, each individual's conscience is blended together with all the members of his or her collective group to form a moral force or moral order that is greater than the sum of its parts. The collective consciousness is the social "force field" formed by the power of the group as it acts together.

collective representation: a term suggested by Durkheim to denote the concepts and symbols that have a common meaning to the members of a particular group. For example, the American flag is a symbol to which most Americans show at least a modicum of respect because it is a symbol which represents a collective ideal and a consciousness of certain commonalties in belief.

Naturally, Americans who dislike the idea of nationalism are going to feel less internal respect for symbols that represent ideals to which they do not subscribe -- flags, for example. But in a social situation, even these people will pay some small homage to the rest of the collective's acts of respect to the symbol in question. For example, when you go to a sporting event, you may not feel like standing up and acting respectful when the national anthem is played, but most people, at least, will stand, out of a sense of deference or respect for the power of the collective, and, often times, out of respect to other people who have a stronger feeling for certain collective representations. One thing to keep in mind: a collective representation can be an abstract concept (such as the idea of freedom or democracy), as well as a concrete symbol, such as a flag. What kind of collective representations seem to capture your hearts and minds?

profane: as contrasted with sacred; when used sociologically, profane generally denotes that which is not given the special power of the force of the collective consciousness or of being regarded as a collective representation. If the power of the collective consciousness does not imbue an object or symbol with special social meaning, the object or symbol is not seen to be sacred in the Durkheimian sense. When used in this fashion, the word **profane** is synonymous with the term **secular.** In other words, when the term profane is used sociologically, it does not mean that the object or symbol to which it is applied is "bad" (as in the implication of the word "profanity"). When used sociologically, the term profane only means that which is "not sacred." Durkheim was the sociologist most known for dividing the social world into those things and concepts that were labeled as sacred and profane.

subculture: refers to "little cultures" based on certain unique folkways and mores (norms) developed by a subgroup in society, largely for the membership of that group. Groups with common interests (e.g., professional, recreational, sexual preference, age, etc.) evolve behavioral patterns that differ, at least in part, from those of general societal conventions or norms without necessarily challenging the conventions or norms of the larger society.

For example, you might become a quilter, or a square dancer, or a biker, or a "Deadhead," or a "gun nut," or a "surfpunk," or a "garage saler," or whatever . . . . you get it. Even the university or academic subculture has its own "ways."

However, when a subculture deliberately develops norms that differ dramatically from those of the general society, these are called deviant subcultures or countercultures. How does one determine the difference in a subculture that is merely different than the "accepted subcultures" and those subcultures that would be considered "deviant subcultures?"

social facts: a term that was coined by Durkheim in **The Rules of Sociological Method** to indicate a type of phenomena that are *sui generis* (in a category by themselves), social, rather than individual. Specifically, Durkheim believed that social facts are things that **only can be known from without**, that is, not intuitively. In **Suicide**, Durkheim says: "Sociological method as we practice it rests wholly on the basic principle that social facts must be studied as things, that is, as realities external to the individual . . . if no reality exists outside of individual consciousness. Thus, Durkheim believed that social facts are the appropriate subject matter for sociological inquiries.

According to Durkheim, **social facts: 1)** are external to the individual (that is, they are collective sentiments)**; 2)** exercise a constraining power on the individual (the individual typically obeys the dictates of the collective sentiment)**;** and **3)** can be explained only by making reference to other social facts (for example, the incest taboo exists because it keeps the family -- which is itself a social fact -- functioning more smoothly).

incest: sexual relations between individuals who, in a given society, are defined as being the type of close kin for whom such relations are taboo. Taboos between mother-son, and father-daughter are universal, although there are variations on sexual taboos among various other kin in different cultures.

taboo: the socially-prescribed prohibition of some action. The incest taboo is a good case in point of something that is highly negatively sanctioned when it is broken. What are some of the other taboos of our society? Are any old taboos breaking down? Are any new taboos developing? It may prove very interesting for you to think about the connection between taboo and myth.

nuclear family: a couple and their children (including those who are adopted, but generally excluding those children who are themselves married). The nuclear family is sometimes referred to by other terms such as: biological family, conjugal family, immediate family, primary family, etc.

mechanical solidarity: the social bonds prevailing between people and groups in a largely homogeneous society where there is a minimum of division of labor and little individualism. In other words, in such a society the "social glue" that keeps society together (gives it solidarity) is based upon a great deal of like-mindedness and a very "mechanical" (almost machine-like or automatic) compliance with fairly rigid social rules. People comply because that is all they know to do. Moreover, there is little diversity in the division of labor because the society is not sufficiently developed for there to be much specialization. Thus, most people take care of the production of their own fundamental needs rather than specializing in making one thing and trading it with another person who makes a different and specialized thing. **There would be mechanical solidarity during Comte's theological stage of his Law of Three Stages.**

organic solidarity: the social bonds prevailing between people and groups in a heterogeneous society where people are dependent on one another because of the way the division of labor has developed. Implicit in organic solidarity is the organicistic view (see organicism) of society as being very much like an organism such as the human body, with each organ developing differently, functioning to do different things, and with each organ's health dependent, to a significant extent, on the health of the other organs. So, just as organisms, societies develop a division of labor in which different people do different things, and some sociologists believe that if any portion of the network of interdependency of individuals or groups on each other breaks down, the whole system can break down

Protestant Reformation: a religious movement within Christianity that originated in the early 16th century in Europe and was lead by **Luther, Calvin, Knox, and Zwingli.** It gave rise to many "reformed" denominations and churches. **The major branches in this regard were Lutheranism, Calvinism, Anabaptism, and Anglicanism. The Reformation was a revolutionary effort to substitute the authority of the Bible for that of the Roman Catholic Church and its Pope.** There was an emphasis on the believer's direct communication with God, without the need of a mediating priest, as was the case with Catholicism. To a significant degree, the Reformation was also an attempt to assert the rights of the non-aristocratic classes against the social class elitist abuses under the feudal system.

bureaucratization: the inclination for organizations to adopt bureaucratic principles and procedures, ostensibly in the interests of efficiency. Bureaucratization is most likely to occur wherever large numbers of people have to be "rationally" coordinated in pursuit of the common objectives of the social organization. Sometimes the process of bureaucratization is called the "rationalization process" by sociologists. (See the next definition of **rationalization**.) The use of the term "rationalization" can be confusing because the term means quite different things to sociologists and psychologists.   Just remember, when sociologists are using the term rationalization in the context of a sociological organizing principle, they mean bureaucratization.

They do not mean to imply the kind of rationalization Freud talks about as one of the human psychological defense mechanisms. The Freudian term has only the most peripheral relationship to the sociological term.

anomie: a social condition characterized by a general breakdown or absence of norms governing group or individual behavior -- a condition of normlessness, a moral vacuum, the suspension of social rules. **Anomie exists: 1)** if social norms break down; **2)** if there is a conflict of social norms so that in complying with some norms, the individual unavoidably will violate other social norms; or **3)** if the individual is detached from his/her moral relationships with other persons in the society such that the individual has no sense of the acceptable boundaries of individual self-indulgence in relationship to the rights of others in the society. (GOO)

typology: **a typology is a scheme of classification containing two or more categories [types] based on features of the things being classified that are considered to be of importance to the person doing the classifying, and to the persons interpreting the scheme of classification.** We can group people or things into typological classifications according to thousands of different criteria, such as age, gender, height, eye color, preference for flavor of ice cream, etc.

If you were constructing a typology for analytic purposes, you would try to achieve two things: **exhaustiveness and mutual exclusiveness.** What are these? Well, let's construct a typology. Let's make it a typology of musical tastes. First, we'd have to define the population we were analyzing. So, let's say we are going to build a typology of all the musical tastes of everybody in the United States.

Now, if we want the typology to be **exhaustive,** we have to make sure that every musical taste of any people living in the United States would be included. So we would have to have classical, jazz, metal, reggae, hip-hop, country, blues, soul, rhythm and blues, rock, rock 'n' roll, space, new age, easy listening, rap, pop, bluegrass, Broadway, soundtrack, gospel, country and western, surf, thrash, punk, grunge, international, alternative, dance, opera, disco, house, military, doo-wop, barbershop, techno., industrial, polka, big band, new age, calypso, contemporary Christian, rave, classical rock, folk, mountain, and so on. In other words, we would have a very big typology, indeed. And the list above is not even close to exhaustive. Let's say that we are trying to study the music that is the most popular in the United States.

The other criteria that marks a good typology is **mutual exclusiveness,** or, the absence of overlapping between categories. Here is where we really would be in trouble with our typology. We know that most people like more than one kind of music; thus, it would be impossible to put each person in the U.S. into a particular category of musical tastes. Some would only like one kind of music, but what would we do about the person who absolutely liked speed metal and thrash, equally? Well, you get the picture, our typology could have been made exhaustive, but, for analytic purposes, it created real problems of mutual exclusivity. Some of these kinds of music -- or some players -- just defy categorization in one category. Where, for example, do you put Beck? He seems to be in about six categories. Some scholars study or analyze phenomena mainly by classifying them according to types, although that probably is the least sophisticated mode of analysis.

Definitions pertaining to CHAPTER SIX:
"The Wellspring" of Elements of Sociology Through Theory --
(WORD LIST #7)

asceticism: a doctrine which asserts that through moderation or renunciation of the desires of the flesh and not seeking pleasure in worldly things, one can discipline oneself to reach a high state, either spiritually or intellectually. Self-denial to reach higher ideals. A person who believes and practices this doctrine is called an **ascetic**. Do you know any ascetics?

Calvinism: in Protestant Christianity, a special set of interrelated, ascetic doctrines that were first systematized by the 16th century theologian **John Calvin,** which center on beliefs in: **1) predestination** (e.g., God alone elects who shall be saved from eternal damnation, thus no amount of "good works" will save a person); **2)** humanity's natural depravity (humans are steeped in original sin); and **3)** the idea that each person has a task set by God -- **a "calling"** -- the "calling" actually being a concept borrowed from **Martin Luther.**

Calvinism was very important to Weber's idea in **The Protestant Ethic and the Spirit of Capitalism,** that capitalism really sprung from the Protestant Ethic, and more specifically, from Calvinism. The view of the "calling" freed humans from feeling that they had to live the ascetic life of a monk, nun, or some other cleric to be viewed favorably by God, insofar as God viewed successful participation in any worthy calling equally. Hence, if business were one's calling, that became a legitimate goal to pursue.

The belief in predestination thrust the Protestants of the time into what has been described as a state of "brooding individualism." They would enter this state of mind because they had no way of knowing if they were among the saved or the damned. However, as history unfolded, many of the Protestants reasoned that God would not allow worldly success to those persons who had been predestined for eternal damnation. Hence, many of the Protestants interpreted success in their calling as a sign both to themselves and to their neighbors that they were among the "saved." **Of course, one way to succeed in one's calling was to engage in the highly productive new economic system called capitalism. Thus, we see the relationship between the Protestant Ethic and the development of capitalism.**

Protestant Ethic: the complex of Calvinistic-Puritanical ideas and norms which stress: **1)** the positive value of diligent work at an occupation that is socially and individually beneficial ("the calling"); **2)** frugality in living style and the productive use of time; and **3)** the notion that adversity is the test of individual character.

The Protestant Ethic was said by Max Weber to be one of the fundamental motivating factors behind the development of capitalism. Although the Calvinistic belief was that a person was predetermined (predestined) to salvation or damnation, and that no amount of good works could change that state, there was an accompanying belief that if one were successful (particularly in "the calling"), this success was a sign the person was one of those predestined by God to be saved. The Protestant Ethic thus glorified success, accumulation, and work for work's sake (if not always for God's.)

Because the Protestant Ethic said that income from hard work was not to be used for self-indulgence, the righteous individual was supposed to live frugally and accumulate savings (which was an ideal source of investment funds). The combination of hard work, high productivity in a calling, frugality, etc. acted as a strong impetus for the development of capitalism, although there are authors -- especially a fellow named **Tawney** in a book called, **Religion and the Rise of Capitalism** -- who disagree with Weber's notion that capitalism found its genesis in The Protestant Ethic.

secularization: refers to the manner in which religious institutions and beliefs have been largely replaced by secular, nonreligous, or "worldly" institutions and beliefs. Whereas in small-scale folk societies, religion is at the core of most beliefs and activities, most activities and beliefs in the modern industrial world are based on much more secular concepts (e.g., trade, profit, power, comfort, consumption, etc.) Even many churches themselves have become less religious and more secular in their outlook. (Look at TV evangelists and the seeming lust some of them display for money.) As a matter of fact, don't you think it is peculiar, if Weber is right about the religious origins of capitalism, that capitalism has become such a secular system, and that it even has secularized religion? Or do you think that really has happened?

value freedom: Weber's way of describing what we have already defined as "objectivity." Weber believed a social scientist was acting in a "value free" way when she or he conducted scientific studies in such a manner that personal opinions and values did not distort the scientist's findings. Of course, most scientists recognize that value freedom is an ideal that we strive for, rather than a reality that we reach.

verstehen: The term means "understanding" in German. It is Weber's concept of empathetic (based on empathy) understanding of the motivations and behaviors of others. It is a sociological method that consists of attempting to obtain an objective understanding of the social behaviors of others through an empathetic, intuitive (intersubjective) interpretation. **In other words, one does not have to be another person to put oneself in that person's place and to obtain some kind of understanding of why that person thinks and does what he or she thinks and does.**

Weber argued that ***verstehen*** was particularly important because so much social action is nonrational action -- wherein people do not use the most obvious means to achieve their desired ends, or, they may not even know their desired ends. In any event, where social action is nonrational, it does not make sense to measure or analyze the action sociologically by making use of objective, highly rational, social methods. Thus, understanding of the social action must depend to some degree on an understanding of the subjective experience of the social actors involved. In other words, through an act of empathy, the scientist has to "try to get inside the heads" of these social actors, to see the world as they see it, to feel the world as they do.

The paradox of ***verstehen*** is, of course, that we **can be more objective scientists** by allowing ourselves **to be more subjective scientists** under certain circumstances. It is important to remember, though, that Weber insisted that all hypotheses that came from the use of ***verstehen*** still had to be tested by more objective scientific means either to verify or to falsify them. **Thus, it** is **very** **important** **to** **remember** **that** **Weber** **did** **not** **believe** **that** *verstehen* **was,** **in** **itself,** **a** **sufficient** **scientific** **procedure** **to** **verify** **the** **principles** **derived** **from** **its** **use.**

symbolic **interactionism**: a branch of social theory which contends that the most distinctive features of human behavior emit from the fact that humans have developed conventionalized symbols that have become organized into languages which are the vehicle for the transmission of culture and the definition of reality. This is not to imply, though, that symbolic interactionists think that symbols, once conventionalized, remain completely static (don't change). Indeed, one of the major beliefs of symbolic interactionists is that the meaning of symbols are constantly negotiated and reinterpreted, and it is these processes of negotiation, interpretation, and reinterpretation that are the basis of all social interaction, and the basis of what we call social reality. **In** **other** **words,** **social** **reality** **is** **a** **process** **rather** **than** **a** **structure.**

Another important aspect of symbolic interactionism holds that our sense of self is a social construct which is symbolically negotiated with individual others and/or with the collectivity. **In** **other** **words,** **our** **sense** **of** **self** **is** **a** **process** **rather** **than** **a** **structure.**

Perhaps **the** **most** **important** **aspect** **of** **symbolic** **interactionism** **is** **the** **view** **that** **symbols** **(which** **usually** **are** **abstract** **or** **intangible** **things** **such** **as** **words)** **can** **create** **tangible** **realities.** For example, can you think of any words that a person could say to you that would cause your blood pressure to rise? If so, you have a case of something abstract or intangible causing a tangible change in reality.

An interesting concept . . . the idea that reality is negotiated. Does that mean that reality is not just there to be accepted as is? But what about the power of the collective, and the fact that most of the direct manifestations of that power are prior to the individual; i.e., developed before he/she is born? Is reality really so pliable as to be changed by altering our view of it symbolically? And if it is, why would sociologists waste their time studying something that is just going to change everyday anyway?

psychosis: a severe personality disturbance in which the ego disintegrates and the person loses touch with the world as others know it. An **organic** **psychosis** is primarily physiological in nature, while a **functional** **psychosis** is believed to be a purely psychological disorder.

ideal **types**: a term coined by Max Weber which denotes a hypothetical phenomenon in which that phenomenon's most characteristic features are exaggerated, or in which the most frequently observed aspects of a phenomenon are put together to create the ideal form or ideal image of the phenomenon. (Feeling a little lost? Maybe the following will help.) Remember Durkheim's typology of Suicide? In reality, we probably rarely ever would see forms of suicide fall exactly into the categories Durkheim created. It was just a typology that he created to help us in our understanding of suicide. Or, what about Weber's three forms of authority? Which you will be learning about very soon. Chances are, we would see some forms of authority that are different from, or combinations of, **traditional,** **charismatic,** **or** **legal-rational** **authority.** But the typology Weber created helps us to understand authority, even though we all know the real world never unfolds in exact accordance with the typologies we make up -- although those typologies may give us a picture quite close to reality.

In short, we could create an ideal type for any category of phenomena, although no phenomenon would be likely to appear in society in its ideal form. So, an ideal type is an imaginary standard that Weber used to attempt to isolate facts and compare social situations in a world in which everything changes so quickly it is difficult to study unless we create models to help our understanding of it. "Ideal" as used here carries no connotation of better or best; an ideal type is merely a standard against which we can measure social realities.

authority (**Weber's Typology**): A form of "power" based on the acceptance of the authority's legitimate right to exercise power by those persons over whom the power is exercised. As you will remember from an earlier portion of the dictionary, authority is distinguished from coercion -- a form of power based on the capacity to reward or punish. Obviously, the moment coercive power is resorted to, authority has broken down.

Max Weber was the first sociologist to distinguish three modes by which authority can be legitimated (See **legitimation** in the next definition below.) **First,** there is **traditional authority.** Here, the legitimation is based on the acceptance of very traditional, often ancient, institutional arrangements that give certain persons the authority to exercise power. The chief of a tribe, or, the king or queen in a system of monarchy would be examples of traditional authority. Of course, if the institution were under challenge -- say that of the monarchy during the French Revolution -- then there would be a considerable erosion in the exercise of authority because the tradition is breaking down.

Second, Weber identified **charismatic authority.** Here, the legitimation of a person's right to exercise authority is based on the perception of exceptional qualities in a particular individual (such as might be seen in a revolutionary leader who has special oratorical prowess, and/or abilities to galvanize followers around his/her ability to do things such as performing "miracles," or the like.) A leader such as Jesus would have had great charismatic authority.

Third, Weber identified **rational-legal authority.** Here, the legitimation of authority is based on a belief that the institutional system functions in accordance with general rules applicable to all and provides for needs essential to all. For example, persons in society legitimate the authority of a judge because the judicial system is seen to work in the best interests of the society. Another example would be the rational-legal authority granted to professionals such as physicians. We all know there are good physicians and others who are not so good at what they do; but we tend to give all of them authority in medical matters because they all go through a training and licensing procedure that makes them full-fledged members of a medical system that, for the most part, we trust to be in the interests of the society.

And, of course, the primary applicability of **rational-legal authority** is that variety we see in **bureaucratic social structures,** which I am sure you will get more than your fill of in life.

legitimation: the condition of general acceptance that is accorded persons, groups, and behaviors that are judged to be compatible with the prevailing values of a group or society that allow certain persons and groups to exercise specific types of authority. Thus, nearly any person, group, or behavior can be legitimated by society to perform legally (with the society's blessing) certain social roles.

One should not confuse the concept of morality with the concept of legitimation. For example, once Hitler had been legitimated by the German people as their leader, he was viewed by them and the rest of the world as the German State's legitimate leader. This legitimation permitted him to perform all the duties that any other head of state would have had. That notwithstanding, did his legitimation make his decision as leader to exterminate Jews (and many other groups) moral? Obviously not.

Each of Weber's types of authority requires legitimation. Each type typically requires a somewhat different type or configuration of legitimation.

charisma: Literally translated, charisma means **"the gift of grace."** In the sociological sense, charisma is the purported possession by some individual of exceptional powers, genius, and/or extraordinary merit that draws persons to the charismatic individual. Charismatic persons frequently are accepted as leaders, prophets, or the like, of major social movements (a revolution would be an example), with followers giving the leader absolute trust and devotion. A charismatic person may lead a social movement for "good," although that need not be so in all cases, as is apparent from examples of persons who were said to have had great charisma (e.g., Jesus, Hitler, JFK, Ghandi, Einstein, etc.) -- Hitler being an obvious exception.

Max Weber believed charisma to be the root of mass social movements, especially in their early stages. However, as the social movement itself becomes more stable, Weber says that there tends to be **a routinization of the charisma.** What does he mean by this?

As a social movement develops an administrative apparatus (often times, a form of bureaucracy) and achieves material success and influence, coercive power and other incentives can be used on followers to get them to do what the "power structure" of the social movement desires. Thus, the charisma of the leader is no longer the sole basis of authority.

In fact, even the process of charismatic leadership can become routinized as procedures for selecting new leaders are institutionalized. And if this process of institutionalization of the means of choosing new leaders occurs during the period of the original charismatic leader's life and/or leadership, that leader may become something of a problem to the very organization that he or she helped to forge. This is easy to understand if you realize that the charismatic leader's initial appeal to the masses is the threat that she or he poses to the established order or to established way of doing things. **However, once that old order and its practices have been overthrown or replaced, there is an immediate tendency to replace the old routines with new routines. Frequently, the very thing that made the charismatic leader an excellent leader for change, makes him or her a very poor leader for routinization -- routine leadership being exercised on a "legal" rather than a personal basis. This might cause you**

to ask yourself if it is at all surprising that societies, or social movements within them, kill their greatest charismatic leaders.

rationalization: the use of highly impersonal criteria to regulate human relationships within modern social organizations -- usually the organizations we call bureaucracies. **One purpose of rationalization is to create a maximally efficient environment in which only those things that are essential to achieving the goals of the organization are stressed in assessing the probable (and later) actual performance of members of the organization.**

Rationalized relationships are very different than those one sees in more traditional societies, where individuals are evaluated on the basis of personal qualities (and sometimes, family lineage). In modern societies, however, individuals who are being hired to become part of an organization are supposed to be evaluated on the basis of objective criteria such as the credentials they have. Once hired, these individuals are supposed to be evaluated on the basis of their objective performances in complying with certain well-defined standards, which may be abstract (loyalty to the organization) or concrete (e.g., a specific level of expected productivity such as number of cars built in a day).

Rationalization also may refer to the organization of production and the distribution processes for goods and services. Production and distribution are seen to be rational when they maximize efficiency and optimize output. To many people, the term rationalization is synonymous with the idea of bureaucratization.

bureaucracy: the formal organization of most large-scale enterprises such as those associated with governmental, military, religious, corporate, or educational institutions. Bureaucracies typically are characterized by: **1)** a clearly defined division of labor, including a careful specification of the decision-making power of each bureaucrat so that there is an unambiguous chain of command among the **hierarchy** (see definition) of officials; **2)** responsibility and authority residing in the office one holds, not in the person who holds the office; **3)** credentials (one's degrees or paper qualifications) being more important than human characteristics; **4)** a pervasive attention to implementing the goals of the organization, which typically are considered more important than the welfare of the individual members of the organization; **5)** an impersonal application of rules that are regarded as inviolable even if the situation may warrant it; **6)** a routinization of tasks to the extent that personnel are seen to be easily replaceable with other persons who quickly can be taught the routines that go along with a particular job; **7)** a reluctance on the part of bureaucrats to engage in activities outside the bounds of their particular office or sphere of influence (in other words, a person is very reluctant to step on someone else's "turf"); **8)** considerable accountability (keeping track in a traceable manner, usually on papers or forms) for activities; **9)** an absence of ownership of the means of production by bureaucrats; and **10)** a promotion system based on merit or seniority (or both) so that officials typically anticipate a lifelong career in the organization or one like it.

Bureaucracy is one way of socially organizing a complex organization. One of the major reasons given to legitimate bureaucracy as a means of social organization is that it creates social structures that lead to maximum efficiency when attempting to organize highly complex social activities. Based upon the characteristics of bureaucracies listed above, can you think of ways in which bureaucratic organization undermines the very efficiency it is supposed to create? Can you think of forms of organizing complex organizations that would be alternatives to bureaucracy?

irrationality: a circumstance in which there is a significant inconsistency between the means (ways of getting to goals) and the ends of social actions (the goals themselves). Irrationality, in this sense, is especially likely to be present if either means or ends are based on purely emotional rather than logical or rationally sound considerations. For example, committing genocide (destroying virtually a whole population of people) to bring peace is irrational; it cannot help but to sow the seeds for future wars, unless one side completely obliterates the enemy.

If we employ means which cannot possibly achieve their desired ends, our actions can be said to be irrational. Or if we aim at ends which cannot possibly be met by the means at our disposal, our actions are irrational. Is possible for behavior to be both rational and irrational at the same time?

status groups: political, economic, or cultural groups (sometimes overlapping) that Weber thought were even more important in understanding human interaction and social life than social class. You will remember that Marx thought social class was the most important of any of these concepts.

Definitions pertaining to **CHAPTER EIGHT:**
"Symbols and Society" of <u>Elements of Sociology Through Theory</u> --
(<u>WORD LIST #8</u>)

<u>**self**</u>: according to Mead, that reflexive part of us that comes from our participation in society and which, in turn, perpetuates society. The self can be both the subject and object of its own scrutiny. In other words, when we think about our self, it is the self doing the thinking.

tabula rasa: literally means an "erased tablet" or "clean slate." It was the metaphoric basis for John Locke's image of the mind of humans at birth. The implication was that we are born into this world with no predispositions and that our social experiences write on the blank tablet of our minds, transforming us into whatever we become. Such a philosophy, of course, gives testimony to a view of the virtually infinite malleability of human beings; i.e., to the notion that society can write anything on the slate it wants to. Such a concept would disagree with the notion that there is something called "human nature."

<u>**significant others**</u>: people who are most important to an individual in determining his or her self-concept and behavior. Usually, the significant others in our lives include parents, siblings, friends, spouses, opinion leaders in peer groups, and so on. Ask yourself who are your most significant others? Is it possible for there to be a significant other in your life who you do not even know?

<u>**generalized other**</u>: taking the role of the generalized other is the final stage in the development of the self as proposed by George Herbert Mead. The concept of the generalized other is complicated, but it is easy to understand if you take it a step at a time. Let us have a look:

One of the first things we have to learn to do as a child is to have a sense of how others are viewing and assessing our actions. In order to do that we have to try imagine what is going on in the other person's mind on the basis of the verbal and other symbolic cues he or she gives us. Thus, in that act of imagination, we symbolically look at ourselves and try to see ourselves as the other person is seeing us.

As we become older, we usually meet more and more people. And the more people we meet, the more different kinds of views of ourselves we are likely to have reflected. For example, the view of ourselves we get from our boyfriends or girlfriends tends to be different than the view we get from our siblings, or our least favorite teacher, or the man who sells us our first used car, or the town bully, etc. **William James, the renowned psychologist, called this phenomenon "the pluralism of selves."** In other words, if we rely on others, in any way, for our view of ourselves, we will have many selves because we will have taken the role of many others in relation to us.

Finally, according to Mead, in the process of taking the role of the other, we progress to the final stage of taking the role of numerous others in society, many of whom we do not know, and with whom we may have no direct contact. In other words, we have enough experience taking the role of particular others, that we begin to be able to imagine what it is like to see ourselves as we see the collectivity of all individuals to be seeing us and assessing us. In short, taking the role of the generalized other is achieved through the imaginative symbolic act of relating one's self to innumerable other people. And, in this act the whole society becomes incorporated within the individual.

Norms help us become social beings. The socialization process helps us to become social beings. Taking the role of individual others helps us to become social beings. But, it is not until we have taken the role of the generalized other that we become fully realized social beings.

looking glass self: **Charles Horton Cooley's** term for the three-stage process whereby an individual develops an idea of what type of person he or she is, i.e., develops a self. **The three stages are: 1)** an individual's imagination of how he or she appears to others; **2)** an individual's internal assessment of how the others are judging his or her appearance and behavior; and **3)** the resulting feelings that provide a person with a sense of what kind of person he or she is. Looking glass self is the way in which we come to see ourselves as we see others to be seeing us. And, the more significant the other person is to us, the greater the impact their reflected view of our self will have on us.

Does it make us some kind of a phony to define ourselves in terms dictated by others? How do we decide when to internalize the image reflected in the "looking glass self?" Are we just a bunch of other-directed sheep, willing to play nearly any social role certain people in society script for us? If society really molds us in the way Cooley suggests, perhaps one of the worst things we can do is to give other people an inaccurate view of themselves. Thus, being polite or diplomatic with someone about something we find repellent about them may be the cruelest thing we can do. Does the society seem to be geared to providing people with an accurate version of themselves in acts of social reflexivity? Think about false consciousness?

"I" and "me" concepts: concepts originally advanced in their very specific meaning by William James. Mead expanded the discussion in his developmental theory of self. According to Mead, the self consists of two parts. First, there is an objective component Mead called the "me." Second, there is a subjective component Mead called the "I." To understand this better, imagine that you are thinking about yourself. When you think about yourself, there is the part of you doing the thinking -- the self as knower, or the "I." Further, when you think about yourself, there is the part of you about which you are thinking -- the part that is the object of your own thoughts. This objective component -- the self as known, is the "me."

There are other ways Mead distinguished the "I" from the "me." The "I" is the aspect of the self that initiates thought and action, acts out social roles, and experiences the consequences of these actions. The "I" is the unique, creative part of your self.

In contrast to the "I," there is the "me" component of the self. The "me" consists mainly of the internalized set of others' attitudes. It tends not to initiate action; rather, it tends to respond to what it knows it should do. Thus, it is not creative, but tends instead to conform. It is not unique because it is primarily a collection of normative social attitudes. Thus, the "me" is passive; it is conservative. It is a mirror of culturally approved values and norms.

The fact that the "I" and the "me," must be taken together to form as a totalized self, is what Mead says distinguishes humans from other animals. It is highly unlikely that most animals have self-reflexivity; that is, it is difficult to imagine a turtle or a cow internalizing the attitudes of others, and then stepping back to ponder, understand, and assess themselves as an object who has internalized these social attitudes, all the while, being aware of their own feelings and behaviors.

The aforementioned definitions of "I" and "me" are very simplistic. Moreover, the concepts are reified; in other words, they are abstract mind constructs that we might find easy to treat as though they were real. Are they? Do you have an individual self and a social self? Do they know each other? Would they invite each other over for dinner? Think about the "I" and "me" concepts in relation to other ideas, such as: the id, ego, and superego; the generalized other; and the looking glass self.

autokinetic effect: this effect was identified in the classic studies conducted by the social psychologists **Muzafer Sherif and Solomon Aush in 1948.** Sherif and Aush put groups of people in a darkened room that had a spot of light projected on a screen. The researchers discovered that the perceived movement of the spot of light on the screen depended on "group norms." In other words, some research subjects who overheard judgments about the movement of the light made by other people in the same room (who, in some cases, were deliberately trying to mislead the research subject), abandoned their own perceptions about the movement of the light and adopted the group perceptions. The experiments showed that social pressure can alter a person's perception of an objective reality, or can alter a person's report of what actually is being perceived.

exchange theory: a theory that tends to be based on an economic metaphor; exchange theory views human interaction primarily as a phenomenon in which participants look for a fair exchange with others of something that is valued such as services or benefits. Thus, there are at least two preconditions for exchanges to continue. First, both partners who are engaged in exchange must value the service or benefit (this could include such disparate things as wealth, power, prestige, attention, flattery, affirmation of the person's worth, etc.) provided by the other partner. Second, the partners need not exchange a service for a service or a benefit for a benefit; just so long as the partners equate what the other person gives them with what they are giving the other person, a successful exchange can take place. Indeed, to an outsider, the differentiation in what is exchanged may look completely unfair; what is important is that the benefits or services being exchanged seem fair to those engaged in the exchange.

One of the places in which we see apparently differential exchange relations is in large organizations where certain individuals have great power, and therefore, have control over resources valued by others in the organization who have less power. In these cases, the only thing the less powerful person may have to exchange is his/her compliance with the more powerful person's expectations. Indeed, the only thing the less powerful person may be required to exchange is his/her willingness to accept that the more powerful person has the legitimate authority to ask for compliance with expectations (even though he/she may never do so). Such reciprocity forms one aspect of the basis of legitimate authority that is believed to be essential to the functioning of organizations. Try to imagine your world strictly in terms of the exchange theory metaphor. Is there anything about it that bothers you? What happens to a concept such as altruism in the world of exchange theory?

ethnomethodology: the study of the methods people employ in their everyday living practices. Ethnomethodology is the systematic study of the formal properties that underlie the informal methods through which people engage in ordinary, commonplace, commonsense, everyday actions and activities.

One of the central tenets of ethnomethodology is that the most powerful norms that motivate human behavior are also the most untested and least understood norms. This probably explains why we answer many of the ethnomethodologist's questions about why society works the way it does by saying: "Because that is just the way things are."

You saw that Durkheim believed society to be "invisible." The ethnomethodologists seek to make visible those aspects of society that are invisible. They do so, not by superimposing their own categories of analysis on the social situation, but instead, by trying to get inside of the social actor's own frame of reference.

One of the primary interests of ethnomethodological studies is to understand "routine grounds" that are the basis of how people formulate commonplace courses of action in daily life. The problem here is that because these methods of formulating action are so routine (essentially automatic), people often cannot even begin to tell the social scientist how they formulate their actions. For example how do most of us make decisions?

One of the major findings of many ethnomethodological studies holds that when there is no commonsense, taken-for-granted solution to a problem, and no previous experience to draw upon that is comparable, a person will become very suggestible, taking almost any source of guidance that seems to them and to other social observers to be socially correct. Thus, most ethnomethodologists believe that one of the primary concerns of social actors is figuring out the correct action in situations for which there is no pat (normatively correct) response.

Perhaps the most immediate contribution of ethnomethodology has been to compel sociologists to examine the extent to which they **impose** a view of social reality on the world they study, rather than endeavoring to understand the often strange, sometimes illogical, ways in which social actors really act. Perhaps the most important contribution of ethnomethodology has been to let us know that, often times, we have no idea why people do the little, everyday kinds of things they do, and that perhaps we had better figure these out before we go on to bigger questions. An example of an ethnomethodological type of interest would be, "Why do people have children?"

eclecticism: an approach to knowledge that selects what appears to be the best aspects of various doctrines, theories, methods, or styles and then makes an effort to resolve the contradictions that occur between different doctrines, theories, etc. The problem with an eclectic view is that, in finding the merit in all theories, it becomes very easy not to commit oneself to a "best" point of view. The problem here is that it becomes difficult to know whether an eclectic view is a manifestation of tolerance, or a sign of a lack of fortitude or conviction. The advantage of eclecticism is that all theories used for looking at the social world probably have some merit, even if it is only because there is truth that accompanies every illusion.

*****SAMPLE EXAM FORM *****

STUDENT NAME: _____

<u>Sociology 100</u>   <u>Introductory Sociology</u>
                                                      <u>Purdue University</u>

Sample Exam Number 1

****** READ THESE INSTRUCTIONS ******

<u>1</u>. Start this sample exam by counting the pages to make sure you have all 8 of them. If you are missing a page, you will be supplied with another exam.

<u>2</u>. There is only one correct answer to each of the following questions.

<u>SPECIAL</u> <u>NOTE</u>: To those students using this sample quiz to help you study for the real thing: Please keep in mind that the sample exam is designed primarily to show you <u>the form</u> the questions on the real exam will take, <u>not necessarily the content</u>. That is certainly not to say that there is not content on the sample exam that will appear on the real exam. Quite the contrary. <u>However, if you only study the content on the sample exam, you will be missing a great deal of the of the content that will appear on the real exam. Thus, refer to your study guides; they will gave the material you need to know for the examination.</u>

***** QUIZ FORM *****

<u>1</u>. <u>True-False:</u> One of the most important concepts associated with sociology and the study of society is the **socialization process.** All of us probably have been at the supermarket and watched various parents yell at their children and threaten them. Let's say, the child really is acting against the prevailing cultural standards for supermarket behavior and continues to act up. Finally, the parent hits the child in the head with a frozen pizza because the child has been disobedient. The child, who really knows what proper supermarket behavior is, stops being disruptive because of a parental threat that any further disruptive behavior will result in another rap to the skull -- perhaps with an even more lethal object such as a bottle of apple juice. In obtaining the child's compliance with the socially desired form of supermarket behavior through threats and corporal punishment, has the parent created the "ideal" form of compliance with the social norms related to supermarket behavior? In other words, the **socialization process has worked in the <u>most ideal</u> way it can?**

        a. True.   b. False.

1

2. True-False: The dynamic aspect of **social role** is social status.
  a. True.   b. False.

3. Of the **models of social change** we studied, which one could most aptly be described by saying, **"The more things change, the more they stay the same."**?
  a. conflict theory.   d. random theory or "chaos."
  b. linear theory.   e. cyclical.
  c. dialectical theory.

4. If you see a child trying to do her or his mathematics by counting on her or his fingers, and they would not be able to do the mathematics without such finger counting, you might conclude that the child has difficulty in:
  a. conceptualizing the subject-object dichotomy.
  b. understanding and explaining teleological (from teleology) concepts.
  c. abstracting.
  d. expressing their fundamental sense of ontology
  e. concretizing.

5. We discussed three basic models of social change: **1) linear models; 2) cyclical models; and 3) dialectical models.** Which one of these models would be most closely associated with **equilibrium theory?**

  a. linear models.
  b. cyclical models.
  c. dialectical models.
  d. random models.
  e. All of the aforementioned models of historical change can be equally said to be associated with equilibrium theory.

6. True-False: The concept of **behaviorism** is discussed in the **Dictionary of Sociological Terms**. Based on that discussion, generally speaking, it is safe to say that "feelings," "emotions," "unconscious motivations" and the like are not the basis of how behaviorists evaluate the psychological world?
  a. True.   b. False.

7. Social class, social caste, the antiquated concept of estate, SES, etc. are all parts of the study of:
  a. metaphysics.   d. social stratification.
  b. social transmigration.   e. cosmological valuation.
  c. the socialization process.

8. True-False: By definition, **society is much more specialized** than most other forms of social organization?
  a. True.   b. False.

2

9. True-False: A caste system is a system of **social stratification** based almost completely on **achieved status**?

    a. True.   b. False.

10. The branch of philosophy dealing with what is **"good," "bad," "right," wrong,"** etc. is called :a. Metaphysics.   d. Ontology.

    b. Ethics.   e. Cosmology.

    c. Epistemology.

11. Empiricism is a system of inquiry that:

    a. tells us that knowledge comes from the use of our Reason and the things that can be discovered through Reason.

    b. holds that knowledge can be based only upon those things about which we can make absolute, positive statements.

    c. says that the ultimate source of knowledge depends upon the logical constructs that we can formulate with our minds.

    d. seeks the ultimate realities that underlie the world of appearances — the basis of empiricism being that appearances are deceiving.

    c. None of the aforementioned answers is correct because empiricism is a concept that suggests that we have to use every way of knowing to obtain even a very limited understanding of a social phenomenon, including using the knowledge that comes from our imaginations and dreams.

12. The meaning of the word *Weltanschauung* most closely resembles the meaning of which one of the words below?

    a. Mordant Skewer   d. conflict theory.

    b. Utopia.   e. secondary group (as opposed to primary group).

    c. A paradigm.

13. "**Speculative philosophy**" is another name for:

    a. Aesthetics.   d. Ontology.

    b. Cybernetics.   e. None of the aforementioned.

    c. Epistemology.

14. So-called **Gemeinschaft** societies are most closely associated with:

    a. contractual groups and relationships.

    b. secondary groups and relationships.

    c. socially intimate (primary) groups and relationships.

    d. large national groups with very specific purposes such as The National Rifle Association, or The American Association of Retired Persons.

    e. None of the aforementioned answers is Correct.

15. True-False: Hegel is credited with naming **sociology**?

    a. True.   b. False.

16. **True-False:** A sociologist wants to study the changes that go on in criminal activities as a result of the changes brought about by an economic depression in a society. In this study, the changes in crime rates would be the **independent variable**, whereas the economic depression would be the **dependent variable**?

        a. True.   b. False.

17. If one were to summarize **Comte's** views on society, which one of the following statements would be correct?

        a. As human society grows and becomes more complex, it becomes less efficient due to communication problems which result from great **diversification.**

        b. As societies grow larger and more complex, individuals increasingly come to rely on **traditions** in order to keep a "sense of themselves" belonging to "something" in an ever fragmenting world.

        c. Although all societies will go through certain stages of development, the time at which a society enters a certain stage and the amount of time it takes to proceed through each stage may vary.

        d. When all societies finished going through the three essential stages of development, there would be a decline into complete chaos because the most powerful societies would fight for control.

        e. All the possible selections above are correct.

18. Let's pretend it is the year 2020. Let's pretend that **Comte's** utopian vision has been attained. Which one of the following selections **does not agree** with **Comte's** visualization of his **utopia?**

        a. Humanism replaces religion as heaven on earth is achieved.

        b. All citizens would be expected to obey the universal social truths which are uncovered by the positivistic method of science.

        c. Sociologists would be the educators of the young in accordance with the discovered universal social truths.

        d. The "ruling power" in terms of political and economic might will stem from the Temple of Sociology, where the "High Priest" resides — directing even the most powerful secular individuals.

        e. Responsibilities might have to outweigh rights; but that would be a small price to pay for a smoothly operating society.

19. In society, there is a continuum of **norms.** Three major varieties of these norms were discussed in the text. All of the norms are important to the society, but some are considered more important to the maintenance of the society and are much more rigidly enforced than others. Going from the **least rigidly enforced** and socially important norms to the **most rigidly enforced** and socially important norms (reading from left to right), choose the most appropriate answer below?

        a. Folkway, More, Law.   d. Law, Folkway, More.
        b. Law, More, Folkway.   e. More, Law, Folkway.
        c. Folkway, Law, More.

20. **True-False:** Pretend that you are a researcher. You are interested in discovering what is the most popular display of art at The Art Institute in Chicago. You ask the curators if they have any sense of exactitude about this issue. They do know which is the most popular exhibit in terms of numbers of people viewing it, but for reasons of their own they say that they prefer not to tell you. As a good researcher, you decide to use good sense and your senses in discovering which is the most popular exhibit. You discover that all the flooring in the Institute was changed at the same time twenty years ago. Naturally, it is beginning to show signs of wear. You conclude that the best ways to discover the most popular display is to observe for a month and count the number of people who come to see the various displays. Then you conclude, if the flooring is most worn in the area in which you count the most people, you have discovered the most popular exhibit. Would this evidence be sufficient in **Comte's positivistic** view to satisfy the conditions for you to conclude that your findings are valid?

      a. True.   b. False.

21. Sanctions typically are used to enforce societal norms. There are different kinds of sanctions -- positive sanctions that reinforce appropriate normative behavior, and negative sanctions that penalize or punish inappropriate or nonnormative behavior. **Imprisonment** represents:

      a. Informal sanctions.   d. Positive Sanctions.
      b. Diffuse sanctions.   e. None of the aforementioned
      c. Organized sanctions.   answers is correct.

22. What is the second stage in **Comte's "Law of Three Stages?"**

      a. the theological.   d. the metaphysical.
      b. the metaphorical.   e. the positivistic.
      c. the methodological.

23. A young person decides to go "bar-hopping" in West Lafayette. The person is "underage" and thus is not legally old enough to get into bars in the State of Indiana. However, this person has a fake I.D. This person doesn't know whether his fake I.D. is good enough that the bars will let him in. In other words, **he doesn't really have a theory or hypothesis about whether he will get into the bars.** He goes to the first bar. He can't get in because the person working the door sees that the I.D. is a forgery. The would-be drinker goes to another bar. The same thing happens; he is not admitted. This happens several more times. He tells his friends to go on without him; it is no use. The young man concludes that his fake I.D. is just too bad to get him into any bars and he will try to get another better ID. This bit of informal research in which the man took several specific instances before arriving at a general conclusion shows that the young person in question is engaging in:

      a. Operationalization.   d. Deductive Reasoning.
      b. Inductive reasoning.   e. Relativism.
      c. Nihilism.

24. **True-False:** In the **Dictionary of Sociological Terms**, the concept of value or human values is discussed. It is clear from this discussion that the notion of **value** and the notion of **utility** are not exactly the same thing.

      a. True.   b. False.

25. True-False: For his whole life and in all his writings, **Karl Marx** was an **idealist** in the sense **Hegel** was.

      a. True.   b. False.

26. Of the things listed below, which one **would not** be an example of the **means of production?**

      a. A large factory.   d. A new Cadillac El Dorado.
      b. A 4,000 acre farm.   e. A group of 200 robots used
      c. A cross-country freight railroad.   for welding trucks in a GM plant.

27. True-False: A **planned economy** is much more likely to rely on the automatic functioning of the laws of supply and demand than a **market economy.**

      a. True.   b. False.

28. True-False: Marx did not like to talk about consciousness of any kind. As a **materialist**, he found **discussions of consciousness to be irrelevant reifications** and to cloud the issues associated with the **material (economic) world** with a lot of psychological sentimentalism.

      a. True.   b. False.

29. Thomas Malthus is known for having studied:

      a. False Consciousness.   d. Population and economic resources.
      b. Mass Culture and Consumerism. e. Atheism and Communist Societies.
      c. The relative differences in the wage rates of men and women.

30. "**The Reserve Army of the Unemployed**" was, to **Marx**, just another way of referring to the   a. petit bourgeoisie.   d. the owners of the means of production.
              b. the proletariat.   e. the lumpen proletariat.
              c. the haute bourgeoisie.

31. *Laissez Faire* means:

      a. "Take it easy."   d. "Stop the Presses."
      b. "Get Involved."   e. "The Gift of Grace."
      c. "Let Them Do."

32. True-False: Marx **hated technology** in any form. Not only did it take jobs away from people, but it polluted the planet, and could never be put to any useful purpose in a truly advanced society. a. True.   b. False.

33. True-False: Even though **Marx** is a very controversial character, every one of his predictions has come true.

      a. True.   b. False.

34. True-False: Marxist theories view **imperialism** as a necessary outcome of **capitalism.**

      a. True.   b. False.

35. There are several important quotes from **Marx** that most educated people know. Which one of the quotes below can be accurately attributed to him?

    a. "God's in His heaven and all's right with the world." (This in relation to his communist utopia.)

    b. "Capitalism is the bane of the petit bourgeoisie."

    c. "I am a part of all that I have met."

    d. "I'd rather have a bottle in front of me than a pre-frontal lobotomy."

    e. "Religion is the opiate of the people."

36. Marx:

    a. Liked the State and thought it would always be necessary.

    b. Felt the same way about the State that most Socialists do; to wit, that the State ought to administer the means of production on behalf of the people.

    c. Hated the State but thought it would always be with humans in their societies.

    d. Thought the State was an ill-fated idea that must be wiped out immediately in the revolution of the proletariat.

    e. Thought it was possible, even probable, for people to outgrow their need for the State.

37. **True-False:** In addition to being described as a **materialist**, a **dialectical thinker**, a **conflict theorist**, an **activist**, and a **communist**, **Marx** could be accurately described as an **Anarchist**.

    a. True.   b. False.

38. **True-False:** People who follow **Marx's** ideas or ideas similar to his are considered to be **right-wing, reactionaries**.

    a. True   b. False.

39. How did **Marx** feel about the concepts of **objectivity and subjectivity**?

    a. He thought scholars should be completely objective.

    b. He thought all people were completely objective.

    c. He thought all scholars and other people should be completely objective.

    d. He thought all scholars should be subjective and that other people were subjective in their consciousness.

    e. He thought scholars could and should be objective, but that other people could not help but perceive the world subjectively.

40. **True-False:** **Marx** thought that **false consciousness** was essential for workers to keep from going insane in the capitalist world and that, as alienating as it was, **false consciousness** was what propelled the **proletarian** revolution against the **bourgeoisie**.

    a. True.   b. False.

41. **True-False:** It is much easier to understand **Marx's** radicalism when we consider that, during his life, **capitalism** had already become a **global** economic phenomenon.

    a. True.   b. False.

42. True-False: Empirical generalization is the highest of the three levels of social theory in terms of providing social scientists the broadest, most integrated, precise explanations of society.

      a. True.   b. False.

(If this statement is not true, **what is the highest of the three levels of social theory?**)

43. **Marx** believed that in a capitalist system, **surplus** is created from:

      a. constantly installing new **technology.**

      b. the dynamics of the **Law of the Rate of Falling Profit.**

      c. **raising wages** as an incentive for increased managerial and proletarian productivity.

      d. **labor.**

      e. All of the above choices contributed to the creation of surplus in **Marx's** mind; they are all correct.

44. True-False: The **Wealth of Nations,** written by **John David Rockefeller,** is considered to be the **primary early text** which establishes the theories about the workings of **capitalism.**

      a. True   b. False.

45. Stereotypes have all but one of the following characteristics; what is that erroneous characteristic?

      a. They are usually negative.

      b. Typically, stereotypes are one of the few things an "out-group" has that gives the stereotyped group an accurate portrayal to the rest of the members of society.

      c. Stereotypes are typically not tested in the world of empirical realities.

      d. Stereotypes are usually caricatures or exaggerated versions of the people to whom they are applied.

      e. Stereotypes normally give us a fixed mental image about a group.

46. True-False: If one looks at **Mannheim's Ideology and Utopia,** it becomes obvious that the **utopian** thinker always seeks to preserve the existing order (**status quo**) in his or her thinking or writing.

      a. True.   b. False.

47. True-False: An **historicist** is, by definition, a **determinist.**

      a. True.   b. False.

48. There are different kinds of **power.** Which variety of power listed below is the kind in which people let others exercise control over them because the people accept the right of the others to exercise power over them?

      a. legitimation.   d. authority.

      b. coercive power.   e. Paretoian Power.

      c. ideological power.

STUDENT NAME: _____

Sociology 100   Introductory Sociology
                                                  Purdue University

Sample Exam on Spencer, Durkheim, and the last part of Marx

****** READ THESE INSTRUCTIONS ******

As you will remember, these are the typical instructions on our exams.

<u>1</u>. Start this exam by counting the pages to make sure you have all 6 of them. If you are missing a page, you will be supplied with another exam.

<u>2</u>. Make certain your name is on both the "EXAM FORM" and the "ANSWER SHEET."

<u>3</u>. You must use a Number 2 lead pencil to fill out the examination. If you do not have a #2 pencil, one will be available at the front of the hall.

<u>4</u>. Make sure you put your STUDENT I.D. on the ANSWER SHEET. If you don't do this, it slows down the grading process by about two days.

<u>5</u>. There is only one correct answer to each of the following questions. Each question is worth five points.

<u>6</u>. If you are in the 1:30 class, your section number is 0001; if you are in the 3:30 class, your section number is 0002.

<u>7</u>. After you have completed the examination, leave the ANSWER SHEET in the appropriate folder on the tables in the front of the hall. Put your ANSWER SHEET in the folder that is marked with the first letter of your last name.

<u>8</u>. SPECIAL NOTE: To those students using this sample exam to help you study for the real thing: Please keep in mind that the sample exam is designed to show you the form the questions on the real exam will take, and part of the content. That is certainly not to say that there is not content on the sample exam that will appear on the real exam. Quite the contrary. However, if you only study the content on the sample exam, you will be missing at least half or more of the content that will appear on the real exam. You will be responsible for all the material on the last part of Marx (starting with and including the "law of the rate of falling profit"), Spencer and Durkheim in the Textbook and all the terms related to Spencer and Durkheim in the Dictionary, and the class lectures.

<u>1</u>. **True-False:** Marx hated technology in any form. Not only did it take jobs away from people, but it polluted the planet, and could never be put to any useful purpose in a truly advanced society.

        a. True.   b. False.

2. <u>True-False</u>: Marxist theories view **imperialism** as a necessary outcome of capitalism.
  a. True.   b. False.

3. Thomas Malthus is known for having studied:
  a. False Consciousness.   d. Population and economic resources.
  b. Mass Culture and Consumerism.   e. Atheism and Communist Societies.
  c. The relative differences in the wage rates of men and women.

4. <u>True-False</u>: Even though Marx is a very controversial character, every one of his predictions has come true.
  a. True.   b. False.

5. <u>True-False</u>: In addition to being described as a materialist, a dialectical thinker, a conflict theorist, an activist, and a communist, Marx could be accurately described as an Anarchist.
  a. True.   b. False.

6. <u>True-False</u>: **Herbert Spencer was not a very altruistic** fellow.
  a. True.   b. False.

7. The idea that the **"greatest good should be done for the greatest number of persons in a society"** is known as:
  a. Liberalism.   d. Social Darwinism
  b. Utilitarianism.   e. Totalitarianism
  c. Eugenics.

8. <u>True-False</u>: **Herbert Spencer** liked the concept of **individualism.**
  a. True   b. False.

9. A **monist**:
  a. Only knows one thing.
  b. Thinks that only two or three rules guide the whole universe.
  c. Would argue strongly for cultural relativity.
  d. Typically has a very eclectic view of what makes the social world function.
  e. None of the aforementioned answers is correct.

10. <u>True-False</u>: **Herbert Spencer** was "the father of the **eugenics** movement."
  a. True.   b. False.

11. Buck v. Bell:
  a. Set the tone for the Equal Rights Amendment.
  b. Resulted in handgun regulation that banned so-called "Saturday Night Specials."
  c. Was both an outcome of and a catalyst for the eugenics movement.
  d. Regulated the workplace such that a minimum wage had to be paid.
  e. Put an end to the "Free-Speech" Movement in Durkheim's France.

12. True-False: The middle class typically has **much less of a role** in the development of **fascism** than the **bourgeoisie or the proletariat.**

    a. True.   b. False.

13. True-False: **Herbert Spencer** was a strong **proponent of social planning.**

    a. True.   b. False.

14. Herbert Spencer:

    a. Didn't believe the State was negative a force as someone like Marx.

    b. Thought that society was very close to reaching a utopian state.

    c. Didn't put much stock in the activities of social reformers.

    d. Was a liberal.

    e. All of the aforementioned answers are correct.

15. Emile Durkheim was:

    a. An Atheist.

    b. anti-Semitic.

    c. A good Catholic gone "Bad"

    d. An Agnostic.

    e. Completely disinterested in religions and religious concepts because he believed they contributed to a sloppy, anti-scientific mood in both the natural and social scientists.

16. True-False: One of **Durkheim's** most famous books was called **The Sacred and the Profane**.

    a. True.   b. False.

17. True-False: The **Declaration of Independence** of the United States is **a social fact.**

    a. True.   b. False.

18. Which one of the following books did **Durkheim not** write?

    a. **The Division of Labor in Society.**

    b. **Principles of Sociology.**

    c. **Suicide**.

    d. **The Elementary Forms of Religious Life.**

    e. **The premise of the question is false.** Durkheim wrote all of the books mentioned in the choices above.

19. True-False: **Durkheim** had a very low regard for **individualism.**

    a. True.   b. False.

20. True-False: **Agnostics** could have **sacred** objects in the Durkheimian sense?

    a. True.   b. False.

21. True-False: **Sociologism** is a form of sociological **reductionism.**

    a. True.   b. False.

__22.__ Which one is not one of the characteristics of a **social fact** as **Durkheim** explained them?
    a. They are external to the individual.
    b. They are constraining.
    c. They can only be understood by making reference to another social fact.
    d. They are "things."
    e. The premise of the question is wrong; all of the aforementioned answers are correct.

__23.__ True-False: **Durkheim** believed that **there was only one kind of solidarity** that held modern societies together and that there would always only be one.
    a. True.   b. False.

__24.__ True-False: **Durkheim** scarcely agreed with **Marx** on anything -- one being an **equilibrium theorist** and one being a **conflict theorist.** One would think that they could agree on at least one thing relating to working people. That one thing they might have agreed upon was Durkheim's concept of "**occupational associations.**" After all, this would lead to better working relations between the bourgeoisie and the proletariat. As one looks at occupational associations, it is clear that Marx would have thought them to be a very good idea.
    a. True.   b. False.

__25.__ Durkheim was an equilibrium theorist. Thus, he would be "happy" if:
    a. The "normal rate" of homicide in France stayed pretty much the same over the years.
    b. The "normal rate" of homicide in France suddenly went up dramatically in a single year.
    c. The "normal rate" of homicide in France took a precipitous drop in a single year.
    d. He would never have viewed homicide as "normal," so the premise of the question is wrong.
    e. As an equilibrium theorist, Durkheim would never have studied deviance such as homicide.

__26.__ True-False: **Durkheim** believed that there was an order of social explanation that was _Pulvis et Umbra Sumus_ sociological.
    a. True.   b. False.

__27.__ True-False: Generally speaking, in **Durkheim's typology of suicide, a "loner"** who didn't want to be a loner would be most likely to commit **egoistic suicide.**
    a. True.   b. False.

__28.__ True-False: A prisoner in a maximum security prison -- in which his **every move was watched** -- his every utterance reported to the warden -- his every piece of mail opened by the prison guards suddenly commits suicide. That probably would be considered a **fatalistic suicide** in **Durkheim's typology.**
    a. True.   b. False.

__29.__ We know that **Durkheim** was the kind of man who liked to see society in a good state of equilibrium. Then, one day: Wham! The stock market crashes; the military takes over the society; the thugs go wild looting in the middle class neighborhoods; the cities burn; and there is no gasoline to get to the country. Durkheim decides to commit suicide. What kind of suicide would that be most likely to be in his typology?

a. Samsonic.
b. Altruistic.
c. Anomic.

d. Egoistic.
e. Fatalistic.

30. Several years ago in Japan, many people were killed when deadly gas was released into the subway system. Most of the people who released the gas got away with the help of gas masks. But say there was one of these devotees of the guru who ordered the attack who knew that at least one of the devotees would have to die in the gas attack if it were to be successful. The person to be sacrificed assumes this responsibility for the group and dies. What kind of suicide would this be in Durkheim's typology?

a. Samsonic.
b. Altruistic.
c. Anomic.

d. Egoistic.
e. Fatalistic.

STUDY GUIDE

Study guides are basically assignments. They are just assignments I do not collect. They are the most relevant assignments I can give you in a class with as many students as ours has. However, I will know if you have done your assignments by how well you do on the examination. If you study your study guides, you would have to work very hard not to earn at least a "C" on the exam. A person really has to work at not working to earn a grade lower that a "C" in this class. However, you also have to work at working to earn a "B" or an "A."

1. The so-called "Law of the Rate of Falling Profit" is very important to understand. You need to go over each point regarding it in the text. It is THE thing that is important about Marx because of its potential ramifications for modern-day capitalism. What are these ramifications?
2. What is the relationship of the Labor Theory of Value to the Law of the Rate of Falling Profit?
3. Does Marx think that the economic infrastructure of the capitalists needs to be destroyed in the event of a class war in which the proletariat wins?
4. You will have to know the qualities of imperialism, not only for what it is, but the environments in which it thrives.
5. Is American Society a pluralistic society?
6. You will need to know the ways described in the text of how an overproductive capitalist economy tries to ward off major crises (such as a depression) in capitalism .

13

7. Does Marx believe there is a 100% chance their will be a class revolution by the proletariat against the bourgeoisie? The answer has to do with determinism versus historicism.

8. Look on page 93, last paragraph, to see if Marx is a materialist, even in his belief regarding who would be the victors of a class war.

9. What on earth is a "dictatorship of the proletariat," and did Marx think it would last forever in the wake of a successful proletarian revolution?

10. Look over very carefully the critique of Marx. Then consider with great care those criticisms that are presented as being legitimate.

11. Who wrote The Wealth of Nations and what political-economic viewpoint does it represent?

12. Consider what would be an altruistic act. Have you done one today?

13. There were several levels of political economy mentioned in the beginning of the Spencer chapter. Going from "the Right" to "the Left," what are these forms of political economy and who were the advocates mentioned in the text of each type mentioned in the text.

14. Is there a difference in liberalism and Liberalism?

15. Obviously, you will be expected to know who wrote The Origin of Species.

16. What is monism and how does it differ from uniformitarianism?

17. What is the precise nature of natural selection and how does it relate to evolutionism.

18. Did Spencer think sociologists should do the same things as Marx or Comte; if they did differ in what they thought sociologists should do, was is the exact nature of these differing expectations about what sociologists should do?

19. You need to know what a social reform is, whether Spencer was a social reformer, and what specific social reforms Spencer felt strongly about as explained in your text.

20. Did Spencer like the State? Did Marx?

21. How did Spencer see the moral order in relation to the material order? How did Marx?

22. Would most *laissez faire* capitalists like Social Darwinism? In other words, did capitalist ideology and Social Darwinist philosophy have "cozy" parallels? If so, what were these parallels?

23. Who was Francis Galton; what famous relative did he have; and what social movement is he usually given credit for initiating?

24. Would Spencer have liked the eugenics movement?

25. You will need to know the names of the three primary eugenics books mentioned in the text.

26. You will need to know the basic methodology of Goddard's Kallikak family study. 27. You have to have a very specific understanding of fascism and the kind of environment in which it thrives.

28. Going back to the Marx chapter and its dictionary portion, you have to know what Critical Theory is.

29. What is demography?

30. What is sociobiology and who is its primary proponent?

31. There was a film shown in which two "ghosts" debate each other. Who are these debaters?

STUDY GUIDE

This study guide is designed to help with your preparations for the examination on part of the Karl Marx chapter and its Dictionary component, and the Chapters on Spencer and Durkheim and their Dictionary components.

Study guides are basically assignments. They are just assignments I do not collect. Study guides are the best assignments I can think of to share with students in a class with as many students as ours has. This is based on the idea that assignments ought to be for the good of students, not primarily for the good of somebody else who has to assess the work done.

STUDY GUIDE ABOUT DURKHEIM

1. Look at the differences in agnosticism and atheism. Which one of these was Durkheim in his latter life.
2. Make sure to understand the relationship of conservatism, organicism, equilibrium theory, and functionalism.
3. What does it mean when one is sociologically reductionistic.
4. It is essential for this exam to understand Durkheim's definition of religion.
5. Durkheim defined many terms in unconventional ways. Know these ideas such as "the sacred," "the profane," his concept of God, his position that religious rules are social rules, his use of the term "functionalism," and "normalcy" as it relates to deviance.
6. Does Durkheim believe we can make virtually anything sacred or profane?
7. What did Durkheim believe about the concept of a "group mind?"
8. What do the words *sui generis* mean and how do they relate to Durkheim's concept of the development of sociology as a social science?
9. Four qualities regarding "social facts" are discussed in the Durkheim chapter; what are those four qualities?
10. To Durkheim, deviance plays an important role in society in that it is functional; what does Durkheim mean by the word "functional?"
11. What are the three major qualities, as presented in the text, that Durkheim thought were identifying factors of "deviance?"
12. How does the suicide study conducted by Durkheim relate to every aspect of his overall theoretical viewpoint?
13. What groups did Durkheim study in the suicide study and how did they vary in terms of what would come to be called "egoistic" suicide by Durkheim?
14. How is the suicide study important to the development the idea of sociology as a social science? (Consider your answer on study question number eight on this form.)
15. Know very well the four kinds of suicide which came out of Durkheim's study, what characterizes them, and make up examples of your own of the different types of suicide.
16. Which religious group did Durkheim think would have the greatest rate of egoistic suicide and why did he hypothesize this group rather than others he studied would have this higher rate?
17. What is anomie?
18. What is "Samsonic Suicide?"

19. What is a typology?

20. Does Durkheim have any typologies in his sociology as presented in the text?

22. In the critique of Durkheim presented in the text, what do you think is the most unfair criticism; and, what criticisms do you think should have been leveled at Durkheim that were not?

STUDENT NAME: _____ _____

Sociology 100

Introductory Sociology
Purdue University

Sample Test for the ___ Examination on Durkheim and Weber

1. **True-False:** Sociologism is a form of sociological reductionism.
    a. True.   b. False.

2. Which one is not one of the characteristics of a social fact as Durkheim explained them?

    a. They are external to the individual.
    b. They are constraining.
    c. They can only be understood by making reference to another social fact.
    d. They are "things."
    e. The premise of the question is wrong; all of the aforementioned answers are correct

3. **True-False:** Durkheim believed that there was only one kind of solidarity that held modern societies together and that there would always only be one.
    a. True.   b. False.

4. **True-False:** Durkheim scarcely agreed with Marx on anything -- one being an equilibrium theorist and one being a conflict theorist. One would think that they could agree on at least one thing relating to working people. That one thing they might have agreed upon was Durkheim's concept of "occupational associations." After all, this would lead to better working relations between the bourgeoisie and the proletariat. As one looks at **occupational associations**, it is clear that Marx would have thought them to be a very good idea.
    a. True.   b. False.

5. Durkheim was an equilibrium theorist. Thus, he would be "happy" if:

    a. The "normal rate" of homicide in France stayed pretty much the same over the years.
    b. The "normal rate" of homicide in France suddenly went up dramatically in a single year.
    c. The "normal rate" of homicide in France took a precipitous drop in a single year.
    d. He never had viewed homicide as "normal;" the premise of the question is wrong.
    e. As an equilibrium theorist, Durkheim would never have studied deviance such as homicide.

6. **True-False:** Generally speaking, in Durkheim's typology of suicide, a "loner" who didn't want to be a loner would be most likely to commit egoistic suicide.
    a. True.   b. False.

7. <u>True-False</u>: A prisoner in a maximum security prison -- in which his every move was watched -- his every utterance reported to the warden -- his every piece of mail opened by the prison guards suddenly commits suicide. That probably would be considered a fatalistic suicide in Durkheim's typology.

    a. True.   b. False.

<u>8</u>. We know that Durkheim was the kind of guy who liked to see society in a good state of equilibrium. Then, one day: Wham! The stock market crashes; the military takes over the society; the thugs go wild looting in the middle class neighborhoods; the cities burn; and there is no gas to get to the country. Durkheim decides to commit suicide. What kind of suicide would that be most likely to be in his typology?

    a. Samsonic.   d. Egoistic.
    b. Altruistic.   e. Fatalistic.
    c. Anomic.

<u>9</u>. Several years ago in Japan, many people were killed when deadly gas was released into the subway system. Most of the people who released the gas got away with the help of gas masks. But say there was one of these devotees of the guru who ordered the attack who knew that at least one of the devotees would have to die in the gas attack if it were to be successful. He assumes this responsibility to the group and dies. What kind of suicide would this be in Durkheim's typology?

    a. Samsonic.   d. Egoistic.
    b. Altruistic.   e. Fatalistic.
    c. Anomic.

10. <u>True-False</u>: **Durkheim** believed that there was an order of social explanation that was <u>*Pulvis et Umbra Sumus*</u> sociological.

    a. True.   b. False.

<u>11</u>. **Emile Durkheim** was:
    a. An Atheist.   d. An Agnostic.
    b. anti-Semitic.   e. Completely disinterested in religions and
    c. A good Catholic gone "Bad"   religious concepts.

12. <u>True-False</u>: One of **Durkheim's** most famous books was called <u>**The Sacred and the Profane**</u>.

    a. True.   b. False.

<u>13</u>. <u>True-False</u>: The <u>**Declaration of Independence of the United States**</u> is **a social fact**.
    a. True.   b. False.

<u>14</u>. <u>True-False</u>: **Agnostics** could have **sacred** objects in the Durkheimian sense?

    a. True.   b. False.

15. **True-False:** Max Weber was responsible for the Protestant concept of "the calling."

    a. True.   b. False.

16. Which one of the following was not one of Weber's types of authority?

    a. Traditional.   d. Metaphysical.
    b. Charismatic.   e. The premise of the question is wrong;
    c. Rational-Legal.   Weber had no typology of authority.

17. **True-False:** Weber though capitalism would work a lot better if it were paired with a different type of social organization than bureaucracy. Moreover, he thought it would be relatively easy for capitalism to escape from rationalization.
    a. True.   b. False.

18. The **definition below** that most closely approaches **Weber's** meaning of the word *Verstehen* is: a.   the notion that if one does not "use" a skill, one will "lose" the skill -- for example, learning to speak Spanish and then not putting oneself in environments where it is spoken.

    b. based on sociological understandings that are possible only for individuals who have minds trained to ignore the personal (subjective) factors that make up other people's beliefs.

    c.   an empathic (from the word empathy) understanding of other persons and their behaviors based on an effort to put oneself in another person's place, but not lose the important sense of subjectivity that comes from following one's own basic philosophical outlook.

    d.   the idea that scientific objectivity is possible to achieve because, if a scientist looks carefully enough, he/she will discover that all human behavior is based on rational action, despite the fact that it is often difficult to see this rationality.

    e.   a scientist can be subjective; or, a scientist can be objective; or, a scientist can be neither; but a scientist has to specify in advance of a study, what **theory** he or she is using -- whether the person is a social scientist or a natural scientist.

19. **True-False:** In terms of his personal life, Weber had a peculiar relationship with his parents. Weber's very **ascetic father** and his **"party-prone" mother** created an air of tension in the house, and this was worsened by Weber's rivalry with his father for the love (Platonic variety) of his mother.
a. True   b. False.

20. Which of the following is **not a characteristic of bureaucracy** according to the way it was presented in the textbook for this course?
    a. Allegiances and conflicts are **concretized** in a bureaucracy so we can discover who our friends and foes are with precision.

    b. The individual is dealt with **legalistically** rather than **personally.**

    c. The **goals of the organization are paramount** -- "paramount," meaning "**most important.**"

    d. **Responsibility and authority** reside in the **office not the person.**

    e. **All** of the above are characteristics of bureaucracies.

21. True-False: When **John Calvin** introduced the concept of **predestination** into his form of reformed religion, it had the effect of throwing many believers into a state of brooding individualism and isolation because of their inability to be able to know their fate before God.

    a. True.   b. False.

22. True-False: Typically, the charismatic leader's first and primary concern is to maintain the equilibrium of the current society.

    a. True.   b. False.

23. Max Weber and **Emile Durkheim** both focused on comparative studies of **Catholic and Protestant** populations in Europe. **Durkheim** studied the differences in suicide rates of the two groups; **Weber** focused his attention on the differences in their:

    a. mores regarding willingness to kill the enemy during wartime.
    b. differential efforts to utilize coercive power.
    c. mortality (death) rates associated with work-related diseases.
    d. willingness to create and dispense negative propaganda about other religions.
    e. None of the choices above is correct.

23. Literally translated, **charisma** means:

    a. the gift of "gab." (a good and persuasive talker.)
    b. the gift of intelligence.
    c. the gift of grace.
    d. the gift of mystical connections such as Extra Sensory Perception, precise prediction of events based upon little or no information.
    e. Guns don't kill people. People kill guns . . . people? . . . something like that?

24. Tawney wrote a book that directly contradicted what **Weber** had said in his writings about **capitalism and Calvinism.** What was the name of **Tawney's** book?

    a. The Trivialization of Basic Economic Concepts: The Weberian Myth.
    b. Religion and the Rise of Political Economy.
    c. The Ghosts of Capitalism in Weber's German Ideology.
    d. On Max Weber: Truth, Fiction, and the Protestant Ethic.
    e. None of the aforementioned choices is correct.

25. True-False: Weber believed that **status groups** were completely **mutually exclusive.** In other words, by definition a person who belongs to one status group **cannot** and should not belong to another different status group.

    a. True.   b. False.

1. **<u>True-False</u>:** Georg Simmel was the first Professor of Sociology at The University of Berlin.

    a. True.   b. False.

2. **<u>True-False</u>:** Georg Simmel never met Max Weber, but was aware of Weber's ideas and disagreed with virtually all of them.

    a. True   b. False.

3. **<u>True-False</u>:** Simmel tended to write in a range of periodicals that was much wider in scope and style than typical academics of his time.

    a. True.   b. False.

4. Georg Simmel wrote all but one of the following books. Which one did he not write?

    a. **<u>The Problems of the Philosophy of History</u>.**
    b. **<u>The Philosophy of Money</u>.**
    c. **<u>Economy and Society</u>.**
    d. **<u>Conflict and the Web of Group Affiliations</u>.**
    e. The premise of the question is wrong. Simmel wrote all of the aforementioned books.

5. **<u>True-False</u>:** Simmel was most interested in the study of social microprocesses as opposed to social macroprocesses.

    a. True.   b. False.

6. **<u>True-False</u>:** Like Marx, Simmel's conflict theory led to a utopian vision of society.

    a. True.   b. False.

7. Which one of the following principles did Simmel not believe?

    a. Socialism is a bad political ideal to bring about social equality.
    b. Equality is easier to achieve in a small group than a large group.
    c. Large groups are authoritarian.
    d. Large groups are always hierarchical
    e. The premise of the question is wrong; Simmel believed in all of the aforementioned ideas.

8. True-False: According to the text, to Simmel, conflict is the only "engine" that drives social history.

      a. True.   b. False.

9. In the text, there were a limited number of forms of interaction in which Simmel believed. Which one below was not on that list?

      a. subordination.
      b. exchange.
      c. competition.
      d. division of labor.
      e. The premise of this question is wrong all of the aforementioned concepts were considered fundamental forms of interaction by Simmel.

10. True-False: Durkheim had seen society as a thing or organism. (That is true.) Simmel saw society much in the same way.

      a. True.   b. False.

11. True-False: Simmel believed in three levels of sociology. Which one below is not one of those levels?

      a. Pure Sociology.
      b. General Sociology.
      c. Existential Sociology.
      d. Philosophical Sociology
      e. The premise of the question is wrong. Simmel had four levels of sociology.

12. True-False: In his study of sociology, Simmel was so anti-structuralist that he never showed any interest in the social structure of societies.

      a. True.   b. False.

13. We studied several different levels of the theory of social change early in the semester. Which one of those theories of social change did Simmel subscribe to?

      a. linear theory
      b. cyclical theory.
      c. dialectical theory.
      d. random theory.
      e. the theory of "higher powers."

14. __True-False:__ Simmel talked about Objective Culture and Subjective Culture. Objective Culture was the form of culture that was most closely associated with the idea of the individual or individualism.

a. True.   b. False.

15. __True-False:__ Simmel was not particularly optimistic about the outcome of human society.

a. True.   b. False.

16. In the text, a list of aspects of Objective Culture according to Simmel are given. Which one of the factors listed below was not on that list?

a. Tools.
b. Arts.
c. Wisdom.
d. Philosophical Systems.
e. Legal Systems.

17. __True-False:__ To Simmel, although people always retain the capacity to create and re-create culture, the long-term trend of history is for culture to exert a more and more coercive force on the actor (people).

a. True.   b. False.

18. __True-False:__ It was Simmel who came up with the idea that society becomes trapped in the "iron cage" of bureaucracy.

a. True.   b. False.

19. In sociology, a group with two persons is called:

a. a biad.
b. a triad.
c. a dyad.
d. a monad.
e. a crawdad.

20. __True-False:__ Simmel was interested in the social effects of the addition of individuals to a social group. Simmel thought the addition of a third member to a group was much more dramatic than the addition of a tenth member.

a. True.   b. False.

21. In the Simmel chapter in the text, there is a discussion of an experiment that is concerned research subjects being shocked. Who conducted that experiment.

    a. Zimbardo.
    b. Mead.
    c. Cooley.
    d. Milgram.
    e. Cooley.

22. True-False: In the experiment that is the basis of question #21, it was discovered that research subjects will resist the authority of a researcher if that authority could result in danger to other research subjects.

    a. True.   b. False.

23. True-False: According to Coser, conflict sharpens the sense of a group's boundaries.

    a. True.   b. False.

24. True-False: Simmel believed individuality in being and action generally increases to the degree that the social circle encompassing the individual expands.

    a. True.   b. False.

25. True-False: Simmel believed that the greater our dependency on others becomes in a bureaucracy, the less likely we are to really know the actual individuals upon whom we become more dependent.

    a. True.   b. False.

1. George Herbert Mead is considered a:

    a. Political Economist.
    b. Symbolic Reactionist.
    c. Critical Theorist.

    d. Positivist.
    e. None of the aforementioned answers is correct.

2. True-False: Mead believes that society influences people in it so powerfully that there is no reciprocal effect these people have on society.

    a. True.
    b. False.

3. The dynamic aspect of status is:

    a. rites of passage.
    b. self.
    c. role.

    d. ego.
    e. None of the aforementioned is correct.

4. Which one of the following books is most associated with the name of George Herbert Mead?

a. **Mutual Aid**.

    b. **The Presentation of Self in Everyday Life.**
    c. **Mind, Self, and Society.**
    d. **The Journeying Self.**
    e. None of the aforementioned choices is correct.

5. The psychologist credited with first using the term "the pluralism of selves" is:

    a. W.I. Thomas.
    b. Sigmund Freud.
    c. Charles Horton Cooley.
    d. William James.
    e. It actually was not a psychologist at all who identified the concept; it was the social psychologist, George Herbert Mead, who identified this concept.

6. The concept of "looking glass self" was developed by?

    a. William James
    b. Charles Horton Cooley.
    c. John Dewey.

    d. W.I. Thomas.
    e. George Herbert Mead.

7. True-False: According to George Herbert Mead, a symbol (as opposed to a sign) provides a stimulus to which there is a set, predictable response?

    a. True.
    b. False.

8. SI advocates believe all except one of the following. Which one is that?

    a. Humans have developed conventionalized symbols that have become organized into languages which are the vehicle for the transmission of culture and the definition of reality.
    b. Symbols, once conventionalized, remain static concepts.
    c. Social reality is a process rather than a structure.
    d. Symbols have tangible or material consequences.
    e. The premise of the question is incorrect. All of the choices above are correct.

9. In Mead's terms, the incorporation of the society within the individual is achieved through taking the role of:

    a. the collective conscience.
    b. the significant other.
    c. the particularized self.
    d. the generalized other.
    e. Trick question. Mead's whole point was to illustrate the incompatibility of having an individual self and a social self; he believed that people either had to be directed inwardly (individual self) or outwardly (other-directed, social self).

10. The experiments on autokinetic effect were concerned with the perceived movement of:

    a. Populations of people.
    b. Waves of traffic on large freeways..
    c. Light.
    d. People's hands when they touch objects which frighten them (snakes, in the case of some people for example.)
    e. Political sentiments in polls taken before elections.

11. Mead would say that a child who is unable to participate in a baseball game (because of the cognitive inability by the child to understand the rules) has not yet reached the **play stage** of development of self.

    a. True.   b. False.

12. Which of the following is not discussed in the last part of the concluding chapter of the book?

    a. Fordism.
    b. Post-Fordism.
    c. The Fast Food Society
    d. The Homogenization
    e. The premise of the question is wrong; all of these factors are discussed in the last chapter.

STUDY GUIDE NUMBER TWO FOR EXAM NUMBER THREE IN SOCIOLOGY 100

Study guides are basically assignments. They are just assignments I do not collect. Study guides are the best assignments I can think of to share with students in a class with as many students as ours has. This is based on the idea that assignments ought to be for the good of students.

1. How is Max Weber's name pronounced?
2. What is asceticism and who was the ascetic in Weber's house?
3. What are the two major books Weber wrote that are mentioned in the chapter.
4. What did Weber think the relationship was between Protestantism and Capitalism?
5. Did Weber think Protestants or Catholics were more economically productive?
6. What are the ideas that make up the "Weber Thesis?"
7. What was the difference in engagement in ritual by Protestants and Catholics at Weber's time?
8. What are the links between capitalism, Protestantism, and bureaucracy to Weber?
9. How did Tawney feel about the "Weber Thesis?"
10. What is the Theory of the Preponderance of the Means Over the Ends; who named it?
11. Read very carefully the last half of page 150 and the top of page 151.
12. What was Weber's view on objectivity in the different phases of scientific study?
13. What is *Verstehen*?
14. What did W.I. Thomas think about "the definition of the situation?"
15. Understand the eleven qualities of an "ideal type" in the Weber chapter.
16. Weber's three types of authority are very important; know them and their characteristics.
17. What is a gerontocracy, primary patriarchalism, and patrimonialism?
18. What is charisma and how does the charismatic leader typically act?
19. What does rationalization typically mean to a sociologist as opposed to a psychologist?
20. Very Important: know what the characteristics of bureaucracies are.
21. What are the components of Weber's typology of rational action?
22. What does Weber mean when he talks about people finding themselves in an "iron cage?"
23. Weber believes that people in society are motivated by what three primary human drives?
24. What are status groups and how do they relate to the motivations in #23?
25. Of the three status hierarchies Weber identified, which one did he think was the most important?
26 Who named Symbolic Interactionism?
27 Who was the focal person in the development of SI at the "Chicago School" and the book of his main writings compiled by his students?
28 What are the differences in macroprocesses and microprocesses?
29. What did Mead think was the importance of the symbolic order of society?
30. Self and society as processes, not things.
31. Very Important: Mead's concept of the development of the individual self and the social self in society.

32. What is "looking glass self" and who is responsible for it?
33. What is the "pluralism of selves" and who is responsible for it?
34. What does *tabula rasa* mean?
35. In Mead's terms, what is the difference in the "me" and the "I?"
36. What were the experiments about autokinetic effect about?
37. What was Mead's view on the relationship of "being" to "doing?"
38. Very Important: Know SI's view on the material consequences of abstract symbols.
39. What are Fordism and Post-Fordism?
40. What is the meaning of cultural homogenization?